T. S. Eliot's Dialectical Imagination

Hopkins Studies in Modernism
Douglas Mao, *Series Editor*

T. S. Eliot's Dialectical Imagination

Jewel Spears Brooker

Johns Hopkins University Press
Baltimore

Printed in the United States of America on acid-free paper
9 8 7 6 5 4 3 2 1

Johns Hopkins University Press
2715 North Charles Street
Baltimore, Maryland 21218-4363
www.press.jhu.edu

Library of Congress Cataloging-in-Publication Data

Names: Brooker, Jewel Spears, 1940– author.
Title: T. S. Eliot's dialectical imagination / Jewel Spears Brooker.
Description: Baltimore : Johns Hopkins University Press, 2018. | Series: Hopkins studies in modernism | Includes bibliographical references and index.
Identifiers: LCCN 2018002315 | ISBN 9781421426525 (hardcover : acid-free paper) | ISBN 9781421426532 (electronic) | ISBN 1421426528 (hardcover : acid-free paper) | ISBN 1421426536 (electronic)
Subjects: LCSH: Eliot, T. S. (Thomas Stearns), 1888–1965—Criticism and interpretation. | Modernism (Literature)
Classification: LCC PS3509.L43 Z64547 2018 | DDC 821/.912—dc23
LC record available at https://lccn.loc.gov/2018002315

A catalog record for this book is available from the British Library.

Frontispiece: Paul Gauguin (French, 1848–1903). *Le Christ jaune* (*The Yellow Christ*), 1889. Oil on canvas, support: 36 1/4 x 28 7/8 inches (92.07 x 73.34 cm); framed: 50 x 42 3/4 x 3 inches (127 x 108.59 x 7.62 cm). Collection Albright-Knox Art Gallery, Buffalo, New York; General Purchase Funds, 1946 (1946:4). Photograph by Tom Loonan.

Johns Hopkins University Press uses environmentally friendly book materials, including recycled text paper that is composed of at least 30 percent post-consumer waste, whenever possible.

Mae Johnson (1919-97) and William Burnside Spears (1917-99)
Judy Lee Spears Reed (1942-2014)
William Burnside Spears, Jr. (1944-2015)

And what the dead had no speech for, when living,
They can tell you, being dead: the communication
Of the dead is tongued with fire beyond the language of the living.

Eliot, *Little Gidding* I

Ralph, Emily, Mark, and Rachael
Tamara, Ken, and David

We shall not cease from exploration
And the end of all our exploring
Will be to arrive where we started
And know the place for the first time.

Eliot, *Little Gidding* V

The life of a soul does not consist in the contemplation of one consistent world but in the painful task of unifying . . . jarring and incompatible ones, and passing, when possible, from two or more discordant viewpoints to a higher which shall somehow include and transmute them.

Eliot, *Knowledge and Experience*

Contents

Acknowledgments

I have accumulated innumerable debts in the course of working on *T. S. Eliot's Dialectical Imagination*. The most immediate is to my editors at Johns Hopkins University Press, Matthew McAdam, Juliana McCarthy, and Catherine Goldstead; to Barbara Lamb; and to Douglas Mao, editor of the Hopkins series Studies in Modernism. Their attention to my argument and their suggestions have made this a stronger book. My deepest long-term debt is to Valerie Eliot, who, for more than four decades, collected and preserved her husband's papers.

For assistance in securing permission to quote from Eliot's writings, I am grateful to Clare Reihill of Set Copyrights Ltd. and Alex Baldwin of Faber & Faber Ltd. My quotations, which are from a variety of works and span a number of decades, consist of extracts ranging in length from single lines to brief paragraphs. All are reproduced by permission, as follows: © Set Copyrights Ltd. © Estate of T. S. Eliot: © Faber & Faber Ltd. and Johns Hopkins University Press. Extracts of Eliot's poetry are quoted from *The Poems of T. S. Eliot* (2 vols., 2015), edited by Christopher Ricks and Jim McCue; extracts of his prose are from *The Complete Prose of T. S. Eliot: The Critical Edition* (volumes 1-6; 2014, 2015, 2017), edited by Ronald Schuchard and his coeditors (listed below and in the bibliography). Extracts of Eliot's correspondence are from *The Letters of T. S. Eliot* (vols. 1-7; 2009, 2012, 2013, 2014, 2016, 2017). The first two volumes were edited by Valerie Eliot and Hugh Haughton and all subsequent volumes by Valerie Eliot and John Haffenden. Extracts from *Murder in the Cathedral* and *The Family Reunion* are from *The Complete Poems and Plays* (1969). I am also grateful to Kate Goldkamp of the Department of Special Collections at Washington University Libraries (St. Louis) for assistance in securing permission to quote from "Philosophy the

Science of Truth," an oration given at the university by T. S. Eliot's father in 1863.

My principle recent debt to institutions is to Merton College (University of Oxford), where, as a Research Fellow in 2014, I completed drafts of the final chapters. I will long savor the hospitality and courtesy of the warden, Sir Martin Taylor, the librarian, Dr. Julia Walworth, and Professor Richard McCabe. I am also grateful to the Fulbright Program for sponsoring me as a senior specialist in humanities over the past decade, a position that enabled me to lecture on Eliot in Israel and South Africa. I am also indebted to Dr. Kelly Brown of the Missouri History Museum for assistance in locating materials related to the Eliot family. The foundation for all of my work on Eliot was formed in conversation with my mentor and first collaborator, Joseph Bentley, and in archival research at King's College Library (University of Cambridge), the Houghton Library (Harvard University), and the New York Public Library (Berg Collection). I will always be grateful to the archivists of those splendid collections of rare books and literary manuscripts.

I am indebted to my collaborators in the Eliot Prose editorial project, above all, Ronald Schuchard (Emory University), but also Anthony Cuda (University of North Carolina, Greensboro), Frances Dickey (University of Missouri, Columbia), Jennifer Formichelli (Boston University Academy), Jason Harding (Durham University), David Chinitz (Loyola University, Chicago), Jayme Stayer, SJ (John Carroll University, University Heights, Ohio), and Iman Javadi (Cambridge, UK).

My argument crystallized in conversation with other scholars, chiefly Leona Toker (Hebrew University of Jerusalem), Ricardo J. Quinones (Claremont McKenna College), and Adam Lausch-Holuboquicz (School of Oriental and Asian Studies, University of London). In a more general way, I am indebted to Lyndall Gordon, John Haffenden, Tatsuo Murata, and especially to Michael Edwards, whose work has been a source of inspiration over the years. Finally, I am pleased to acknowledge a debt to the many students who have passed through my classes, chiefly at Eckerd College, where I was supported by my dean, Dr. Lloyd Chapin, and a dear colleague, Carolyn Johnston, but also at Hebrew University of Jerusalem, North-West University (Potchefstroom, South Africa), and the International T. S. Eliot Summer School in London.

Although the present book builds on my previous scholarship, the overall argument, informed by recent archival work, is presented here for the first time. Earlier versions of chapter 2 (on Eliot and Bergson) and chapter 5 (on Eliot's criticism) appeared in whole or part in *Partial Answers* (Hebrew University of Jerusalem). Threads in other chapters were prefigured in articles published in Eliot Society journals (Korea, Japan, and England), in compilations of scholarship (including the Blackwell *Companion* and several *Cambridge Companions*), in collections of essays by several hands (including *T. S. Eliot and the Concept of Tradition*, *Julian of Norwich's Legacy*, and *Eliot, France, and the Mind of Europe*), as well as in journals such as *Modern Philology*, *ELH*, *Modernism/Modernity*, *South Atlantic Review*, and *Religion and Literature*.

In the course of my activities as a lecturer, I have been privileged to meet with scholars throughout the United States and from around the world. They listened, offered suggestions, and helped me to hone the argument underpinning this book. Some of my lectures were addressed to literary associations—MLA, SAMLA, American Literature Association, Modernist Studies Association, and Christianity and Literature; most, however, were presented to friends in organizations devoted to scholarship on Eliot and modernism, including the T. S. Eliot Society of St. Louis and sister associations in other countries, including England, Japan, and South Korea. In the last few years, I have discussed various strands of my emerging thesis with audiences in Florence, Italy and at Burnt Norton, Little Gidding, and Cambridge. My lectures outside of the United States and England have enabled me to appreciate other perspectives on American and English poetry. I am grateful to audiences in Canada (Vancouver, Toronto), China (Beijing), Denmark (Odense, Aarhus), France (Paris, Angers), Germany (Halle, Bamberg), Israel (Jerusalem, Tel Aviv), Italy (Florence, Milan, Loppiano, Rome), Japan (Kyoto, Tokyo, Sendai, Nagasaki), Malta (Valletta), Scotland (Glasgow), South Africa (Potchefstroom), South Korea (Seoul, Andong), Sweden (Lund), and Switzerland (Lausanne, Fribourg, Basel, Bern).

My greatest debt by far is to my parents, who nurtured me physically and spiritually, teaching by precept and example how to love, how to pray, and how to work. In a different way, I am indebted to my siblings, my children, and my granddaughter, for delighting and amazing me through the years. Most immediately and most practically, I am grateful to my husband, who helps me in a hundred ways every day. These dear ones are named in my dedication.

Abbreviations

Works by T. S. Eliot

AW	*Ash-Wednesday*
BN	*Burnt Norton*
CPP	*The Complete Poems and Plays*
DS	*The Dry Salvages*
EC	*East Coker*
HM	*The Hollow Men*
KE	*Knowledge and Experience*
LG	*Little Gidding*
OPP	*On Poetry and Poets*
Poems 1, Poems 2	*The Annotated Text of the Poems of T. S. Eliot*
TCC	*To Criticize the Critic*
WL	*The Waste Land*
WLF	*The Waste Land: A Facsimile and Transcript of the Original Drafts*

The Letters of T. S. Eliot

L1	*1898–1922*
L2	*1923–1925*
L3	*1926–1927*
L4	*1928–1929*
L5	*1930–1931*
L6	*1932–1933*
L7	*1934–1935*
L8	forthcoming (1936–1938)

For complete bibliographical data, see the Bibliography.

The Complete Prose: The Critical Edition

Prose 1	*Apprentice Years, 1905–1918*
Prose 2	*Perfect Critic, 1919–1926*
Prose 3	*Literature, Politics, Belief, 1927–1929*
Prose 4	*English Lion, 1930–1933*
Prose 5	*Tradition and Orthodoxy, 1934–1939*
Prose 6	*The War Years, 1940–1946*
Prose 7	*A European Society, 1947–1953*
Prose 8	forthcoming (1954–1965)

Related Works

A&R	F. H. Bradley, *Appearance and Reality*
M&M	Henri Bergson, *Matter and Memory*
TFW	Henri Bergson, *Time and Free Will*

T. S. Eliot's Dialectical Imagination

Introduction

Logic and Longing in T. S. Eliot

This thought this ghost this pendulum in the head
Swinging from life to death
Bleeding between two lives . . .

Eliot, "Song" (1921)

And all shall be well . . .
When the tongues of flame are in-folded
Into the crowned knot of fire
And the fire and the rose are one.

Eliot, *Little Gidding* V (1942)

The hallmark of T. S. Eliot's early poems is the dramatization of painful psychological and social conflicts. His characters, typified by J. Alfred Prufrock, are thought-tormented figures who are paralyzed by the disjunction between mind and body, thought and action. The need to address the impasse is part of what drew Eliot to philosophy, and the failure of philosophy to assuage his disquiet is the reason he gave for abandoning it.[1] Eliot's exploration of the epistemological dimension of his discontent, however, was not fruitless. As a PhD student at Harvard and Oxford between 1911 and 1915, he considered various ways of dealing with dualism in the realm of ideas. My thesis is that two of the principles that he absorbed in his graduate studies in philosophy became permanent features of his mind and art, grounding his quest for wholeness and underpinning most of his subsequent poetry. The first, at the heart of his work on F. H. Bradley and idealism, is that contradictions are best understood dialectically, by moving to perspectives that both include and transcend them. The second, basic in his work on James G. Frazer and the social sciences, is that no one truth is self-sufficient, that all truths exist in relation to other truths. What relativism recommends is "not to pursue any theory to a conclusion, and to avoid complete consistency" (*L*1.88).[2] Together or in tandem, these two principles—dialectic and relativism—constitute the basis of a continual reshaping of his imagination. The dialectic serves as a kinetic principle, undergirding his impulse to move forward by looping back, and the relativism supports his ingrained ambivalence.

Although Eliot's early cogitations, like those of the young narrator of "La Figlia Che Piange," troubled his midnights and agitated his noons, they proved to be a major source of power in his poetry. He continued to be haunted, at times tormented, by double vision, by an awareness of fragmentation within and without. In 1910, the dissociation was between intellect and feeling; in 1914, between refinement and desire; in 1925, between the idea and the reality; in 1928, between asceticism and sensuality; in 1934, between time and the timeless; and in 1942, between the fire and the rose. This evolution of self and style, which he later diagnosed as part of a religious quest, is in itself dialectical, for it inevitably involves moving forward by looping back, with nothing abandoned en route. Thus, the existential sensibility of the early poems is countered by the philosophical thrust of the postwar work, which is followed by a religious turn that both includes and transcends the conflict between feeling and intellect.

The point of departure for this study includes two positions that have long been part of the critical consensus on Eliot's work. The first, dating from the early 1920s and hardening after his conversion in 1927, is the observation that there are "two Eliots" and, moreover, that this self-division is dramatized in his poetry. The perception that the poet was divided within himself was noted by his earliest reviewers, including friends such as Conrad Aiken, Paul Elmer More, and W. H. Auden,[3] and has been explored in biocritical volumes by scholars such as Ronald Bush and Lyndall Gordon. Most of the characters in Eliot's first book of poems, *Prufrock and Other Observations*, are intellectuals paralyzed by intelligence, thinkers who, in Dante's phrase, have "lost the Good of the intellect" (*Inferno* III.18). Unwilling or unable to say yes or no, they conceal themselves in shades of gray. The second position, which formed in the mid-1940s, is that Eliot's poetry falls into three blocks, each defined by a signature masterpiece—"The Love Song of J. Alfred Prufrock," *The Waste Land*, and *Four Quartets*. The first position is the *point de repère* for my analysis of the disjunctive imagination, and the second the framework for my discussion of his development as a poet.

My argument has several elements. The first is that the three stages in Eliot's life as an artist correspond to three overlapping stages in the development of his intellectual and spiritual life—disjunction, ambivalence, and transcendence—with bursts of creativity followed by exhaustion and then by revitalizing interventions. The first block in his poetic oeuvre dates from 1909 to 1911, the second from the end of the Great War in 1918 to the mid-1920s, and the third, from the late 1920s to the early 1940s. The second part of my argument is that these stages are dialectically related. In the early phase, Eliot's poems are dominated by entrapment in binaries, by "either/or" thinking; in the second, by the "both/and" thinking of relativism; and in the third, by triadic thinking that reformulates both, resulting in a pattern that is "new in every moment" (*EC* II.35).[4] The first phase, which emphasizes feeling and self-consciousness, is deeply personal; the second, which privileges analysis and detachment, includes an attempt to depersonalize his poetry and criticism; and the third, which includes the unification of flesh and spirit in the Incarnation, is both impersonal and ultrapersonal at the same time. These stages evolve organically, with each both including and transcending those previous. The third element in my argument is that the stages are punctuated by ideological interventions that in retrospect can be seen as decisive in that they become the means of recovery in life and renewal in art. The primary intervention between the first and second stages is his graduate work in philosophy, a break supported by the disruptions of war and marriage. The primary intervention between the second and third stages is his conversion to Christianity, an event clarified by his return to America in 1932. The heart of my argument is that the invisible hand shaping Eliot's poetry is the tension between his personal life and his philosophical inclinations, with the two principles—dialectic and relativism—serving as the instruments for a continuous process of invention and fine-tuning.

Scholars have been attending to Eliot's work for almost a century. Unfortunately, few if any have had access to the full range of his writing for the simple reason that much of it has been secluded in archives and private collections, where it was only available to scholars with special permission. We are in the dawn of a renaissance in Eliot studies because the long-restricted archival material is now being published in critical editions. The poetry, including work that Eliot chose not to print, has now been published, edited by Christopher Ricks and Jim McCue; six of eight volumes of the complete prose have appeared, with Ronald Schuchard as general editor; and a multivolume collection of the poet's letters is being edited by John Haffenden. The present study is offered as a contribution to a conversation with colleagues and readers based on decades of working with archival material and teaching Eliot's writing in the context of literary and intellectual history.

Eliot's philosophical work is an essential reference point in this study, not because philosophy is important in itself, but because the philosophical positions that he first considered and later abandoned are congruent with his chronic anxiety about psychophysical dualism. In various guises, the early formulations endured and reappeared in all of his subsequence work, including his poetry and literary criticism. Following the publication in 1964 of his doctoral dissertation on F. H. Bradley's epistemology, several scholars turned to the relevance of his philosophical grounding to his poetry and criticism. At first, these studies focused on Eliot's early poetry, but over time they expanded to consider the postmodern theories of language reflected in *Four Quartets*. In 1982, one of the first and best studies to mine Eliot's philosophical work was Piers Gray's *T. S. Eliot's Intellectual and Poetic Development*. Gray secured permission to read and quote from Eliot's graduate essay on primitive ritual and used it to interpret his poetry from "The Love Song of J. Alfred Prufrock" through *The Waste Land*. In *Discovering Modernism*, published in 1987, Louis Menand placed Eliot's preoccupation with objects in the context of imagism and early modernism. In *Skepticism and Modern Enmity*, a brilliant study published in 1989, Jeffrey Perl connected Eliot's philosophical work to an exposition of his relativism as it shaped his concept of tradition. In 1999, M. A. R. Habib published *The Early T. S. Eliot and Western Philosophy*, a study of the poet's three essays on Kant, relating them to the early Eliot's mode of irony. In *Mystic, Son, and Lover* (1997) and *From Philosophy to Poetry* (2001), Donald Childs drew on the dissertation and unpublished prose to discuss Eliot's mystical imagination and his rejection of a career in philosophy. Scholars with a broader interest in literary modernism, including Michael Levenson, Michael Bell, and Sanford Schwartz, have discussed Eliot's work in philosophy in the context of the revolution in culture and style that occurred in the early twentieth century. The purpose of the present study is to illustrate the coherence between Eliot's mind and art based on a reading of virtually all of his philosophical and religious writings and to reveal, through readings of major poems, what Henry James refers to as the "figure in the carpet" of his creative life.[5]

My analysis of the pattern in the carpet follows Eliot's evolving ideological and spiritual proclivities as woven into his poetry. The ideas are explored primarily through an analysis of two interventions in his intellectual life—his formative work in philosophy in the mid-1910s and his reevaluation of Christianity in the mid-1920s. The poetry is explored through close readings—from the "First Debate between Body and Soul" in 1910 to *Ash-Wednesday* in 1927-30 to *Little Gidding* in 1942—which reveal the shaping influence of the philosophical and religious materials. The poems are approached through the lens of his palpable sense of disjunction and his recurring attempts to cope with his divided self. My first chapter documents his disjunctive imagination, which he refers to as the "pendulum in the head." My last traces his attempt in *Four Quartets* to address the problem of evil, a meditative process ending with a return to poetry, not as a religion, as in aestheticism, but as a Virgil who escorts the reader to the gate of an "unimaginable zero summer" (*LG* I.19-20). The intervening chapters are devoted to an analysis of relevant prose and major poems that connects the swinging pendulum and the flaming rose.

My argument is developed on two tracks representing two structural principles. The first, reflecting the overall arc of Eliot's life, is chronological; the second, revealing the rhythm of dialectic and relativism, is analytical. The dialectical impulse predates his formal study of philosophy and persists long after he has abandoned thinking in philosophical terms. It informs not only individual poems but also his corpus as a whole, which begins with the infernal tongues of flame in "Prufrock," proceeds to the purgative flames of Buddha and Augustine in *The Waste Land*, and returns to the tongues of flame of Pentecost and German bombers in *Little Gidding*. The last image of fire both is and is not the same as the first, for it not only includes the torment, lust, and war of the previous poems but transcends them by moving to the tongues of poetry and of Pentecost. The relativism that is part of *The Waste Land* is reborn as a dance of opposites in *Four Quartets*, and the dialectical shape of Eliot's poetry culminates in the many "returns" of this late masterpiece. The dialectical pattern pervades his literary criticism as well, including the concept of tradition as a dynamic whole, which moves forward by continuously looping back and enfolding the past and present. It is also apparent in Eliot's biography—in his migration from philosophy to poetry to philosophical poetry and in the movement of his forebears from East Coker to Boston, followed by the poet's return to a tomb in St. Michael's Church in East Coker.

Chapter by Chapter

Chapter 1, "The Debate between Body and Soul in Eliot's Early Poetry," analyzes the dramatization of the disjunctive imagination in the poems of 1910 and 1911. Three of these poems—"The Love Song of J. Alfred Prufrock," "Portrait of a Lady," and "Rhapsody on a Windy Night"—consist of quarrels of the self with the self that end in disaster or deadlock. In the work excluded from *Prufrock and Other Observations* but kept in his notebook, Eliot reveals his anguish in stark and sometimes lurid images, ranging from self-division to self-mutilation. To illuminate this psychological fissure in Eliot, I discuss the antagonism of flesh and spirit in the Symbolist poets he most admired—Laforgue, Verlaine, and Baudelaire—and the dialectical whisper in the Primitivism of Gauguin. The antagonism is evident in his notebook poem, "First Debate between the Body and Soul," and in the Hamlet paragraph in "Prufrock." These poems, like most composed before Eliot began his work in philosophy, are written from the point of view of a young man whose powerful feelings and extraordinary intelligence lead to checkmate. Both the antagonism (body and mind, civilization and savagery) and the dialectical impulse are projected in the Prufrock who imagines himself as a "pair of ragged claws" and in the young gentleman caller in "Portrait of a Lady," who hears among the violins the "capricious monotone" of "a dull tom-tom" inside his brain.

Chapters 2, 3, and 4 are devoted to Eliot's grounding in philosophy between 1911 and 1915. The emphasis is on three thinkers whose influence proved to be pivotal in his life and art—Henri Bergson, F. H. Bradley, and Sir James Frazer. All three were to some degree idealists troubled by the post-Darwinian orthodoxy of materialism and evolution, and all three responded by constructing dialectical theories that privilege mind over matter. Chapter 2, "Eliot's First Conversion: 'Rhapsody on a Windy Night' and the 1913 Critique of Bergson," discusses what Eliot referred to as his first conversion. As a student in Paris, he was initially enchanted with Bergson, whose classes he attended in 1911, but he soon became disillusioned, as revealed in two poems, "He said: this universe is very clever" and "Rhapsody on a Windy Night." The chapter includes close readings of the poems and the first detailed analysis of his critique of Bergson's weak idealism, as outlined in a speech to the Harvard Philosophical Club in 1913. The encounter with Bergson was consequential in that it revealed the difficulty of transcending dualism and stimulated Eliot to choose philosophy as a vocation.

Chapter 3, "Eliot's Debt to F. H. Bradley: Reality and Appearance in 1914," discusses Eliot's engagement with neo-idealism at Harvard between 1912 and 1914 and his tutorials under Bradley's disciple Harold Joachim at Oxford in the fall of 1914. Eliot's work on Bradleian idealism is contained in a number of essays and in his doctoral thesis on Bradley's *Appearance and Reality*, completed in draft in December 1914. This chapter includes discussion of these materials, with emphasis on what Eliot absorbed from Bradley, chiefly skepticism and dialectical methodology, and what he rejected, chiefly the notion of an Absolute. His analysis of the relation of theory to life as lived led him to reject philosophical answers to "overwhelming questions" and to identify himself as a relativist. His ambivalence is reflected in a contemporaneous poem on Bradley's epistemology, "Oh little voices of the throats of men," a close reading of which is included in this chapter.

Eliot resumed his life as a poet during the First World War, a circumstance that partially explains an expansion of focus to include the meaning of history. Chapter 4, "The Poet and the Cave-Man: Making History in 'Sweeney among the Nightingales' and *The Waste Land*," includes an analysis of a seminal Harvard essay, "The Interpretation of Primitive Ritual," in which he describes the significance of the fragments of primitive culture that are embedded in contemporary history. In rebutting the claim that religion is a science, he anticipates signature elements of modernist form, notably parataxis and the "mythical method" of *The Waste Land*. This chapter discusses Eliot's adaptation of two principles outlined in the "Primitive Ritual" essay for use in his postwar poetry. The first is that, as material for art, facts (broken, partial) take precedence over interpretations (theories). The second is that attention to internal points of view (part of the "facts") should precede attention to external points of view (part of theory).

Chapter 5, "Individual Works and Organic Wholes: The Idealist Foundation of Eliot's Criticism," explores the tension between realism and idealism, which is one of the defining features of Eliot's modernism. His poetry, notably *The Waste Land*, consists of fragments and is grounded in realism and relativism, whereas his criticism, including "Tradition and the Individual Talent," consists of coherent arguments and is drenched in idealism. In this chapter, I analyze the philosophical foundations of Eliot's postwar criticism, highlighting four principles that are part of classic idealism. The most prominent of these are the concept of an organic whole, in which all writers are systematically connected, and the concept of a dialectical mind, which constantly changes but abandons nothing as it moves. This chapter develops the connection between the dialectical process in criticism and the notion of impersonality in art, illustrating Eliot's position with his criticism of Pound, Joyce, Conrad, and Yeats.

Chapters 6, 7, and 8 contain an analysis of the 1925-27 watershed in Eliot's intellectual and spiritual development, beginning with a reading of the one poem that he designated as blasphemous and ending with an account of his conversion to Christianity. Chapter 6 contains an analysis of *The Hollow Men* and related prose, representing the nadir in Eliot's quest for wholeness in life and art. Chapter 7 deals with his description in the Clark Lectures of the relation between modern despair and Cartesian dualism and his appropriation of Dante and Lancelot Andrewes as models in poetry and piety. Chapter 8 explores Eliot's conversion and his admiration of Pascal. These three chapters trace the implications of dualism, and like the three chapters on Eliot's philosophical studies, they constitute an extended discussion of an ideological (in this case, religious) intervention that enabled the poet to move forward in life and art.

Chapter 6, "Poetry and Despair: *The Hollow Men* and the End of Philosophy," is an analysis of Eliot's frustration with the incongruity between modern philosophy and contemporary life. My argument is that *The Hollow Men* reveals the afterlife of idealism and relativism, the two philosophical positions that Eliot had once considered promising. After years of attempting to reconcile binaries, he did an about-face on dualism by describing the informing principle of the poem as its acceptance in a different form—the ontological dualism of the human and the divine. In a detailed reading of major allusions, I maintain that the presence of Conrad's Kurtz and Shakespeare's Brutus projects a concept of hollowness as high-minded rhetoric, illustrates a belief in the existence of two worlds, and exposes the epistemological and ontological weakness of idealism. I associate the "Shadow" between the idea and the reality with the poet's ineradicable ambivalence, which in the conversion period he came to see as spiritually and intellectually crippling. My reading draws on Eliot's references in correspondence to *The Hollow Men* as a work of religious despair and on a 1924 lecture in which he describes the poem's underlying significance.

Chapter 7, "Love and Ecstasy in Donne, Dante, and Andrewes," contains my reading of Eliot's 1926 Clark lectures on metaphysical poetry and his contemporaneous *Times Literary Supplement* essay on Lancelot Andrewes. In these works, Eliot associates the despair represented in *The Hollow Men* with the separation of subject and object initiated by Descartes. In the lectures, Eliot asks what happens to love poetry, and to love itself, in a world without objects, and he illustrates his answer by contrasting the poetry of Dante, who accepted both subjects and objects, to that of Donne, who privileged intellect, and Crashaw, who privileged emotion—in both cases, to the exclusion of the object. In a world without objects, there is no check on the subjectivity that swallows the beloved. Eliot makes a similar point regarding religious thought in the essay on Andrewes. In a world without objects, what happens to the doctrine of the Incarnation? Without the realms of spirit and flesh, mind and matter, there can be no transcendence; without objects, the Incarnation is exposed as a canard.

Chapter 8, "Eliot's Second Conversion: Dogma without Dogmatism," deals with Eliot's 1927 conversion to Christianity, the milestone that involved reformulating his conflicts and dialectical triads in moral and theological terms. Updating the epistemology inherited from Bradley, he describes the ideal Christian as one who, like Lancelot Andrewes and Pascal, combines intelligence and devotion. Ethically, feeling leads the way; disciplined by intelligence, it moves dialectically toward devotion, conceived of as an enlargement of immediate experience. Doctrinally, the numerous logical and cultural triads are recast in theological terms, bringing him into the company of Trinitarians such as Augustine, Dante, and Julian of Norwich. Theologically, the dialectical foundations of his *vita nuova* are validated by accepting the Incarnation, the Christ event in which the human and divine are both retained and transcended. Epistemologically, the recognition of the gap between the human and divine regrounds his thought in a theology of paradox, preserving space for the struggle between faith and doubt in his Christian life. This chapter concludes with a close reading of "Journey of the Magi," the first poem to appear after Eliot's conversion.

Whereas chapters 7 and 8 deal with the intellectual underpinnings of Eliot's conversion, chapters 9 and 10 deal with a major emotional component —the resurgence of memories of his childhood and youth and the de-idealization that followed his return to America in 1932. In chapter 9, "An Exilic Triptych: *The Waste Land*, *Ash-Wednesday*, 'Marina,'" I discuss these poems as a triptych of the exilic imagination, with "Salutation," the first of the *Ash-Wednesday* lyrics, as the central panel. Pictorially, the panels represent a European river, a mythical desert, and an American seacoast; thematically, they depict the pain of separation, the longing to reconnect, and the return to a lost world. My analysis builds on Eliot's acknowledgment of the dualism of *eros* and *agape* and on his perception of the dialectical structure of exile—exodus/wandering/return. In *The Waste Land* and *Ash-Wednesday*, Eliot draws on the poets and prophets of exile, chiefly Dante and Ezekiel. In "Marina," he re-creates the recognition scenes in Shakespeare's *Pericles* and Seneca's *Hercules Furens* with their dialectic of knowing/forgetting/knowing again. In creating a "crisscross" of antithetical recognitions, Eliot suggests the melancholy undertow in the knowledge that follows experience.

Chapter 10, "'Into our first world': Return and Recognition in *Burnt Norton* and *Little Gidding*," explores the ways in which Eliot's attempt "to redeem the time" by returning to America reshaped his life and his poetry. In "Marina," as discussed in the previous chapter, Eliot presents an idealized version of his "first world," constructed from memories of his youth. The nine months that he spent at home in 1932 and 1933 resulted in a de-idealization that was sealed by his brother's response to his public critique of Unitarianism for a Boston audience that included his immediate family. In *Burnt Norton*, he represents the de-idealization and reconceives his first world as a reality accessed in moments of illumination that function as first fruits of a greater homecoming. The process by which the desire to redeem the time moves from idealization to disillusionment to a religious re-idealization is another version of the reciprocally supporting dialectical patterns in his poetry. The symbol of the exilic journey is the thrush—welcoming in "Marina," deceptive in *Burnt Norton*, and reassuring in *Little Gidding*. This chapter includes an analysis of relevant unpublished correspondence, the Boston address to the Unitarians, and sections of *Murder in the Cathedral* and *Four Quartets*.

Chapter 11, "War and the Problem of Evil in the Wartime Quartets: Reason, Love, Poetry," views the poems that were written during World War II as Eliot's meditation on the dialectical relationship between history and faith. In *Little Gidding*, he places the evil in history (war, the Blitz) in the context of the classic theodicies of Augustine and Julian of Norwich, representatives of the moral and mystical imaginations. Major images, such as the dove descending and the dance, are constructed to suggest the dialectic between good and evil that points beyond both to a reality that is at once imagined and unimaginable. My contention, based on the explicit theodicy in part IV and the meditation on language in part V, is that Eliot's hope for understanding the disjunction between history and faith was reconfigured as an aspect of art, focused on the dialectic between language and Logos and between individual works of art and the patterns of which they become a part. In so doing, he acknowledged the inadequacy of philosophical theodicy and accepted the whispers of transcendence emanating from language. His most beautiful dialectical image, the *Little Gidding* rose with petals of flame, not only contains and transcends beauty and terror, not only circles back to the gardens of *Burnt Norton* and Eden, but also returns to the 1914 philosophical papers, which in turn foreshadow both the dialectical thinking and the elegant relativism of *Four Quartets*.

Eliot's meditations on language in the *Quartets* are a return to one of his earliest concerns—the gap between words and meaning suggested by Prufrock's "It is impossible to say just what I mean" and Sweeney's "I've gotta use words when I talk to you." But as with all of Eliot's returns, this one both is and is not the same. The terror and paralysis once associated with the language gap have been contained and redefined by faith. The opinion that poetry must be considered "primarily as poetry and not another thing" (*Prose* 3.413) has evolved into the view that poetry must be considered both as poetry and as a shepherd of being, a compound shepherd who accompanies the reader to the boundary of "a region where that guide can avail us no farther" (*OPP* 94) and then leaves him to "fare forward," hand in hand with Beatrice.[6]

1 The Debate between Body and Soul in Eliot's Early Poetry

So profound, moreover, and so lasting is our intrinsic dualism . . . so deeply is this dualism rooted in our consciousness, that even when we are . . . alone, we still think as two.

Friedrich von Schlegel, *The Philosophy of Language*

The Conflicted Idealist

The poems that T. S. Eliot wrote at Harvard from 1909 to 1911 are fundamental to understanding his subsequent work, and insofar as they are the response of a poet of genius to a general cultural and intellectual crisis, they are helpful in understanding the modern age. With few exceptions, these poems are written from the point of view of a young intellectual who is preoccupied with the conflict between idealism and materialism, not as an abstraction, but as a psychological and spiritual reality. He is acutely conscious of the split in himself between mind and body (psychophysical dualism), descending from Descartes, and between subject and object (epistemological dualism), descending from Kant; at the same time, he is aware of the mediation of this dualism through Darwin, who changed the focus to the distinction between mind and matter. For Descartes, the rationalist, these opposites meet at the top, in the *cogito*, in which the mental absorbs the physical; for Kant, the idealist, they meet in the unknowable mind of God; and for Darwin, the materialist, they meet at the bottom, where mind collapses into matter. In 1909, fifty years after the publication of *The Origin of Species* (1859), Eliot was among those who were struggling to come to terms with this legacy.[1]

For Eliot, during this period a student in literature and philosophy, this intellectual context was inextricable from a parallel disjunction in himself.[2] In letters to student friends such as Conrad Aiken and Norbert Wiener, he describes himself as hopelessly divided between mind and body, refinement and desire. "In Oxford, I have the feeling . . . that my body is walking about with a bit of my brain inside it, and nothing else . . . [In London], one walks the street with one's desires, and one's refinement rises up like a wall whenever opportunity approaches" (*L*1.81–82). As Lyndall Gordon and others have noted, Eliot, though conflicted, tends toward idealism, and the young man in his early poems is largely a self-portrait of the poet at the age of twenty-one and twenty-two.[3] Like his characters, he yearns for integration, but cannot harmonize the mental and physical parts of himself. In later confirmations of the personal origin of his work, Eliot conceded that his early characters were in part a projection of his own angst. J. Alfred Prufrock, he said in 1962, is a composite figure, "partly an expression of feelings of my own" and "partly a dramatic creation of a man of about 40" ("An Interview," 17)—in part an intellectually precocious, self-conscious, virginal twenty-one-year-old; in part a frustrated forty-year-old, intelligent as ever, even more self-conscious, but still socially and sexually inept, a thinker whose life has been "measured out . . . with coffee spoons" ("Prufrock," 51). In facing what for him was an existential crisis, Eliot was unable to accept either the Cartesian and Kantian granting of ultimacy to mind or the Darwinian reduction of mind to matter. The impasse is dramatized repeatedly in his student poems, often in the form of an inner debate ending in resignation and self-mockery. The conflict was not, as is often suggested, a result of his encounter in late 1910 and 1911 with Bergsonism, for it is evident in poems such as the "First Debate between the Body and Soul" of January 1910 and the Hamlet paragraph of "The Love Song of J. Alfred Prufrock," written the following month.

As an image for the conflict between idealism and materialism, Eliot often uses the gulf separating youth and age. In early poems, the point of view is that of a young man; in later poems, partially as a result of his own aging, it shifts to that of an old man—Gerontion, Tiresias, the Magus, Simeon, Pericles, and Lord Claverton. Most of Eliot's old men are blind, or nearly so, a disability that associates them not only with decay but also, and paradoxically, with poetry and prophecy. For Homer and Tiresias, the loss of sight is compensated by insight; for himself, Eliot feared, blindness promised no compensatory gift: "The thought of possible blindness . . . has always haunted me. . . . For a writer, blindness need not be . . . the end of his activity, as it must be for a painter: but it involves re-adjustments so great as to frighten *me*" (Eliot's italics; "Some Thoughts," 76). In the student poems, the old man has no redeeming qualities. Diseased, demented, and disgusting, he obtrudes himself into the sight line of the young man. As a reminder of both kinship and difference, he is unsettling—an exhibition of mind dissolving into matter and intelligence melting into madness. Eliot's self-division, which can be described in different ways, is part of what he refers to in his review of *Ulysses* as the "lived experience" that forms the bedrock of art. The test for the artist, as he formulates it, is "how much living material does he deal with, and how does he deal with it . . . as an artist?" (*Prose* 2.478).

Initiation of the Poet: Symbolism and Postimpressionism

> I have a peculiar debt of gratitude to your *Symbolist Movement* [*in Literature*] for that was my introduction . . . to a poetry which has been one of the strongest influences on my life.
>
> Eliot to Arthur Symons (1923)

As Eliot was often to acknowledge over the following decades, the seminal event in his life as a poet, the event that enabled him to deal with his material "as an artist," was his accidental discovery in December 1908 of Arthur Symons's *The Symbolist Movement in Literature*. Symons introduced him to Paul Verlaine, Jules Laforgue, and Charles Baudelaire, the precursors who presided over his initiation as a poet. In a 1930 review of Peter Quennell's *Baudelaire and the Symbolists* (1929), Eliot refers to this debt. "But for having read [Symons's] book, I should not, in the year 1908, have heard of Laforgue or Rimbaud; I should probably not have begun to read Verlaine; and but for reading Verlaine, I should not have heard of Corbière. So the Symons book is one of those which have affected the course of my life" (*Prose* 4.11). The debt to Symons stems from his having introduced Eliot to symbolism in poetry, and by stimulating him to study in Paris, to symbolism in the visual arts, specifically to postimpressionism.

The *Symbolist Movement in Literature* resonated with Eliot in large part because Symons emphasized the connection between symbolism and the post-Darwinian clash between idealism and materialism. The basic tension in symbolist poetry, Symons argues, is a debate between body and soul. In the essay on Verlaine, he refers to that "peculiar unity which consists in a dualism, in the division of forces between the longing after what is evil and the adoration of what is good; or rather, in the antagonism of spirit and flesh. Other men 'arrange' their lives, take sides . . . Verlaine hesitates before a choice . . . cannot resign himself . . . to the necessity of sacrificing one to the other" (82). Verlaine and the other symbolists were struggling with a nineteenth-century version of the Pauline conflict between spirit and flesh. Symons argues, paradoxically, that the "peculiar unity" of Verlaine's poetry stems from this dualism, a sentiment approximated in Eliot's discussion of morality (good and evil) in his essays on Baudelaire and in his lines regarding war in *Little Gidding*, where he suggests that antagonists are "United in the strife which divided them" (III.25). The "peculiar unity" of Verlaine's poetry, Symons suggests, stems from the oscillation between the spiritual and the sordid, further maintaining that the plunge into matter—into filth, crime, sickness, and violence—was "needful" for the triumph of his "spiritual vision" (83). Like Laforgue, Verlaine was an idealist who mocked his own idealism as absurd, and like Baudelaire, an aesthete who embraced ugliness as part of beauty and regarded art as a way of transforming not only ugliness into beauty but also evil into good, a theme caught in the title image of *Les Fleurs du mal* (1857). The contraries perceived by these poets were both contained and dialectically transcended in the creation of a poem or painting. Eliot saw in this self-mockery a way of ironizing his despair and insulating his fragile idealism behind a protective mask. Most of his early poems are portraits of idealists in extremis, and most end with a "dying fall"—"The last twist of the knife" in "Rhapsody on a Windy Night"; "And should I have the right to smile?" in "Portrait of a Lady"; "Wipe your hand across your mouth, and laugh" in "Preludes"; and "Till human voices wake us, and we drown" in "The Love Song of J. Alfred Prufrock."

After reading Symons's book, Eliot began reading the poets themselves. In confirmation of Symons's ideas, he found that the symbolists were able to imbue urban images with metaphysical overtones without compromising their sordid materiality. Baudelaire's "Les Sept vieillards" presents a young man on a city street who is confronted by a diseased and decrepit old man who generates undistilled horror by replicating himself seven times. Eliot never forgot the shudder he experienced on first encountering this image, which seems at once literal and hallucinated (*TCC* 126). Another aspect of the French poets that enabled Eliot to find his voice was their interiorization of the monologue. In "Modern Tendencies in Poetry," he remarked that Browning, the "one Victorian poet" worthy of study, had expanded the psychological resources of the monologue by making it dramatic (*Prose* 2.216). In "Donne in Our Time," he grouped Browning with Donne and Laforgue, maintaining that the pattern that emerges in their verse dramatizes "what goes on within the mind" and that Laforgue deserves special credit for moving the monologue from an encounter with the other to an encounter with the self. Instead of focusing, as Shakespeare and Browning often do, on the dialectic between the self and an objective world, Laforgue deals more narrowly with "the play of thought and feeling" (*Prose* 4.376). He does so by using the technique of *dédoublement*—literally, "dividing in two," splitting the self into two parts. In a 1933 reflection on his youth in Paris, Eliot noted Laforgue's adeptness in expressing the "*dédoublement* of the personality against which the subject struggles" (*Prose* 4.516). In "The Essence of Laughter," Baudelaire describes this fissure as "the permanent dualism, the capacity of being both oneself and someone else at the same time" (*Écrits*, 289-90).

Eliot's comments on Laforgue and Baudelaire, spread over several decades, remained remarkably consistent. In a 1950 retrospective, "What Dante Means to Me," he mentions three indispensable influences in his life as a poet—Laforgue, Baudelaire, and Dante. To Dante, he is grateful for cumulative enrichment, stretched over a lifetime, but for the French poets, he is grateful for specific gifts at "a particular stage"—his initiation as a poet. In reading Laforgue, Eliot recognized "a temperament akin to one's own and . . . a form of expression which [led] to the discovery of one's own form." He claimed that he owed more to Laforgue than to any one poet in any language, because he was the "first to teach me how to speak," and in so doing, "to introduce [me] to [my]self" (*TCC* 126). In reading Baudelaire, Eliot learned the poetic possibilities of the "more sordid" aspects of the modern city. As an example of Baudelaire's "fusion between the sordidly realistic and the phantasmagoric," Eliot quotes the opening lines of "Les Sept vieillards" ("The Seven Old Men"), lines that he alludes to in the first "Unreal City" section (line 60) of *The Waste Land*.

> Fourmillante Cité, cité pleine de rêves,
> Où le spectre en plein jour raccroche le passant![4]

In a revealing aside, Eliot says, "I knew what *that* meant, because I had lived it," adding that these lines epitomize Baudelaire's significance for him (Eliot's italics; *TCC* 126-27).

A secondary aspect of Eliot's indebtedness to Symons is that by shaping his preunderstanding of symbolism and stimulating him to study in Paris, Symons prepared him to benefit from avant-garde painting. The importance of his encounter with symbolist art can be gauged by focusing on his interest in Paul Gauguin, a leading postimpressionist and the founder of synthetism. When Eliot returned to America in 1911 to begin work in the Harvard Philosophy Department, he brought a Gauguin print acquired in Paris. One of his closest friends at this time and for the next two or three years was Conrad Aiken, with whom he regularly met for dinner and conversation about poetry and the arts. According to Aiken, the post-Paris Eliot was "perceptibly Europeanized"; he was interested in French poetry and in a "kind of sophisticated primitivism" represented by a "Gauguin Crucifixion" ("King Bolo," 21). The Gauguin in question was *Le Christ jaune* (*The Yellow Christ*), which Eliot proudly displayed on the wall of his room on Ash Street. Aiken proposed featuring the print in a fin-de-siècle caricature of his friend. On 23 February 1913, he informed Eliot that he was working on "a caricature . . . entitled 'Decadence' . . . a caricature worthy of Beerbohm." The subject of this ironic portrait was "T. S. Eliot Esq. . . . It has you and your poems (the earlier Lamia kind as well as the later Prufrock variety) and your hoisted Jesus, and all; a complete composite photograph" (*Selected Letters*, 25-26).[5]

Critics have had nothing to say about Gauguin's influence on Eliot. Crawford notes that he brought back a "disconcerting" Gauguin Crucifixion (*Young Eliot*, 165); Hargrove comments briefly on his possession of *The Yellow Christ* (146-47); and the editors of the *Edinburgh Companion to T. S. Eliot and the Arts* refer to Gauguin in passing: "References to visual art and artists enter into Eliot's poetry to register a cultural attitude or aesthetic sensibility, earnestly or with ironic effect: . . . Hakagawa bows among Titians in 'Gerontion' (1919); and Gauguin maids make a cameo appearance in *Sweeney Agonistes* (1927)" (3). In contrast to these critics, I suggest that Eliot's "hoisted Jesus" (hoisted on the cross, but also on the wall of his room) was vitally important, especially in the formative years between 1911 and 1914. There is no doubt that Eliot encountered Gauguin's paintings in Paris, where the vogue for his work began soon after his death in 1903 and accelerated, due to major posthumous exhibitions. Gauguin's work was introduced in London by Roger Fry, who coined the term *postimpressionism* and mounted the first postimpressionist exhibition in England in December 1910, and in the May 1911 *Fortnightly Review* printed his gallery lecture. The Grafton Street exhibition featured more than forty works by Gauguin, and when Eliot visited London in April, Gauguin and his fellow postimpressionists were at the center of the art scene.[6] Given that the mind of the poet "abandons nothing *en route*" (*Prose* 2.107), and given the likelihood that Eliot faced an iconic Gauguin over his morning coffee for years on end, it is reasonable to assume that both the image and the theory were part of his developing aesthetic.

Gauguin was in the vanguard of those who rebelled against impressionists who, in their obsession with copying nature (light and water), neglected the emotional and spiritual aspects of reality. In the late 1880s, he founded synthetism, a style in which the appearance of the object, highly valued by impressionists, is synthesized with feeling in order to create a new work of art. His aim was not to abandon the object, but to subjectify it, in the process projecting two levels of reality—the tangible world of everyday life and the intangible world of dreams. Like his friend Van Gogh (a lay preacher), he was searching for a religious idiom, in pursuit of which he retreated from Paris to rural Brittany, and later, to Tahiti. In regard to technique, he recommended a two-dimensional arrangement of bold colors and heavy lines and a return to simpler times and characters.

According to the Gauguin website, *The Yellow Christ*, painted in Pont Avon in 1889, "is the apogee of Gauguin's early 'synthetist' style" (www.gauguin.org). This striking painting, which is the frontispiece for this book, pictures a gaunt and yellow Christ hanging on a cross. Instead of the two Marys (the mother of Christ and the Magdalene) at the foot of the cross, one finds nineteenth-century Breton peasant women, and instead of the rocky hill of Golgotha, one sees the lush landscape of rural Brittany bathed in yellow with splotches of reddish-rust. The crucifixion is closely modeled on an anonymous wooden crucifix in a small church near Pont Avon, and the women are modeled on local Christian believers. In keeping with the tenets of synthetism, the appearance of the wooden crucifix, the women, and the landscape is respected, but decontextualized and infused with feeling through strong colors, heavy lines, and the use of the painter's own face as the model for the head of the Christ. The radical decontextualization of the crucifixion generates the double vision that conveys the reality of two worlds, one that is here and now and another that is timeless.

Whether or not Eliot was familiar with Gauguin's theory of synthetism, he would have quickly identified with several formal features in *The Yellow Christ*. The dialectical nature of the composition—its synthesis of the subject and object to project feeling, its return to primitive elements in the quest for truth, its projection of two related but unreconcilable worlds—is visible even to an untrained eye. Of perhaps greater importance to Eliot would have been the topic. As Gordon observes, Eliot in 1911 was on a spiritual quest (85-92). The crucifixion had been at the heart of the Christian story from its beginning; at first an image of shame, it became in the fifth century a major symbol of sacrifice in European art. It is clear from Eliot's letters and notebooks that he was particularly drawn to religious subjects, especially to representations of crucifixion and martyrdom. When, in July 1914, he returned to Europe for graduate work in philosophy, he wrote to Aiken that, in passing through Belgium, he had visited art museums in Ghent, Bruges, Antwerp, and Brussels. "The paintings are *stunning*," he exclaims, describing works of Memling, Van Eyck, Mastys, David, Breughel, and Rubens as "really great stuff." Hardly able to contain his enthusiasm, he adds "And O a wonderful Crucifixion of Antonello of Messina." He saw Hans Memling's St. Sebastian in Brussels, and adds that it is one of "*three* great St. Sebastians," the other two being Mantegna's in Venice and Antonello of Messina's in Dresden, which he mistakenly says is in Bergamo, an error that suggests he also saw the St. Sebastian by Raphael that hangs there. Unlike these works by old masters, the Gauguin crucifixion is associated with the modernist revolution.

Eliot's fascination with crucifixion is evident in his poetry and plays. In "He said: this universe is very clever" (1911), the third stanza reads:

> He said: "this crucifixion was dramatic
>   He had not passed his life on officechairs
> They did not crucify him in an attic
>   Up six abysmal flights of broken stairs." (9-12)

The continuing power of the religious art that Eliot first encountered in Europe, including the crucifixion he saw every morning on the wall in his room, is also evident in his plays. In *Murder in the Cathedral* (1935), the multiple swords piercing the body of Thomas recall the arrows piercing the flesh of St. Sebastian. In *The Cocktail Party* (1949), the revelation dropped in the middle of a cocktail party that the heroine has been crucified near an anthill is an image of decontextualization worthy of Gauguin himself.

One other point, to be taken up in a later chapter, is Eliot's mindfulness about two worlds—one that is material, the other supernatural. The two worlds that one sees in paintings by Gauguin are represented in literature by Dostoevski. While in Paris, Eliot read *Crime and Punishment*, *The Brothers Karamazov*, and *The Idiot*, and he later said that the characters in all three seem to be distracted by an awareness of another world, a world behind the screen. In a lecture at Cambridge in 1924, Eliot revealed that he identified with these characters and incorporated Dostoevski's insights into his own self-analysis. The importance of this identification will be discussed in my chapter on *The Hollow Men*.

"First Debate between the Body and Soul" (January 1910)

> Ah! Seigneur! donnez-moi la force et le courage
> De contempler mon coeur et mon corps san dégoût![7]
>
> Baudelaire, "Un Voyage à Cythère"

Within months of reading Laforgue and Baudelaire, Eliot found his voice and was able to deal with his "living material . . . as an artist." His early experiments to cope with his intrinsic duality are on full display in poems he excluded from his personal canon. They survived in his notebook and were published in 1996 in *Inventions of the March Hare*. Consisting primarily of uncensored fragments and unburnished drafts, they present a post-Romantic *Weltschmerz* in which a young idealist oscillates between mind and matter and a thought-tormented Hamlet is unable to decide who or what he is. Although deemed unworthy of publication by the poet himself, these texts are valuable for the glimpse they give of his workshop at a crucial moment in his development and for the access they offer to the sanctuary in which he was struggling with personal identity and the conflict between spirit and flesh. Two of the rejected poems were conceived of as debates between body and soul. The earliest, which Eliot dated January 1910, is entitled "First Debate between the Body and Soul."[8] In Gordon's view, the "First Debate" reveals "Eliot's state of mind more clearly than any other poem of the undergraduate period." She suggests, moreover, that it is the prelude to "Silence," a lyric that describes a terrifying moment of stillness that justifies human existence and anticipates the timeless moments represented in *Four Quartets* (23-24, 34).

Although Eliot found his voice as a poet through his encounter with the symbolists, he did not simply imitate them. In entitling his poem "First Debate between the Body and Soul," he became part of a tradition that predates the nineteenth century. The debate genre was used in earlier times to present the relation between natural opposites (summer and winter, earth and sky), which were understood to be both distinct and inextricably bound, each requiring the existence of the other. In the Middle Ages and the Renaissance, the contrast was often freighted with religious significance. Andrew Marvell's "A Dialogue between the Soul and the Body" is typical. The Soul laments being imprisoned and tortured in the Body, and the Body complains of being possessed and controlled by an alien spirit. Each side expresses itself, and from the juxtaposition, there emerges an objective presentation of both their differences and their unity. They are equally paired and perfectly balanced, for the point is not to take sides, but to explore logical and natural relations without doing so.

The traditional debate between body and soul, then, is a means of affirming objectivity; Eliot's debates, au contraire, are a means of exploring subjectivity. Logic is supplanted by a free play of mind, intellect subordinated to feeling. Whereas the former gives equal time and weight to opposing voices, Eliot's debates favor the idealist. In Eliot, there is also a value component, for the soul is pure and prized, and the body is dirty and contemptible. The older debates end in stalemate because the contrasting elements are balanced and appreciated as essential parts of a larger whole.[9] In Eliot, the debate also ends without resolution, but in self-mockery rather than equipoise. In the older poems, irony is seldom used, for it would tip the scales; in Eliot's debate, beginning with the title and ending with the "falling off" at the end, irony is ubiquitous.

The original title of "First Debate" was simply "Debate between the Body and Soul." Eliot tinkered with the title, first writing and then canceling "Reflections in a Square" above it, and at some later point adding "First" to indicate his intention to write a sequel.[10] The hesitation about the title is illuminating. The use of "reflections" points to subjectivity, a single voice, whereas the use of "debate" suggests objectivity, a presentation of conflicting views. Both are important, for although Eliot settles on a minidrama in the theater of the mind, he undercuts the dramatic element by mediating it through the reflections of an idealistic youth who feels compelled to linger in the red-light district of Boston (or Cambridge).

> . . . devoted to the pure idea
> One sits delaying in the vacant square
> Forced to endure the blind inconscient stare
> Of twenty leering houses that exude
>
> The odour of their turpitude (8–12)

The "debate" has two aspects—the first is the conflict between idealism and materialism shown in the contrast between the "pure idea" and the prurient environment; the second is the conflict between soul and body represented by the young narrator and an old man who stumbles into the square.

A blind old man who coughs and spits sputters
Stumbling among the alleys and the gutters. (2-3)

This diseased and disfigured old man, a descendant of Baudelaire's proliferating phantoms in "Les Sept vieillards," appears in many of Eliot's notebook poems. Like some of his later characters, such as the woman who keeps the kitchen in "Gerontion" and Madame Sosostris in *The Waste Land*, he suffers from influenza, and like Gerontion and Tiresias, he is blind and malodorous. He soils the pure idea of the young man simply by appearing on the scene. Later in the poem, he is described as senile, a word that extends the decay of his body into his mind. The association of Eliot's phantom with decay is reinforced not only by the setting but also by the season. Stumbling through the square, the old man is accompanied by an "August wind . . . shambling down the street" (1). The narrator's idealism is undermined by his awareness of the wind, which, in ancient and modern poetry, from the Bible to the Romantics, is identified with presence.[11] But this square is "vacant." Here, as in "Preludes" and "Rhapsody on a Windy Night," wind is a symbol of absence, of a purely natural force that mindlessly redistributes leaves and scraps of paper in "vacant lots."

The *dédoublement* of the self into youth and age, idealist and materialist, is supported by the structure of the poem. There are three stanzas of approximately ten lines and a refrain of four. The stanzas present the voice of the idealist, who is focused on the discrepancy between the "pure idea" and the material objects in and around the square. Aware of houses with prostitutes peering through windows, he fears contagion—"the cosmic smudge of an enormous thumb/Posting bills/On the soul" (27-29). The youth reflects that in this situation the very existence of the Absolute is imperiled. In the third stanza, he suddenly turns, mocking the Absolute and chiding himself as a "super-subtle peasant in a shabby square" (39).

The refrain, by contrast with the stanzas, is associated with materialism and, in its first appearance, with the dirty old man. The refrain does not reflect the old man from his own point of view, but from that of a youth attempting to shelter his high ideas. The first two lines vary in each refrain, but the last two are always "The withered leaves/Of our sensations." In keeping with his disabilities, the old man finds his way by using a walking stick.

He pokes and prods
With senile patience
The withered leaves
Of our sensations— (4-7)

The old man's offense is intruding himself into the view of the young man; simply by being a fellow human being and existing in the same space, he disturbs the composure of the young man: "Imagination's/Masturbations/The withered leaves/Of our sensations" (18-21). The refrain returns as "Imagination's/Defecations" and "Imagination's/Poor Relations" (49-51). This is part of a debate about the source of ideas. The young man believes they are innate, given, pure. The presence of the old man suggests that ideas arise from matter, that they are the waste residue of sensation. One thinks of Yeats, who, mindful of approaching death, tries to remember the source of his images. In "The Circus Animals' Desertion," he reflects:

> Those masterful images because complete
> Grew in pure mind, but out of what began?
> A mound of refuse or the sweepings of a street
> Old kettles, old bottles, and a broken can . . .
> Now that my ladder's gone
> I must lie down where all the ladders start
> In the foul rag and bone shop of the heart. (33-36, 38-40)

The old Yeats concedes what the young Yeats denied, that the pure idea originates in the foul rag-and-bone shop of the body.

The image of the street piano, one of several that Eliot took from Laforgue, occurs in every stanza as part of a couplet that functions as a secondary refrain.

> The street pianos through the trees
> Whine and wheeze. (16-17)

In Laforgue, as Piers Gray points out, the piano is "symbolic of the lyric and the lyric evocative of the tragic" (20). In Eliot, the image is deromanticized, serving primarily as a mediator between mind and matter, the young man and the old. Mechanical and out of tune, it has the musical equivalent of influenza, an affliction that connects it with the old man who is coughing and spitting. As with other images in the notebook poems, the street piano appears in better poems of this period. In "Portrait of a Lady," for example, the sound of a street piano disrupts the narrator's self-possession, becoming a mediator of desire by nudging him to recall "things that other people have desired" (42). In the "First Debate," as in most of the 1909-11 poems, the last lines do not resolve anything. The debate ends with a whimper: "Imagination's/Defecations/The withered leaves/Of our sensations" (48-51).

"The Love Song of J. Alfred Prufrock" (February 1910-Summer 1911)

Ne suis-je pas un faux accord?[12]

Baudelaire, *L'Héautontimorouménos*

The most powerful early presentation of the divided self occurs in "The Love Song of J. Alfred Prufrock," the earliest paragraph of which was contemporaneous with the "First Debate." The poem originated from Eliot's fascination with Shakespeare's Hamlet as mediated through the symbolists, principally Laforgue. In February 1910, he composed the paragraph beginning "No! I am not Prince Hamlet." Over the coming months, as later explained in a letter to John C. Pope, he wrote a few more sections, and when he went to Paris in October 1910, he carried these with him (Pope, 320).[13] He continued to work on the poem during the following winter and spring in Paris, and finished it during the summer in Munich, dating the manuscript "July/August 1911."[14] In September 1914, Eliot showed the poem to Ezra Pound, and soon thereafter Pound submitted it to Harriet Monroe for publication in *Poetry*. She expressed two reservations, the first regarding the Hamlet paragraph and the second regarding the ending, "Til human voices wake us, and we drown." On 31 January 1915, Pound responded: "'Mr. Prufrock' does not 'go off at the end.' It is a portrait of failure . . . and it would be false to make it end on a note of triumph. I dislike the paragraph about Hamlet, but it is an early and cherished bit and T. E. won't give it up" (50). The clash of views here is instructive. Both Pound and Monroe disliked the Hamlet paragraph and recommended deleting it. Eliot demurred—in Pound's view, for sentimental reasons. Be that as it may, it is clear that one hears in this paragraph the voice of the progenitor of Mr. Prufrock.

No! I am not Prince Hamlet, nor was meant to be;
Am an attendant lord, one that will do
To swell a progress, start a scene or two,
Advise the prince; no doubt, an easy tool,
Deferential, glad to be of use,
Politic, cautious, and meticulous;
Full of high sentence, but a bit obtuse;
At times, indeed, almost ridiculous—
Almost, at times, the Fool. (111-19)

Most critics have discussed the two crucial allusions in this verse paragraph.[15] The first is to the "To be or not to be" soliloquy in Shakespeare's play (*Hamlet* III.i), and the second is to the brooding interior monologue in Laforgue's character sketch in *Moralités légendaires* (1887), the latter quoted at length in Symons's book on the symbolists. Like Shakespeare's hero, Prufrock thinks himself into paralysis by brooding on "overwhelming questions." But unlike Laforgue's hero, an idealist depressed by the thought that art and all higher things will return to dust, Eliot's Prufrock is a post-Romantic depressed by the conflict between desire and detachment.

These readings, which are helpful, are insufficiently attentive to the literal meaning (always important in Eliot). The literal topic is the existential problem of conflicted identity—who/what am I? Unlike Hamlet, Eliot's thinker is not the main character in the story of his life. He is a means but not an end, a peripheral presence in a psychic complex where the central position is either vacant or occupied by a fantasy. The form that Eliot uses to deal with the existential question is a version of *dédoublement*. He is and is not the brilliant young Hamlet, and he is and is not Polonius, the dithering old fool who is "full of high sentence, but a bit obtuse." From there, Prufrock disintegrates into a string of insignificant Shakespearean characters, in turn becoming an interchangeable nobody paid to swell a crowd, "one that will do/To swell a progress"; the courtier Rosencrantz, "an easy tool, . . . glad to be of use"; and in the last line, Yorick, the Fool. With "I grow old . . . I grow old," the line that follows the Hamlet paragraph in the finished poem, Prufrock melts into his older self, assuming the role of Falstaff in *Henry IV*.[16] Eliot's Hamlet combines and undercuts both Shakespeare's thinker and Laforgue's self-mocking idealist, adding a deeper and darker version of the divided self.

Prufrock's self-division is underscored by his tendency to insert images of suppressed violence into contexts that are highly civilized.

> There will be time, there will be time
> To prepare a face to meet the faces that you meet;
> There will be time to murder and create,
>
> . . . .
>
> And time yet for a hundred indecisions,
> And for a hundred visions and revisions,
> Before the taking of a toast and tea. (26–28, 32–34)

The reference to the ritual of adapting one's behavior for various social roles is immediately followed by a shocking perversion of a passage from Ecclesiastes, the two moments connected by anaphora. Prufrock's "There will be time to murder and create" echoes Ecclesiastes 3: "There is a time to kill and a time to heal." Two Hebrew words—*rasah* and *harog*—are translated in the King James Bible (used by Eliot) as "to kill." The first, which means "to murder," is used in the sixth commandment in Exodus 20:3: "Thou shalt not kill." The second, which means "to slay" (as in battle), is used in Ecclesiastes 3:3: "a time to kill." Prufrock's "a time to murder" reverses the meaning of Ecclesiastes, converting prohibition into permission. Similarly, he absolutizes the second part of the parallel, changing "a time to heal" to "a time to create," thus usurping a divine prerogative.

One troubling aspect of Prufrock's self-portrait is that he sees himself as both subject and object.

> And indeed there will be time
> To wonder, "Do I dare?" and "Do I dare?"
> Time to turn back and descend the stair,
> With a bald spot in the middle of my hair— (37-40)

In this striking image of disjunction, Prufrock positions himself behind and above his own head. A few lines later, he is horrified to see that same head, with its telltale bald spot, as an object on a serving platter.

> But though I have wept and fasted, wept and prayed,
> Though I have seen my head (grown slightly bald) brought in upon a platter,
> I am no prophet—and here's no great matter. (81-83)

This image of decapitation, an allusion to the fate of John the Baptist, is fascinating in a hundred ways, but most relevant here is that Prufrock sees his own head severed from his body, an image of his longing to escape from the tyranny of the intellect.

One of Eliot's more amusing depictions of mind-body dualism is in "Mr. Apollinax" (1914), a satiric portrait of his professor Bertrand Russell. Eliot mythologizes Russell as a mixture of Apollo, God of wisdom, and Priapus, the garden god whose signature is a gigantic phallus. Observing Russell at a Harvard party, the narrator is fascinated by the combination of brilliance and frivolity. He struggles to connect the mind of the famed logician with the surreal laughter "tinkling among the teacups."

He laughed like an irresponsible fœtus.
His laughter was submarine and profound
Like the old man of the sea's

. . . .

I looked for the head of Mr. Apollinax rolling under a chair
Or grinning over a screen
With seaweed in its hair. (7-9, 13-15)

Interestingly enough, others at Harvard, reputedly including George Santayana, also found a disconcerting incongruity between Russell's savage laughter and subtle intellect.

The most elegant dramatization of the conflict between mind and body in Eliot's early poems is in "Rhapsody on a Windy Night." One reason for the clarity of the debate is that the theme and structure of "Rhapsody," unlike that of the "First Debate" and "Prufrock," are anchored in the ideas of a major philosopher, Henri Bergson, who was grappling on a theoretical level with the same issues that troubled Eliot. The role of Bergson in Eliot's intellectual and artistic formation is explored in the following chapter.

2 Eliot's First Conversion

"Rhapsody on a Windy Night" and the 1913 Critique of Bergson

> My only conversion, by the deliberate influence of any individual, was a temporary conversion to Bergsonianism.
>
> Eliot, *A Sermon* (1948)

The state of mind that predisposed Eliot to study philosophy can be seen in the poems composed in 1910, the year he finished his work in language and literature at Harvard. "The Love Song of J. Alfred Prufrock," "Portrait of a Lady," and "Rhapsody on a Windy Night" feature a modern intellectual troubled by an ancient conflict, variously described in different periods and cultures, but always involving a perception of discontinuity. The year following his undergraduate and master's work was one of the most consequential in Eliot's intellectual development. In October 1910, he was a student in the humanities, unsure of his vocation; in October 1911, he was a PhD student in philosophy, on track to become a professor at Harvard or elsewhere. The most important element in the psychological and intellectual pivot was what, in his essay on Pascal, Eliot referred to as a "first conversion," an early enthusiasm that prepares the ground for more mature religious experience. The "first conversion" was precipitated by his infatuation with the philosophy of Henri Bergson, whose fame was related to his focus on the philosophical version of the existential issues represented in Eliot's early poems. During this year, Eliot read Bergson's books, attended his lectures in Paris, and experienced what he would later call a "temporary conversion" (*A Sermon*, 5). As suggested by the term *conversion*, his initial attraction was both personal and doctrinal. The personal element, repeatedly dramatized in the early poems, was distress regarding awareness of a gap between intellect and feeling and between mind and body. The doctrinal was Bergson's claim to have resolved these antinomies. The abrupt collapse of Eliot's enthusiasm is evident in "Rhapsody on a Windy Night" and other poems written during and shortly after his encounter with Bergson. The sudden despair, registered in "Rhapsody" as "the last twist of the knife," is an expression of the pain inherent in the realization that the chasm could not be bridged. Eliot's disillusionment led him to return to Harvard and begin a serious study of philosophy, in the course of which disappointment was replaced by analysis and dissent. In papers written in 1913 and 1914, he outlined the inconsistencies in Bergson's attempt to overcome mind/matter dualism.

This chapter discusses the Bergsonian claim that intrigued Eliot in the winter of 1910 and 1911, the skepticism revealed in poems dated March 1911, and the critique presented in a lecture in December 1913 for the Harvard Philosophical Club.[1] Eliot's dialectical swing from enchantment to disillusionment was followed by decades of mixed comments on Bergson, some favorable, some derogatory. He admired his prose, and in a 1916 review of G. V. Cunningham's study of Bergson, chided the author for neglecting "the many pregnant *aperçus* which make the reading of Bergson a delight." At the same time, he agreed with Cunningham's view that Bergson's account of intelligence and intuition is inherently contradictory (*Prose* 1.425, 427). Similarly, in a debate on Romanticism and classicism with John Middleton Murry, Eliot conceded that, although intuition "must have its place," it "must always be tested" by experience (*Prose* 3.272). In later life, he made a number of inconsistent statements about Bergson's influence. On one hand, he claimed that while writing his first important poems, including "Prufrock," he had been "entirely a Bergsonian";[2] on the other, he insisted that "Bergson had no influence on either my verse or my prose."[3] This ambivalence probably stems from the fact that, whatever he came to think of Bergson's ideas, he cherished the memory of his youth in Paris.

The Siren on the Seine

Bergson is the sweet Siren of adventurous philosophers.

Eliot, "Politics and Metaphysics" (1914)

Eliot earned his BA degree at Harvard in June 1910, and in October he crossed the Atlantic to study in France. He was attracted to Paris in part by its intellectual glamour, vividly recalled in a review of Henri Massis's *Evocations* (1931): "M. Massis is my contemporary, and the period of which he writes includes the time of my own brief residence in Paris." It was a moment, Eliot remembered, when figures such as Henri Matisse and Pablo Picasso, Remy de Gourmont, Émile Durkheim, Paul Claudel, and André Gide could be seen on the streets, and when, hovering over the scene, was "the spider-like figure of Bergson" (*Prose* 5.80–81). Bergson in 1910 was a celebrity whose lectures at the Collège de France were attended by overflow crowds. To get a seat, Eliot later recalled, one had to arrive an hour and fifteen minutes early; it would be difficult, he added, for anyone who had not actually been in the lecture hall to understand *la ferveur bergsonienne* ("What France Means to You," 94).

In the summer and fall of 1910, before leaving for Paris, Eliot began a close study of Bergson's books—*Essai sur les données immédiates de la conscience* (1889), *Matière et mémoire* (1896), and *L'Évolution créatice* (1907). The first two are framed by Bergson himself as critiques of dualism. In the first, he attacks Kant's separation of perception and reality; in the second, Descartes's separation of mind and body; and in both, he claims to have bridged the gap. In the third, beyond the scope of this chapter, he proposes an alternative to the theories of Darwin and Spencer. He accepts the principle of evolution, but rejects its internal mechanism, natural selection, for which he substitutes a spiritual element, the élan vital. Eliot has *Creative Evolution* in mind when, in the course of a discussion of the relationship between metaphysics and politics, he refers to "the two great modern fallacies: the fallacy of Progress, which is the Bergsonian fallacy, and the fallacy of the Relativity of Knowledge, which is the Pragmatic [i.e., Jamesian] fallacy" (*Prose* 1.94).

Bergson: *Time and Free Will*

The groundwork for the whole of Bergson's thought is presented in his first book, *Essai sur les données immédiates de la conscience*, translated in 1910 as *Time and Free Will*: *An Essay on the Immediate Data of Consciousness*. His subject is the debate between free will and determinism, and his argument, formulated as a critique of Kantian dualism, is that an understanding of the debate is contingent upon an understanding of time, and an understanding of time contingent upon an understanding of consciousness (*TFW* 222–40). Bergson dwells on the sharp distinction in *The Critique of Pure Reason* between *phenomena* and *noumena*, that is, between things as perceived and things as they are in themselves. The first is knowable, the second unknowable; the first is associated with cause and effect (and thus determinism) and the second with freedom. Bergson maintains that Kant's mistake was a failure to distinguish between two different aspects of time. The first, anchored in language, assumes identical and thus repeatable units—minutes, hours, years. This concept, associated with speech and clocks, is artificial. The second (*durée réelle*), anchored in consciousness, assumes an undivided continuum of heterogeneous and thus unrepeatable elements. The first treats time, which is a process, as if it were space with parts that could be separated, counted, and placed side by side. The second treats time as an indivisible part of consciousness. Bergson's larger purpose is to undermine determinism by associating it with a lockstep notion of time and to validate freedom by associating it with the unpredictable play of consciousness. In a related move, he argues that, by blurring the distinction between clock time, related to quantity, and the *durée réelle*, related to quality, Kant overlooked the parallel distinction between two modes of knowing—intellectual and intuitive—the first associated with science and the second with philosophy. In *An Introduction to Metaphysics* (1903), Bergson summarizes his critique of Kant, faulting him for analyzing the world in terms of logic instead of entering into it through intellectual sympathy (84-85).

Bergson's basic methodology, evident in *Time and Free Will*, can be thought of in three steps: (1) focusing on well-known pairings, such as mind and body or perception and reality; (2) generating smaller, more subtle binaries, such as clock time and *durée réelle* or intellect and intuition, which can be used to dismantle the larger ones; and (3) sidestepping the dualistic implications of his own theory by claiming that the qualitative subsumes the quantitative. For many readers, the most intriguing feature of Bergson's thought is the second step, namely, the formulation of intermediate binaries.

Bergson: *Matter and Memory*

Bergson's claim to have overcome dualism is even more emphatic in *Matière et mémoire*, translated in 1911 as *Matter and Memory*. His topic is psychophysical dualism, and his stated goal is to show how mind and body are related. He admits that his view is "frankly dualistic" in that it affirms the reality of both matter and spirit, but he promises to deal "with body and mind in such a way as to lessen greatly, if not to overcome, the theoretical difficulties which have always beset dualism" (*M&M* vii). His argument turns on an analysis of memory, which, as Théodule Ribot had contended in *Les maladies de la mémoire* (1881), is situated in the brain and should be identified with matter. Bergson counters that there are two types of memory: motor memory (habit), which is ingrained in the body, and "pure memory," which is part of consciousness (*M&M* 89-105). The first is associated with the mechanical, the second with the *durée réelle*. Bergson's solution to mind/matter dualism is to redefine matter as "an aggregate of 'images,' . . . more than that which the idealist calls a *representation,* but less than that which the realist calls a *thing*," and to redefine memory as "the intersection of mind and matter" (*M&M* vii; Bergson's italics). Memory is important because it is the halfway house in which matter, as redefined, interacts with spirit. He concludes by returning to "the problem towards which all our enquiries converge, that of the union of body and soul," and claims that "consciousness and matter, body and soul . . . meet each other in perception," that is, in the *durée réelle* (*M&M* 292-93). "Spirit borrows from matter the perceptions on which it feeds, and restores them to matter in the form of movements which it has stamped with its own freedom" (*M&M* 332).

Bergson's ideas resonated with those of a broad range of thinkers and writers, in part because they were consistent with a paradigmatic shift in intellectual history, widely discussed as a revolt of the twentieth-century against the seventeenth. Some, such as Thomas Kuhn, saw it as a shift from a Newtonian to an Einsteinian epistemology. In 1921, Eliot argued that the change originated as a decoupling of intellect and feeling, a "dissociation of sensibility" (*Prose* 2.380). In *Mapping Literary Modernism*, an intriguing study of time-consciousness in modernist writers such as Marcel Proust and Virginia Woolf, Ricardo J. Quinones associates the shift with two opposed understandings of time, the "predictive" and the "innovative," roughly equivalent to Bergson's distinction between clock time and *durée réelle*. Quinones argues that the triumph of the mechanistic (predictive) concept in the nineteenth century led, in a "paradox of time," to the early twentieth-century triumph of its opposite, the intuitive (innovative) (7, 38). From the beginning, however, there was vigorous dissent about the Bergsonian binaries, especially intellect and intuition. Well before Eliot's arrival in Paris, Bergson was under attack in France from the left by rationalists such as Julian Benda and from the right by neo-Thomists (Pilkington, 178ff; Marx, 30). In England, he was attacked by realists such as Bertrand Russell, whose 1912 essay in the *Monist* was widely read. In America, the criticism was mitigated by the fact that Bergson was championed by William James, whose studies in psychology had influenced his view of consciousness.

Eliot: "He said: this universe is very clever"

Bergson offered two courses during Eliot's time in Paris, each consisting of twenty lectures and extending from 9 December 1910 through 20 May 1911. One was on the problematics of personality and the other on the epistemology of Spinoza. Eliot attended at least seven of the lectures on personality and took detailed notes in French (1911).[4] It is possible, as Nancy Hargrove assumes, that he attended the entire series (38-40), but it is unlikely, for he ceased taking notes on 17 February. Even if he did continue to attend, he was no longer a disciple. In March 1911, he composed and dated two poems that project skepticism about Bergson's claim that he had overcome dualism. The first—"He said: this universe is very clever"—was left unpublished in his notebook; the second—"Rhapsody on a Windy Night"—is one of the brilliant four of 1910-11 included in *Prufrock and Other Observations*.

"He said: this universe is very clever" is a pencil draft dated March 1911. It has the structure of a sonnet, with three quatrains (abab cdcd efef) giving three approaches to life, followed by a summarizing remark. The sonnet intention is underscored by Eliot's separation of the first eight lines (octave) from the last seven with a horizontal line. The octave presents the traditional antithesis between determinism and freedom and enfolds within it the Bergsonian contrast between intellect and *l'intuition philosophique*.

> He said: this universe is very clever
>   The scientists have laid it out on paper
> Each atom goes on working out its law, and never
>   Can cut an unintentioned caper.
>
> He said: it is a geometric net
>   And in the middle, like a syphilitic spider
> The Absolute sits waiting, till we get
>   All tangled up and end ourselves inside her.   (1-8)

The hypotheses of both science and philosophy are clearly unsatisfactory.[5] The first is pure mechanism; the second, mush in the bloated belly of an infected spider, an image that anticipates Eliot's later association of Bergson with a spider hovering over Paris (*Prose* 5.81). The third quatrain, shunning intellectual distinctions, describes the crucifixion of one who, unlike philosophers and poets, did not "pass his life on office chairs," and whose death occurred on a rocky hill, not in an urban flat "Up six abysmal flights of broken stairs." This sonnet ends with a shift to the first person singular, in which can be heard the cri de coeur of the disintegrating self: "I am put together with a pot and scissors/Out of old clippings/No one took the trouble to make an article" (13-15).

Eliot: "Rhapsody on a Windy Night"

"Rhapsody on a Windy Night," which Eliot also dated March 1911, is a tour de force that deepens the debate broached in "He said." Although both compositions acknowledge the intractability of dualism, "Rhapsody" dramatizes a more profound psychological account of the despair attendant upon the collapse of the Bergsonian promise. Whereas the sonnet concludes with an image of cut-and-paste connections, the rhapsody ends with an image of violent and irreversible severance—"the last twist of the knife."

A number of critics have discussed the presence of Bergsonian elements in "Rhapsody." Given that Eliot embeds an allusion to *Matter and Memory* in the structure of the poem by anchoring it in the antithesis suggested in Bergson's title, and given that the narrator declares that "Memory" holds "the key," it is not surprising that the critical focus has been on Bergson's analysis of memory. In one of the earliest close readings, Piers Gray builds on the distinction between pure memory, associated with consciousness unrestrained by action (fantasy, reverie, dreams), and practical memory, associated with bodily movement issuing in action (habit). He points out that the disjunction between the conscious and unconscious life appears in most of Eliot's early poems, including "Prufrock" (43-52). Manju Jain, similarly, relates pure memory to perception and emphasizes the paralyzing conflict between freedom (consciousness) and automatism (habit) (*Critical Reading*, 70). In a perceptive reading based in part on Eliot's 1913 lecture, Donald Childs also discusses the poem as a dialogue between pure and practical memory (duration and the practical intellect), but his emphasis falls on Bergson's epistemology. He relates Bergson's opposition between intuition and intellect to a conflict in early Eliot between mysticism and logic (*From Philosophy*, 52-54). M. A. R. Habib summarizes Eliot's 1913 paper, placing the objections to Bergson in the context of contemporary philosophical debates between idealism and realism and, in literary terms, Romanticism and classicism (41-42). With few exceptions, critics who discuss Bergson's influence on "Rhapsody" identify the binaries represented in the poem, but also with few exceptions, they either dwell on Bergson's intermediate binaries to the exclusion of his larger thesis regarding dualism, or else they accept his slide into subjectivity.

In "Rhapsody," Eliot dramatizes the complexity of dualism by using the French technique of *dédoublement* (dividing the self in two). His persona, a young intellectual, tests the Bergsonian hypothesis for overcoming psychophysical and metaphysical dualism. Eliot's strategy involves two overlapping and complementary elements: one that is dialogic and prioritizes space, and one that is narrative and emphasizes time. The first establishes a dialogue between *durée* réelle and clock time and uses this as a template for the cognate polarities in *Time and Free Will* and *Matter and Memory*. As the rhapsody begins, a clock announces that the time is "twelve o'clock," but the narrator's mind registers the time as "midnight," the first marking a precise moment in an endlessly repeated series of identical moments, and the second marking a surge in the flow of memory and desire. This jarring juxtaposition of the quantitative and the qualitative introduces the "voices" in the dialogue. The second part of Eliot's strategy attaches the dialogue to a narrative base that gives forward momentum to the back-and-forth between the two types of time. The narrative motion is clear: both the hand of the clock and the mind of the narrator move in time, irreversibly, from twelve to four and from the streets to a furnished flat. The overall effect of Eliot's two-pronged strategy is that of a tedious debate superimposed on a parody of the Homeric motif of *nostos* (homecoming).

In the first stanza of "Rhapsody," the speaker is heading home at midnight; in the last, he arrives four hours later at his urban flat. In the intervening stanzas, he moves step by step, minute by minute, as consciousness and its other (both internal and external) mutter and sputter, cogitate and recollect, against the background of a relentless clock. The narrator's mantra is pure Bergson: in *Time and Free Will*, the French philosopher replaces Descartes's "I am a thinking thing" with "I am a conscious automaton" (*TFW* 168). In a striking parallel, Eliot's thinker is represented as an automaton aware of himself. His body has a mind of its own, his feet know the way home and move in tandem with the clock, not with the perceptions tussled by disgust and desire on a windy night. By conceiving of matter (a "twisted branch," a "crab with barnacles," the "hand of a child") as neither a thing nor an idea, but rather as a series of overlapping images, Eliot is probing the Bergsonian hypothesis. If it is valid, then the intellect will melt into consciousness, leading to transcendence of the divided self.

The narrator's journey takes him through streets separated into spaces illuminated alternatively by lamp light and moonlight.

> Twelve o'clock.
> . . . . . .
> Every street lamp that I pass
> Beats like a fatalistic drum,
> And through the spaces of the dark
> Midnight shakes the memory
> As a madman shakes a dead geranium. (1, 8–12)

This opening stanza is replete with juxtapositions of quantitative and qualitative elements. The clock is ticking, the streets are divided into blocks, the lamps emit steady drum-like sounds, and a body moves forward in measured steps. At the same time, an "I"—consciousness—muses, aware of midnight, madness, darkness, and fate. The split between the automatic movements of the body and the random oscillations of the mind is supported by the musical analogy suggested in the title. In this rhapsody, the bass line corresponds to the beats of a primitive drum and the treble to the improvisations of modern jazz. The drum beats are parallel to mechanical time, and the improvisations to the free play of consciousness.

In the middle stanzas, Eliot explores the Kantian distinction between perception and reality that is critiqued in *Time and Free Will* and the Bergsonian distinctions devised to overcome it. The conversation launched in the first stanza is developed, and the "remarks" of the lamp, associated with scientific observation, and the emergent memories, associated with feeling, alternate for the rest of the poem. The second and third stanzas establish the pattern.

> Half-past one,
> . . . . .
> The street-lamp said, 'Regard that woman
> Who hesitates toward you in the light of the door
> Which opens on her like a grin.
> You see the border of her dress
> Is torn and stained with sand,
> And you see the corner of her eye
> Twists like a crooked pin.' (13, 16–22)

In the next stanza, memory responds to the twisting eye by casting images of other twisted things upon the beach of consciousness.

> The memory throws up high and dry
> A crowd of twisted things;
> A twisted branch upon the beach
> . . . .
> A broken spring in a factory yard, . . . (23-25, 30)

Like the prostitute's dress, these twisted things are "torn and stained with sand"; like them, she is "Hard and curled and ready to snap." The images surface automatically from the depths of experience stored beneath consciousness. They surface, Bergson argues in *Matter and Memory*, because without them it would be impossible to interpret one's perceptions. "Perception is never a mere contact of the mind with the object present; it is impregnated with memory-images which complete it as they interpret it" (*M&M* 170).

The fourth stanza continues the pattern of structured oscillation between the Kantian world of appearance and reality and the Bergsonian world of intellect and intuition.

> Half-past two,
> The street-lamp said,
> 'Remark the cat which flattens itself in the gutter,
> Slips it out its tongue
> And devours a morsel of rancid butter.'
> So the hand of the child, automatic,
> Slipped out and pocketed a toy that was running along the quay.
> I could see nothing behind that child's eye. (33-40)

The analogy between the tongue of the cat and the hand of the child is explicit, and as Gray, Jain, and others have remarked, what the two have in common is that both are reflex actions, examples of Bergson's practical memory (Gray, 42; Jain, *Critical Reading*, 74). The conflict represented by the dialogue between perception and reality, Bergson argues, is a delusion that can be dispelled by thinking of matter as an "image" existing between what is normally thought of as mind and as matter (*M&M* vii-viii). The tongue of the cat, which exists between the mind of the narrator and the gutter in the street, pulls from the memory bank the claws of the crab and the hand of the child. Spatially understood, these things are quantitative; understood as part of *durée*, by contrast, they are qualitative, constantly in flux, interpenetrating, and melting into what Bergson's friend William James, in *Principles of Psychology* (1890), referred to as the stream of consciousness.

At half-past three, the lamp directs the eye of the narrator to the moon. The image points to Romanticism, but this is subverted by association with smallpox, nocturnal odors, and paper roses. The odor and disease, however, are characteristics, not of the moon in the sky, but of the moon in the mind. The external moon is a discrete material object; the moon within, by contrast, is an aging prostitute who "winks a feeble eye" and "twists a paper rose." Both the sullied wench in stanza two and the cosmic cocotte in stanza five are images mediated by literature, the former in large part by novels Eliot was reading at the time, including Charles Louis Philippe's *Bubu de Montparnasse*, and the latter by nineteenth-century poems and songs. Like the woman in the doorway, the moon is an image, but whereas the woman is diminished and dehumanized, the moon is humanized and enlarged. Unlike the prostitute in the street, however, she is a phantasm, which is why she harbors no memories and no resentment: "La lune ne garde aucune rancune." As the stanza concludes, the idea fades into the reality; the image of the moon as celestial flirt is supplanted by images of entrapment in narrow squalid spaces.

> The reminiscence comes
> Of sunless dry geraniums
> And dust in crevices,
> Smells of chestnuts in the streets,
> And female smells in shuttered rooms,
> And cigarettes in corridors
> And cocktail smells in bars. (62–68)

In the last stanza, the narrator arrives at his "home," a numbered flat in a series of similar or identical flats.

> The lamp said,
> 'Four o'clock,
> Here is the number on the door.
> Memory!
> You have the key,
> The little lamp spreads a ring on the stair.
> Mount.

> The bed is open; the tooth-brush hangs on the wall,
> Put your shoes by the door, sleep, prepare for life.'
>
> The last twist of the knife. (69–78)

The startling final image has been read in different ways, depending on whether or not the reader believes that Eliot remained a disciple of Bergson. Childs, who believes that he was "still a full-blown Bergsonian," suggests that the image confirms the French philosopher's critique of the practical intellect. "The life of the practical intellect is death; the death of the practical intellect is the immortality of Life everlasting." The image of the knife is "not the expression of dissatisfaction with Bergsonism, . . . but frustration with the inadequacy of his own intuitive ability. . . . The point of the poem is to acknowledge how difficult a task it is to escape the confines of the practical intellect" (*From Philosophy to Poetry*, 52–53, 62, 63).

Gray, on the other hand, sees the image as undermining Bergson's distinction between practical and pure memory. Practical memory has enabled the narrator to reach his door, find his key, brush his teeth, and get into bed. In sleep, Bergson claims in *Matter and Memory*, practical memory is replaced by pure memory; in sleep, there occurs "a relaxing . . . of the tension of the nervous system" that will enable him to replenish himself "in the life of dreams" (*M&M* 199–200). Gray argues, however, that the images that return in sleep will be those from which the narrator is seeking to escape, the images of "the lonely street inhabited by sterile unthinking life." He reads "The last twist of the knife" as the ironic realization that his dreams will consist of an endless replay of the images of his waking hours (50–51).

In the context of Bergson's optimism regarding the reintegration of intellect and feeling, the image of "the last twist of the knife" emerges as the interpretive crux of "Rhapsody." For the agonized narrator, the discontinuities remain painfully intact, and the "last twist" is the recognition that this is necessarily so. There is no escape—neither upward into high-minded ideas nor downward into the rubble of history. An additional twist comes from the realization that mechanism is ingrained in life itself, which consists of the repetition of identical hours, days, and years. Confined by what Quinones calls the "predictive" aspect of existence, the speaker is left with the horror of unmitigated ennui. The final image, as suggested by Gray and Childs, is triggered by the immediately preceding line, "sleep, prepare for life." But the last line is also set apart. As indicated by spacing and the disappearance of the quotation marks, it functions as a coda reflecting retrospectively on the overall experience of this ironic *nostos*. It is the "last" in a series of "twists"—on the street and in the mind, all tinged with physical and moral decay. The corner of the prostitute's eye "twists like a crooked pin," the memory tosses up "a twisted branch upon the beach," and the moon "twists a paper rose." It is, however, one thing to remember the shape of a motionless dead branch and quite another to imagine the twist of a plunging knife. As the "last twist," it subsumes the others and augurs catastrophe. The disquietude evident in "Rhapsody" anticipates the critique Eliot was to give in his 1913 lecture at Harvard.[6]

Eliot: "Inconsistencies in Bergson's Idealism"

> By the seduction of his style we come to believe that the Bergsonian world is the only world, and that we have been living among shadows. It is not so.
>
> Eliot, "Politics and Metaphysics" (1914)

In September 1911, Eliot returned to America, and in October, he began work at Harvard on a PhD in philosophy. In a seminar paper written in the spring of 1913, he defended Kant's position that the mechanical and the moral cannot be merged or reconciled. Kant's "permanent virtue" is to have seen that dualism is embedded in the human condition, to have recognized that "the twofold aspect is irreducible" (*Prose* 1.53). In December 1913, Eliot presented a critique of Bergson for the Harvard Philosophical Club, of which he was then president.[7] As a reexamination of books he had recently studied, "Inconsistencies in Bergson's Idealism" is retrospectively illuminating in regard to the poems composed in 1910–11, especially "Rhapsody on a Windy Night." Eliot's thesis is that Bergson's claim to have mediated between idealism and realism, in the process overcoming dualism, is too weak to warrant assent. En route to this conclusion, he considers three interrelated steps in Bergson's methodology: (1) the focus on received antinomies such as idealism and realism, (2) the use of a distinction between quantity and quality to generate his own more nuanced binaries, such as the two aspects of time, and (3) the use of his pairings to overcome the larger ones with which he had begun.

Eliot begins by scrutinizing the sine qua non of Bergson's philosophy: the assumption of a clear distinction between "extrinsic and intrinsic multiplicity," that is, quantity and quality. "If this antithesis breaks down we get a doctrine essentially absolutistic as well as idealistic" (*Prose* 1.67). The quantitative, as has been noted, assumes that reality is composed of parts that can be separated and counted, the qualitative that it consists of indivisible interpenetrating states of consciousness. One is associated with exterior objects immobilized in space, the other with interior states fluctuating in time. Eliot examines the examples that Bergson presents in support of this distinction and finds that most actually subvert his argument. He points to Bergson's claim that there are two ways of knowing that a bell has tolled four times. One is by counting the strokes; the other is "not by counting, but because *four* strokes is a *quality*, different from three, five, and the rest" (*Prose* 1.69; Eliot's italics). The notion that a specific number of strokes can be perceived purely as a quality, Eliot says, is not only inherently contradictory, but inconsistent with Bergson's concession that qualitative perception "contains number *en puissance* [in potential]" (*Prose* 1.70). Eliot shows that, even for Bergson, qualitative perception is never pure, that it inevitably includes an element of number and thus of spatiality. "I cannot recognize, as Bergson does here, any essential difference between the . . . physical world . . . and the world of introspection. Number exists in the latter as in the former" (*Prose* 1.70). Number exists, then, in both the extrinsic world where the bell tolls and intrinsic one in which it is heard. This conclusion had been anticipated in "Rhapsody." As the narrator moves into the dark, he is visited by memories of "twisted things" (plural, as separate items)—a "twisted branch upon the beach," "a broken spring in a factory yard." Admittedly, they are perceived qualitatively, as a disintegrating world, but they are also perceived quantitatively, as a list of objects with spatial locations.

In undermining Bergson's antithesis between quantity and quality, Eliot discredits the most famous part of his thought—his signature binaries; in further analysis, he delivers a collective coup de grace. His task is simplified because all of these dichotomies (clock time and *durée*, intellect and intuition, habit and pure memory) are at bottom different versions of the distinction between quantity and quality, so in discussing any one of them, he is commenting on all of the others. In regard to the theory of time, Eliot interrogates the identification of *durée réelle* with reality. In *Time and Free Will*, Bergson associates *durée* with consciousness, consciousness with temporality, temporality with motion or change, and finally, all of these cognate entities with reality. In *Matter and Memory*, on the other hand, he connects reality to stasis and spatiality by declaring that perception of reality depends on immobilization: "To perceive means to immobolise" ("Perçevoir signifie immobiliser") (*M&M* 275). Regarding this contradiction, Eliot asks, "Where again is the reality—in the consciousness or in that which is perceived?"

(*Prose* 1.77). Regarding Bergson's insistence that the *durée* consists of interpenetrating moments in flux, Eliot responds, "It is only as the moments *do not wholly* interpenetrate, that we can be said to have . . . change at all" (*Prose* 1.79; Eliot's italics added). That is because the perception of change depends on the perception of difference (number, spatiality, exteriority). He concludes by rejecting one of Bergson's foundational theories: "We cannot rest at the *durée réelle*. It is simply not final" (*Prose* 1.79). The contradictory nature of the *durée* is all too evident in "Rhapsody." Reality is not synonymous with consciousness; it exceeds consciousness, encompassing the tongue of the cat and the toothbrush on the wall.

The overall purpose of Eliot's 1913 critique, announced at the top of his lecture, was to evaluate Bergson's intervention in the long-standing quarrel between idealism and realism. Building on his demonstration of the weakness of the *qualité/quantité* antithesis and the contradictions of the *durée*, he analyzes Bergson's "attempt to occupy a middle ground between idealism and realism" (*Prose* 1.67). He concludes that "the crux of the *affaire Bergson* seems to me to be in his attempt to invest with the title of reality this middle territory. . . . This territory cannot be regarded as *selbststandig* [self-sufficient]" (*Prose* 1.78). Twice in the lecture Eliot quotes Bergson's explicit identification of reality with something existing between space and time, between things and perceptions: "What is given, what is *real, is something intermediate between the divided extension* [space] *and the pure inextension* [time]" (*Prose* 1.71, 74; M&M 326; Eliot's italics).[8] He remarks that he does not think "one could find a more significant passage in the whole of Bergson's work" than this (*Prose* 1.76).

To support his rejection of the in-between image as a solution to the conundrums associated with dualism, Eliot reviews Bergson's theory of matter and its relation to consciousness. As normally understood, matter and memory would be opposites, but in Bergson's economy, they lose their differentiation. In a passage quoted (and partially translated) by Eliot, Bergson says: "Matter, such as we seize it in a concrete perception which occupies always a certain durée, dérive en grande partie de la mémoire" (*M&M* 200–201; *Prose* 1.75). Stripping matter of its materiality, Bergson redefines it as an "aggregate of images" and defines image as more than a representation but less than a thing (*M&M* vii). This, in Eliot's view, is a sleight of hand, and moreover, in direct contradiction to the notion of "brute matter" in *Creative Evolution*.

The discrediting of Bergson's intermediate or bridge reality leads Eliot back to his overall point—Bergson's claim to be neither a realist nor an idealist. Based on his consistently absorbing the quantitative into the qualitative, Eliot argues that Bergson is fundamentally an idealist. Bergson assumes that "consciousness is a grade of reality above pure space." Space is real, but less real than time; it is "an inferior grade of reality" (*Prose* 1.71); it is first subordinated to and then subsumed by consciousness. Most or all of Bergson's attempts to reconcile oppositions entail this slide into subjectivism—thus time is more real than space, quality than quantity, free will than determinism, consciousness than matter. As Eliot points out, Bergson disposes of quantities by reducing them to qualities (*Prose* 1.71). In a review of Cunningham's book on Bergson, Eliot applauds the author for pointing out a similar discrepancy in regard to intellect and intuition. On the one hand, Bergson assumes that they are opposites; on the other, he insists that intuition subsumes intelligence, and thus "there is no essential difference between the intellect and this intuition" (*Creative Evolution*, 360). Of Cunningham's criticism, Eliot remarks that the "difficulty in Bergson's statements has never been better put" (*Prose* 1.427).

Eliot's rejection of Bergson's claim to have invested with reality a "middle territory between the real and the ideal" (*Prose* 1.78) is part of a larger repudiation of the attempt to connect matter and spirit in humanism, the collapse of which is one of the signature elements in literary modernism and in Eliot's poetry. In "Rhapsody on a Windy Night," he shows that the bridge reality is an illusion, and a decade later, he underscores the point with more detachment in *The Hollow Men*, his brilliant farewell to formal philosophy—"Between the idea/And the reality/. . . Falls the Shadow" (*HM* V). Eliot's immersion in Bergsonism represents a turning point in his intellectual biography, in part because of its organic connection to his existential concerns, in part because it was his initiation into philosophical methodology, and in part because it remained a resource for his poetry. Having discovered the "inconsistencies" of Bergson's idealism, he turned to a consideration of the possible strengths of the idealist tradition in general and of dialectic in particular. In 1911, he returned to Harvard as a PhD student in philosophy in the hope that other and greater thinkers could deliver more coherent responses to the post-Darwinian debate between idealism and realism. His work on Bradley, a more uncompromising idealist, is the subject of the next chapter.

3 Eliot's Debt to F. H. Bradley

Reality and Appearance in 1914

> Metaphysics [is] an attempt to know reality as against mere appearance, or the study of first principles or ultimate truths, or again the effort to comprehend the universe, not simply piecemeal or by fragments, but somehow as a whole.
>
> Bradley, *Appearance and Reality*

Eliot was a student at Harvard from 1906 to 1916, a decade that included a stint at the Sorbonne and an academic year at Oxford.[1] In June 1910, he received his BA degree, and in October, as discussed in the previous chapter, he went to Paris, drawn by the opportunity to attend the lectures of Henri Bergson at the Collège de France. Although his enthusiasm for Bergsonism was brief, it had lasting consequences in that it led him to transfer his allegiance from poetry to philosophy. On his return from Europe, Eliot commenced work at Harvard in modern philosophy and the social sciences. Of the thinkers that he studied at Harvard, he later singled out F. H. Bradley and J. G. Frazer for special commendation, less for their ideas than for the pattern of thinking that shaped those ideas, and that, in turn, Eliot claimed, shaped the sensibility of his generation (*Prose* 2.517). The central strains in his own developing outlook—dialectic and relativism—can be associated with these two thinkers. In Bradley's *Appearance and Reality*, as in all idealism, the dialectical imagination is fundamental. In Frazer's *Golden Bough*, as in most comparative studies, relativism is basic. In this chapter, I explore the relevance of Bradley to Eliot's mind and art, and in the following chapter, that of Frazer.

Context: Temporalization of the Chain of Being

(The lengthened shadow of a man
  Is history, said Emerson
Who had not seen the silhouette
  Of Sweeney straddled in the sun.)

Eliot, "Sweeney Erect"

The essential context informing Eliot's philosophical studies is the late eighteenth-century temporalization of the chain of being, a development that paved the way for breakthroughs in the natural and social sciences. The shift from a view of reality consisting of more or less static entities linked in space to a view consisting of fluid entities moving through time is at the heart of nineteenth-century intellectual life. It was a shift of emphasis from mechanism to organicism and from Being to Becoming. The emphasis on change was liberating for scientists, including Charles Lyell (*Principles of Geology*, 1830–33) and Charles Darwin (*On the Origin of Species*, 1859), who argued that the earth and its inhabitants are immeasurably old and still changing. In subsequent generations, the quest for origins begun in geology and biology led to an explosion of activity in the social sciences, including anthropology, sociology, psychology, and religion.

As indicated in the chapter on Eliot's critique of Bergson, the focus on time in the sciences had an enormous influence on the study of the humanities, including philosophy, which to remain relevant had to deal with the implications of evolutionary models and the dissolution of boundaries between categories. In *The Revolt against Dualism*, A. O. Lovejoy argued that the bedrock assumption of the makers of the modern mind (Descartes, Locke, and Newton) was that the precondition for understanding the world was the strict separation of subject and object. In the post-Hegelian, post-Darwinian, time-drenched reconsideration of the subject/object question, major philosophers rejected the division of the world into irreconcilable parts. Their attempts to overcome dualism typically involved privileging one extreme or the other: the subject absorbing the object (mysticism, idealism) or the object subsuming the subject (materialism, realism) (Lovejoy, 1–5, 83–85). But strictly speaking, as Eliot noted in an essay on the British idealist T. H. Green, this is a sleight of hand: "It is only by an abuse of transcendental dialectic that [one] can reduce the world to the one or the other"

(*Prose* 1.150). Some thinkers, notably Bergson, claimed to be neither idealist nor realist, but they inevitably slipped into a weak version of one or the other. The philosophers to whom Eliot was most indebted included distinguished representatives of the various camps—the idealists F. H. Bradley and Josiah Royce, the realists Bertrand Russell and Ralph Barton Perry, and the fence-straddlers Bergson (vitalism) and William James (pragmatism).

When Eliot read Bergson's *Time and Free Will* in Paris, he was a literature student with an interest in ideas; when he entered the Harvard Philosophy Department, he became part of philosophy proper and joined the professional debate about idealism and realism. The department was then at the pinnacle of its prestige, largely due to the eminence of two philosophers, James and Royce, and to the distinction of visitors such as Russell.[2] James, like Bergson, positioned himself as a bridge figure. His attempt to mediate between idealism and materialism by focusing on results is evident in his definition of pragmatism "as the *attitude of looking away from first things, principles, 'categories,' supposed necessities; and of looking towards last things, fruits, consequences, facts*" (76-77; James's italics). Russell, who taught a course in symbolic logic at Harvard in 1914 (attended by Eliot), had disciples in the department—the neo-realists. In a later comment on the department's ideological fissure, Eliot remarked that the neo-realists were "animated by a missionary zeal against the Hegelian Idealism which was the orthodox doctrine of the philosophical departments of American universities. . . . [They] were on the whole anti-religious and . . . professed considerable respect for Mr. Bertrand Russell and his Cambridge friends" (*Prose* 5.249). Royce was a neo-idealist, and after the death of James in 1910, the department's most influential thinker. In *The World and the Individual* (1901), he addressed the issue that was always at the core of his thought: the attempt to bridge the finite and the infinite, the individual and the Absolute. "The essence of this Doctrine of Evolution," he claimed, "lies in the fact that it recognizes the continuity of man's life with that of an extra-human realm whose existence is hinted to us by our experience of Nature" (242).

T. S. Eliot was not the first in his family to reflect on the intellectual and spiritual implications of Darwin's work. On 18 June 1863, four years after the publication of *Origin of Species*, the poet's father, Henry Ware Eliot, gave the commencement address at Washington University in St. Louis, an institution founded by his father, William Greenleaf Eliot.[3] The nineteen-year-old graduate begins his oration, entitled "Philosophy the Science of Truth," by conceding that truth has to do with evolution: "Truth is the development of the laws of all things, natural and spiritual; of their creation, their existence and their disappearance" (3). The problem is that the biological sciences, no matter how brilliant, cannot reveal the underlying laws of evolution or explain the evolution of spirit or mind. Fortunately, as Eliot explains, there is a higher science: "Philosophy is a science. . . . To philosophize is to comprehend. To comprehend is not merely to know, but to verify what we know" (6, 7). The higher science, as Mr. Eliot describes it, consists of "analysis and synthesis, the dissection and reconstruction of the mental phenomena" (4). He builds his thesis on a careful distinction between appearance and reality, a topic that would later be explored in the magnum opus of F. H. Bradley and subsequently in the PhD dissertation of his own unborn son, Thomas. Decades later, as a student in the Harvard Philosophy Department, the son would refute the position that philosophy or religion could be regarded as a science. Henry's commencement address ends with a flourish, a tribute to Jesus as the thinker who "came to make Philosophy divine" (11), in support of which he quotes Christ's words to Pilate—"To this end was I born, and for this cause came I into the world, that I should bear witness unto the truth" (John 18:37).

Kant, Bradley, and the Limits of the Dialectical Imagination

> The life of a soul does not consist in the contemplation of one consistent world but in the painful task of unifying (to a greater or less extent) jarring and incompatible ones, and passing, when possible, from two or more discordant viewpoints to a higher which shall somehow include and transmute them.
>
> Eliot, *Knowledge and Experience* (1916)

T. S. Eliot's most disciplined search for truth occurred during his years as a graduate student in the Harvard Philosophy Department. As he noted on several occasions, the department was especially strong in idealism, and his courses included work in the major figures—Kant, Hegel, Bradley, Joachim, and Royce. Eliot's engagement with Bradley falls into two blocks—the first in various seminars in 1913 and 1914, and the second, which was far more intensive, in weekly tutorials with Bradley's disciple Harold H. Joachim at Merton College (Oxford) in the fall of 1914. In the first block, Eliot studied Bradley's metaphysics (the nature of reality), and in the second, his epistemology (theory of knowledge). In April 1913, he read Bradley in two Harvard seminars—"The Philosophy of Kant" and "The Nature of Reality." In June 1913, he purchased a copy of *Appearance and Reality*, and by early

1914, he had decided to study with Joachim at Bradley's Oxford college. In the 1914 Michaelmas term, he wrote weekly papers on Bradley's epistemology for Joachim.[4] The following discussion will be informed by these papers and offer extensive comments on two other documents. The first, "O little voices of the throats of men," is a poem focused on Bradley that Eliot composed en route from Harvard to Oxford. The second, *Knowledge and Experience in the Philosophy of F. H. Bradley*, is his doctoral thesis, a draft of which he completed during his Bradley tutorials at Merton.

In the 1913 Kant seminar, Eliot examined Bradley's critique of Kant's dualism in *Appearance and Reality*. The problem with Kant, as Bradley describes it, is the division of reality into two irreducible elements. "The universe . . . falls apart into two regions. . . . One of these is the world of experience and knowledge—in every sense without reality. The other is the kingdom of reality—without either knowledge or experience. . . . On one side, phenomena, . . . things as they are to us, . . . on the other side [noumena], Things as they are in themselves" (*A&R* 110). Bradley dissolves Kant's antithesis by distinguishing between two different meanings of phenomenon, or "appearance"—one related to perception (epistemology) and the other to substance (metaphysics). In the first, associated with Kant, appearance is that which is perceived by the senses and is the *opposite* of reality; in the second, privileged by Bradley, it is that which is partial (incomplete, finite, transient, and limited to a point of view) and is the *essence* of reality (*A&R* 429-31; *Truth and Reality*, 272-73). The second meaning is far more important, and when it is accepted, the wall between unreal and real, phenomena and noumena, collapses. Although no one appearance is reality in its fullness, each is an aspect of reality, which is nothing more than the aggregate of its appearances. Bradley's appearances are finite and knowable; and unlike noumena, which is a catchphrase for the unknowable, his Absolute is an empirical reality known by its myriad constituent experiences. "Reality itself is nothing at all apart from appearances. . . . Reality appears in its appearances, and they are its revelation; otherwise they could be nothing whatever" (*A&R* 488-89).

In the second of three reports for the seminar, Eliot evaluates Bradley's attempt to overcome Kant's dualism by using dialectic. He agrees that "Kant has erected an impassable barrier between the empirical and the transcendental" and, moreover, that this is rooted in a denial of the reality of experience (appearances, the finite). Echoing Bradley, Eliot insists that appearances are real: "The phenomenal is the real, for us" (*Prose* 1.45). Moreover, he praises Bradley's skepticism and applauds his rejection of Kant's concept of an abstract and vacuous thing-in-itself. He agrees, moreover, that insofar as Kant attempts to contemplate the knower and the known from outside of human experience, he fails by definition to understand reality. In this period of his engagement with Bradley, Eliot accepts his critique of Kant but objects to the extension of his argument to its limit in the Absolute, saying that when pushed to its extreme, his position becomes "only the pathetic primitive human *Credo* in ultimate explanation and ultimate reality which haunts us like the prayers of childhood. This Absolute is mystical, because desperate. Ultimate truth remains inaccessible" (*Prose* 1.42). Like all theoretical constructs, idealism has its limits. Eliot's methodological suggestion is "not to pursue any theory to a conclusion, and to avoid complete consistency" (*L*1.88).

Bradley and Poetry: Blowing against the Wind and Spitting against the Rain

> Do I know how I feel? Do I know what I think?
> Let me take ink and paper, let me take pen and ink . . .
> There is something which should be firm but slips just at my finger tips.
>
> Eliot, "Do I know how I feel?"

During his three years as a philosophy student at Harvard, Eliot wrote very little poetry, and he was to write very little in the following year at Oxford. But in the three months between Harvard and Oxford, he wrote a number of poems, most of which he left unrevised and unpublished. The effect of his attention to Bradley is evident in this work. For one thing, as Lyndall Gordon has pointed out, there is a change in the point of view. The paralyzed Hamlet of the early masterpieces "is replaced by a new dominant figure, an almost demented philosopher, keeping all-night vigils in his room" (62).[5] There is, moreover, a shift in setting, from city streets and spacious drawing rooms to furnished flats, and in theme, and from social estrangement to philosophical disenchantment. The central character is still quarreling with himself, but his "overwhelming questions" are now focused on uncertainty about what is real (appearance and reality) and distress about how it can be known (contradictions and dialectic).

At the end of June 1914, Eliot left Boston to attend a summer course at the University of Marburg before proceeding to Oxford. On 19 July, shortly after arriving in Germany, he confided to Conrad Aiken that he had just "written some stuff—about fifty lines" but that he found it to be "shamefully laboured" (*L*1.146). A few days later, he sent Aiken "The Love Song of St. Sebastian" and forty-nine lines of an untitled piece that begins "Oh little voices of the throats of men." The first, the psychomachy of a deranged lover, is linked by its title to "The Love Song of J. Alfred Prufrock"; the second, the meandering thoughts of a disillusioned student of *Appearance and Reality*, is both a sequel to his Harvard work on Bradley and a prelude to his work with Joachim at Oxford.

"Oh little voices" consists of the night-thoughts of a man dozing in an armchair by a window. The thinker is identified as a poet ("singer") troubled by street clamor and a philosopher stymied by "contradictions" and the failure of "dialectic." The poem is divided into three parts. The first and last constitute a frame in which an aesthete ponders questions about the relation of life and art, and a central section in which he considers Bradley's *Appearance and Reality* as a guide though interminable mazes. His conclusion is that intellectuals "who seek to balance pleasure and pain . . . blow against the wind and spit against the rain" (10, 11). The framing elements (1-14, 35-49) are sonnets, and the middle section (15-34) consists of two ten-line stanzas, each beginning with an allusion to Bradley's *Appearance and Reality*. The mise-en-scène is evident in the transition to the closing frame: "He drew the shawl about him as he spoke/And dozed in his arm-chair till the morning broke" (35-36). "As the thin light shiver[s] through the tree," plumes of lilac sweep across the panes and serpentine shadows invade the room.

> Across the floor the shadows crawled and crept
> . . . .
> They crawled about his shoulders and his knees;
> They rested for a moment on his hair
> Until the morning drove them to their lair. (39, 42-44)

In the poem's opening lines, the persona's musings are launched by "little voices" that disturb his composure and undercut his idealism.

> Oh little voices of the throats of men
> That come between the singer and the song;
> Oh twisted little hands of men held up
> To rend the beautiful and curse the strong. (1-4)

The closing frame reveals that the "little voices" are fantasies prompted by the sound of the wind whistling in the chimney and rattling the shutters.

> And had those been human voices in the chimneys
> And at the shutters, and along the stair,
> You had not known whether they laughed or wept. (47-49)

The cries of the phantoms stimulate the budding philosopher to contrast his cerebrations in a closed room with labor in the dust and sun. "For what could be more real than sweat and dust and sun?/And what more sure than night and death and sleep?" (13-14). The questions raise the philosophical issues Eliot himself was dealing with: What is real? What is certain? What is worthwhile? He accepts the brain work of philosophical insomniacs as real, but "blowing against the wind" is not real in the same way and to the same extent as the handwork of the laborer. The persona's questions reveal that he is inclined to believe, contra idealists, that sweat and tears are real in themselves, apart from transcendence to higher entities.

In the body of the poem, Eliot engages in a debate with Bradley. Each of the two stanzas begins with the voice of the eminent philosopher—"Appearances, appearances, he said." In subsequent lines, the student ("I have searched") responds. Eliot's two stanzas are a clear reference to the two sections of *Appearance and Reality*. In the first part, Bradley demonstrates that certain well-known theories describing appearance and reality as opposites are self-contradictory; in the second, he argues that recognizing appearances as finite components of a larger whole dissolves the contradictions. Eliot's first stanza explores part one, Bradley's critique of dualistic theories.

> Appearances appearances he said,
> I have searched the world through dialectic ways;
> I have questioned restless night and torpid days,
> And followed every by-way where it led;
> And always find the same unvaried
> Intolerable interminable maze.
> Contradiction is the debt you would collect
> And still with contradiction are you paid. (15-22)

The quest for clarity ends in the realization that attempts to account for reality in terms of binaries trap one in a circular world. Existing theories, all anchored in dualism, end in an "interminable maze" or infinite regress, with no exit.

The second philosophical stanza takes up the second part of *Appearance and Reality*, with its paradoxical claims that appearances are real and knowable because they are a constituent of experience, but unreal because they are, to use another of Bradley's formulations, mere adjectives of a larger whole (*A&R* 289, 291).

> Appearances, appearances, he said,
> And nowise real; unreal, and yet true;
> Untrue, yet real;—of what are you afraid?
> . . . .
> This word is true on all the paths you tread
> As true as truth need be, when all is said. (25–27, 30–31)

In this stanza, the idealist philosopher seems to be speaking throughout. He repeats the questions raised in the opening frame—What is true? What is real? —and chides the student thinker for his recalcitrance. "O little voices" reflects Eliot's position in the summer of 1914, at the end of his work at Harvard: he is persuaded by part 1 of *Appearance and Reality*, dealing with the contradictions of dualism; he wavers on part 2, in which the contradictions are overcome by appealing to the Absolute.

Knowledge and Experience: Bradley and the Dialectical Imagination

> The token that a philosophy is true is, I think, the fact that it brings us to the exact point from which we started.
>
> Eliot, "The validity of artificial distinctions" (1914)

In October 1914, Eliot began his work on Bradley at Oxford under Joachim's supervision. In the Michaelmas term, he worked primarily on Bradley and his critics, including Russell, and in Hilary and Trinity terms, 1915, he focused on Plato and Aristotle. As noted in his report to the dean at Harvard, the eight Michaelmas essays dealt with "the questions considered in the thesis which I hope to present for the degree of Ph.D." (*L*1.92). The weekly essays, six of which have survived, fed directly into his dissertation, a draft of which was completed by the end of term in early December.[6]

Eliot's dissertation is an analysis of Bradley's dialectical epistemology. Knowledge, Bradley maintains, does not begin with thought but with feeling, which is the primary "fact" in epistemology. He posits a dialectical triad: "immediate experience," "intellectual experience," and "transcendent experience," with the first and third phases made up of feeling, and the intermediate term made up of thought. As Bradley explains in "On our Knowledge of Immediate Experience": "We in short have experience in which there is no distinction between my awareness and that of which it is aware. There is an immediate feeling, a knowing and being in one, with which knowledge begins; and, though this in a manner is transcended, it nevertheless remains throughout as the present foundation of my known world" (*Truth and Reality*, 159-60).

It is the nature of immediate experience to fall apart, to make way for perception in terms of self and not-self. This is the level of analytical (intellectual) experience, the dualistic level of knower and known, subject and object. Although most people never get beyond this level, a few transcend it, achieving a sort of nonanalytical practical wisdom. This empirical wisdom, in Bradley's view, involves a return to the wholeness of immediate experience, but not to its innocence. Whereas immediate experience is characterized by a *knowing and feeling* that comes *before* thinking, transcendent experience is characterized by a *thinking and feeling* that comes *afterward* and is achieved through thought. Transcendent experience is the level that Eliot later refers to as "a direct sensuous apprehension of thought, or a recreation of thought into feeling" (*Prose* 2.379).

Eliot's doctoral thesis is both a critique and a defense of Bradley's thought; more important for his intellectual development, it is a demonstration of his absorption of Bradley's methodology. Three aspects of the approach in *Appearance and Reality* left an indelible mark on Eliot's imagination. The first is Bradley's insistence on the primacy of feeling in the development of knowledge, the emphasis on feeling as the original "fact." The second is his use of a post-Hegelian dialectic in which oppositions are overcome by a process of transcendence that moves forward by looping back. The third is his skepticism, evident in his attack on dualism and his determination to clear away underlying prejudice. These Bradleian attributes, incipient in the 1913 Kant seminar, were full-blown in Eliot's essays by the fall of 1914 and were to carry over into his criticism, including "Tradition and the Individual Talent."

Eliot describes this epistemology in the first chapter of his dissertation (*Prose* 1.243-57). Moreover, in a striking instance of the overlap between the idea and the reality, he mentions in correspondence an experience that reveals an intimate connection between his personal life and Bradley's epistemological triad. Within three weeks of finishing his draft, alone in London on New Year's Eve, 1914, he wrote to Conrad Aiken about his midnight rambles on the city streets. "I have been going through one of those nervous sexual attacks which I suffer from when alone in a city. . . . One walks about the street with one's desires, and one's refinement rises up like a wall whenever opportunity approaches" (*L*1.82). To put this in Bradleian terms: knowledge begins in the ground swell of desire at night on the London street, an immediate experience (a "fact") that is not mediated through the intellect. This feeling is prior to the development of self-consciousness and prior to the distinction between subject and object. This stage melts into a dualistic stage of self-consciousness in which he becomes aware of himself as subject and the prostitute as the object of desire. In this stage, refinement (associated with intellect and class consciousness) rises up and rebukes desire. Ideally, the antithesis between desire and refinement would be transcended in a greater unity, but realistically, as Eliot suggests in his thesis, the third stage is beyond the reach of most people, including the young man who is both attracted to and repelled by the lady of the night. Thus Bradley's epistemology falters at the crucial stage of the return that would complete the dialectical process.

The last of Eliot's 1914 essays on Bradley, "The validity of artificial distinctions" includes an unequivocal statement that his own thinking is dialectical.[7]

> The token that a philosophy is true is . . . the fact that it brings us to the exact point from which we started. We shall be enriched . . . by our experience on the Grand Tour, but we shall not have been allowed to convey any material treasures through the Custom House. And the wisdom which we shall have acquired will not be part of the argument which brings us to the conclusion; it is not part of the book, but is written in pencil on the fly-leaf. For the point to which we return should be the same, but somehow is not, but is a higher stage of reality. (*Prose* 1.191)

Eliot pictures the pursuit for truth as a journey that begins and ends at home. The tourist collects treasures, but in order to return, he has to surrender them to the Customs agent. There are some acquisitions, however, that cannot be taken away—the internal changes wrought by his adventures and the wisdom accumulated en route. In this paragraph, written as he finished his dissertation, Eliot accepts the general principle of Bradley's dialectic —the idea that moving forward always involves moving back. The dialectical intention is clinched by the statement that the point to which one returns is "a higher stage of reality."

In the same essay, Eliot emphasizes the interplay of faith and skepticism in the construction and maintenance of philosophical positions. It is folly, he claims, to try to prove philosophical conclusions. They can "only be maintained by faith, a faith which, like all faith, should be seasoned with a skilful sauce of skepticism. And skepticism too is a faith, a high and difficult one" (*Prose* 1.187). The sauce of skepticism that simmers throughout Bradley's work is carried over to Eliot's dissertation and to his writing of the next decade and beyond. Bradley's skepticism is part of the reason that Eliot associates the British thinker with an unbiased pursuit of truth. But as previously noted, although Eliot absorbed Bradley's methodology and many of his positions, he stopped short of accepting the conclusion that oppositions are overcome in the Absolute. In the last Michaelmas essay, after saying that he accepts Bradley's philosophy "with certain reservations," he scribbles in the margin: "I cannot see my way to the admission that 'Reality is spiritual' " (*Prose* 1.192n7). This is more than a "certain reservation"; it is an unambiguous rejection of Bradley's core principle, as stated in the closing lines of *Appearance and Reality*: "We may fairly close this work then by insisting that Reality is spiritual. . . . Outside of spirit there is not, and there cannot be, any reality" (*A&R* 552).

Eliot concludes by complimenting Bradley for his courage in pursuing truth even when he knows it may be fruitless. The "positive merit" of *Appearance and Reality* is that it presents no "positive result" whatsoever. "When a philosopher pretends to emerge with some 'positive result' which can be formulated . . . some discovery which informs us that anything is anything else than what we supposed it to be before we began to philosophise,—then the philosopher is simply pulling out of his pocket what he put there himself" (*Prose* 1.191). Eliot finished his work at Merton in June 1915. He mood is caught in "Introspection," which according to Rainey was composed between July and August (198).

> The mind was six feet deep in a
> cistern and a brown snake with a tri-
> angular head having swallowed his
> tail was struggling like two fists

interlocked. His head slipped along
the brick wall, scraping at the
cracks.

Eliot's admiration for his Merton tutor, Professor Joachim, was based on the observation that, like Bradley, he combined the deepest skepticism with a relentless quest for truth. In one of his 1913 Harvard essays, Eliot suggests that Joachim's skepticism is even more severe than Bradley's. "Mr. Joachim . . . shatter[s] what little Bradley has left standing, by urging upon us that we have no right to affirm . . . that there is truth at all" (*Prose* 1.42).[8]

Norbert Wiener and Relativism

Almost every philosophy seems to begin as a revolt of common sense against some other theory, and ends—as it becomes itself more developed and approaches completeness—by itself becoming equally preposterous—to everyone but its author.

Eliot to Wiener (1915)

In October 1914, Eliot's friend Norbert Wiener published an essay entitled "Relativism" and shortly thereafter sent a copy to Eliot. Wiener defined relativism as the position that no experience is self-sufficient and no knowledge is certain; terms are meaningless in isolation; to gain plausibility, they must be understood in relation to other terms (567). On 6 January, Eliot acknowledged the essay, admitting that he too was a relativist. "The Relativism I cordially agree with." He confesses that that his own relativism had complicated the work on the dissertation. "My relativism made me see so many sides to questions that I became hopelessly involved, and wrote a thesis perfectly unintelligible to anyone but myself" (*L*1.89). At the time of this correspondence, Eliot was working on a talk to be given a few weeks later in Russell's rooms at Cambridge. In "The Relativity of the Moral Judgment," presented on 12 March 1915, he again describes himself as a relativist and argues that neither realism nor idealism is of any help in ethics. "To reduce the world to a set of formulae is to let it slip through our fingers in a fine dust; but to fly into an emotional orgy or retire into a sunlit stupor is to let the world slip through our fingers in a thin smoke" (*Prose* 1.198). Eliot's correspondence with Wiener documents a watershed moment in his life: the decision to abandon a career in philosophy. "All philosophising," he declares, is a "perversion of reality: for, in a sense, no philosophic theory makes any difference to practice." Eliot now hopes "to avoid philosophy and devote [him]self to either *real* art or *real* science" (*L*1.87, 88; Eliot's italics). Henceforth, instead of committing himself to any theory, he will consider philosophical extremes as two points in a conversation "upon which intelligence feeds" (*Prose* 1.198).

Eliot concluded his formal studies in 1915 with a weekly tutorial on Aristotle. He was thoroughly disillusioned with philosophy, but in deference to his parents, he revised the dissertation and submitted it to Harvard in the spring of 1916. Professor James Woods informed him that Professor Royce considered it "the work of an expert" and that the department had accepted it "without the least hesitation" (*L*1.156). Eliot responded gracefully, saying "I shall try to justify its acceptance by passing a good examination when I come. I don't know at all when that can be" (*L*1.167). In fact, it would never be. In 1915, he married a woman who needed financial and emotional support, and they decided to live in England, then mired down in what seemed to be a never-ending war. In 1929, in a letter to his mother, Eliot reflected on this turning point in his life: "I am sure that I should have made a very poor professor of Philosophy, because, after my first enthusiasm, I found modern philosophy to be nothing more than a logomachy." He assured her that her unstinting support had not been in vain, and indeed, that his work in philosophy had turned out to be "a great advantage" in ways that he "never expected it to be" (*L*4.411-12).

4 The Poet and the Cave-Man

Making History in "Sweeney among the Nightingales" and *The Waste Land*

Primitivism and the Dialectic of History

History has many cunning passages, contrived corridors
And issues, deceives with whispering ambitions,
Guides us by vanities.

Eliot, "Gerontion" (1919)

A few weeks after finishing the draft of his dissertation, Eliot asserted that his intellectual allegiance was to relativism (*L*1.86–88), and two months later, in "The Relativity of the Moral Judgment," he extended his relativism to ethics (*Prose* 1.197–215). In the spring of 1915, he wrapped up his work in philosophy and the social sciences and began the transition from life as an American student to life as an English man of letters. In June, he married an Englishwoman and settled down in war-torn London. In part due to disillusionment with idealism, in part to the horror of living in a city under aerial bombardment, and in part to economic and marital distress, he had become less interested in logic (resolving contradictions) and more interested in history (preserving and connecting fragments). Although many people associate history with objectivity, Eliot associated it with reconstruction from a limited point of view. As he says in his thesis, history is "only relatively true: it must be a history of the object side, postulating the subject, or a history of the subject side, postulating the object side" (*Prose* 1.248). When at the end of the war he resumed writing poetry, he brought to his new work this focus on history, a topic that took him back to his work in the social sciences, virtually all of which were engaged in historical reconstruction. The major thinkers in anthropology, sociology, and psychology were using fragments to understand human development over time. In this project, Eliot argued, Frazer was uniquely influential. In *The Golden Bough*, he "extended the consciousness of the human mind into as dark a backward and abysm of time as has yet been explored" (*Prose* 2.515).

Eliot's first London publications included reviews of landmark works in the social sciences. In 1916, he reviewed Émile Durkheim's *Elementary Forms of the Religious Life* and C. J. J. Webb's *Group Theories of Religion*, and in 1917 Wilhelm Wundt's *Elements of Folk Psychology*, the subtitle of which is *Outlines of a Psychological History of Mankind*. As he transitioned into literary journalism, Eliot focused on the relevance of the social sciences to the situation of modern artists such as Wyndham Lewis and James Joyce. In a review of *Ulysses*, he remarked that "Psychology, . . . ethnology, and *The Golden Bough* have concurred to make possible what was impossible even a few years ago. Instead of narrative method, we may now use the mythical method. It is, I seriously believe, a step toward making the modern world possible for art" (*Prose* 2.479). The title of Eliot's first book of criticism, *The Sacred Wood*, alludes to *The Golden Bough*, and the headnote to *The Waste Land* acknowledges his (and his generation's) debt to Frazer.

One of the major differences in a consideration of binaries in philosophy and in the social sciences is that the latter includes a temporal dimension, as in "the raw and the cooked" of Claude Lévi-Strauss. In Eliot's discussions, the temporal dimension involves not only evolution but also simultaneity. In a 1918 review of Lewis's *Tarr*, he comments on the capacity of the modern artist to benefit from this simultaneity.

> The artist . . . is more *primitive*, as well as more civilized, than his contemporaries; his experience is deeper than civilization, and he only uses the phenomena of civilization in expressing it. Primitive instincts and the acquired habits of ages are confounded in the ordinary man. In the work of Mr. Lewis we recognize the thought of the modern and the energy of the cave-man. (*Prose* 1.747; Eliot's italics)

The coexistence of primitive instincts and "acquired habits of ages" historicizes the dichotomy between feeling and intellect (desire and refinement, body and soul) that was highlighted in Eliot's early poems, including "Prufrock," whose overwhelming questions in decorous rooms coexist with images of dismemberment and murder. In "Prufrock" the instincts of the crab lurk just beneath the abulia of the ultracivilized intellectual. In a discussion of *Le Sacre du printemps*, Eliot makes a similar point in connection with Stravinsky's ballet, the music of which projects primitive energy and modern life in a work of art that transcends both. "The Vegetation Rite upon which the ballet is founded remained, in spite of the music, a pageant of primitive culture," but in "a process of interpenetration and metamorphosis," the music seemed "to transform the rhythm of the steppes into the scream of the motor horn, the rattle of machinery, the grind of wheels, the beating of iron and steel, the roar of the underground railway, and other barbaric cries of modern life" (*Prose* 2.370). In retaining these polarities, the music supports the idea that they are relative and historically determined; in transcending them, it performs a dialectical move that results in the work of art.

The importance of primitivism in Eliot's work and more generally in modernism is a major topic in criticism.[1] In an excellent essay on Eliot's notion of tradition, Viorica Patea argues that primitivism provides a means of piercing the veneer of rationality that blocks encounters with what he refers to as "that vanished mind of which our mind is a continuation" (*Prose* 2.370). For Eliot, she suggests, "the transformation of the personal into the impersonal entailed a mystical process of stripping and purification," of descending into the abysm of time in order to probe the sources of primitive cultural vitality and to discover the foundations of the modern self. This descent enables one to recognize the cultural "other" without which the Western mind would not know itself (Patea, 94). In the following pages, I examine Eliot's seminal essay on primitive religion and discuss its relevance to the modernist form emerging in his postwar Sweeney poems and in *The Waste Land*.

"The Interpretation of Primitive Ritual": Facts, Interpretations, Survivals

> History is largely a mere chronicle without meaning, . . . facts in the long run overpower theory; though without the theory, or without incipient theories, we could hardly say that there were even facts.
>
> Eliot, "Relativity of the Moral Judgment" (1915)

One of the most important contexts for understanding Eliot's criticism and poetry in the years following the war is his work in Josiah Royce's capstone seminar for philosophy students in 1913-14, his last year at Harvard.[2] The announced subject of the class was "A Comparative Study of Various Types of Scientific Method," and the purpose was to compare the meaning of the scientific method in the natural sciences with its meaning in philosophy and the social sciences. The physical sciences, with Darwin's *Origin of*

Species as primary reference, were those associated with the temporalization of the chain of being (see p. 45); the social sciences were those that had emerged by using the theory of evolution to interpret social and religious history. The thinkers discussed in the course included the most eminent social scientists of the previous half-century, beginning with the first major figure to base his work on Darwin, E. B. Tylor, author of the landmark study *Primitive Culture* (1871), and including contemporary figures such as Lucien Lévy-Bruhl, author of the groundbreaking *Primitive Mentality* (1910).

In his main paper for the Royce seminar, "The Interpretation of Primitive Ritual," Eliot articulates principles that were to reappear in his literary criticism and to provide a paradigm for the structure of *The Waste Land.* His essay is an investigation of the claim by sociologists that religion can be understood as a science, and his conclusion is that it cannot: "No 'scientific' definition of religion is possible" (*Prose* 1.106).[3] His underlying criticism, anchored in an analysis of Émile Durkheim's classic *Règles de la methode sociologique* (1895), is that social scientists have diluted or even reversed the traditional understanding of what science is and how it works. For a biologist or geologist, the "scientific method" is inseparable from inductive reasoning—that is, the process begins with facts and generalizes. For a sociologist, on the other hand, reasoning is deductive, moving from theories about primitive people to facts that support those theories. The sociologist begins with definitions that are "never arrived at by a generalisation from the facts; because the facts are never just <u>those facts</u> until we have the definition" (Eliot's emphasis; *Prose* 1.106).

Eliot continues his critique by showing that social scientists also have their own special understanding of what constitutes a "fact." In the natural sciences, facts are material and real—"science deals with objects or with relations of objects"; in science, moreover, facts are independent of the investigator—they are "real because independent, and independent because real" (*Prose* 1.301, 259). In philosophy, on the other hand, facts are intangible and ideal: "A fact is a point of attention which has only one aspect. . . . A fact, then, is an ideal construction" (*Prose* 1.284). Apart from the investigator, such facts do not even exist. In the social sciences, facts are neither real nor ideal; in that they "belong to a place half-way between object and subject"; they are what Eliot calls "half-objects" (*Prose* 1.301). To complicate matters further, in sociology, the meaning of "fact" varies from group to group and age to age. "What seemed to one generation fact is from the point of view of the next a rejected interpretation" (*Prose* 1.109).

Eliot also takes issue with the "deplorable looseness" with which Durkheim refers to the "Evolution of Religion." *Evolution* is a technical term referring to situations "in which there is a continuous relation between organic tendency and environment that can be expressed more or less quantitatively" (*Prose* 1.106). An essential "difference between natural and social evolution is that in the former we are able practically to neglect all values that are internal to the process, and consider the process from the point of view of *our* value, . . . outside the process. While to some extent in a social progress, and to a very great extent in religious progress, the internal values are part of the external description" (Eliot's italics; *Prose* 1.107). In a later *précis* of his paper, he applies the distinction between internal and external values to the issue of interpretation. "Internal" interpretations are those that would have been made by the participants themselves; "external" are those constructed by nonparticipating observers and social scientists.

> Some years ago, in a paper on *The Interpretation of Primitive Ritual*, I . . . attempt[ed] to show that in many cases *no* interpretation of a rite could explain its origin. For the meaning of the series of acts is to the performers themselves an interpretation; the same ritual remaining practically unchanged may assume different meanings for different generations of performers; and the rite may even have originated before "meaning" meant anything at all. (Eliot's italics; *Prose* 2.771–72)

In a 1927 discussion of science and religion, he again draws on the distinction between internal and external interpretations. The point of view of the anthropologist, he points out, and that of the believer are as different as "the appearance of a house to someone who is inside and to someone who is outside of it" (*Prose* 3.262).

In his excellent summary of the "Primitive Ritual" essay, Piers Gray observes that Eliot's conclusion is "that the only *fact* to be found in any past social behavior is the actual *ritual*" (128; Gray's italics). There is no way for social scientists to travel beyond that fact and retrieve elements of consciousness that were not even clear to the participants. Any interpretation that the participants might have had would have been both personal and transient. Eliot uses a literary equivalent of internal and external interpretations in both his criticism and his poetry, a point to be explored in my discussion of *The Waste Land*. In the literary context, internal interpretations are those contained within the text and external interpretations are those constructed by critics.

Eliot supported his distinction between facts and interpretations by examining a number of theories regarding primitive ritual, including those by Tylor and Frazer. In *Primitive Culture*, Tylor extended Darwin's suppositions regarding material remains to beliefs and customs. He begins with a theory of human rationality that leads him to conclude that primitive rituals originated in the attempt of "savage philosophers" (Tylor's term) to make sense of phenomena they otherwise could not understand. Such a conclusion, Eliot suggests, could never have been arrived at by generalizing from facts. The assumption that "this is what we should do were we in the savage's place" came first and the facts emerged to support it (*Prose* 1.107). Frazer, similarly, begins with the theory that religion originated as a primitive form of agricultural engineering, an assumption that leads him to interpret communal acts as fertility rituals. Eliot maintains that "no method, historical or comparative, will give such results" as these, and concludes that "primitive reality . . . cannot be put together out of the abstractions of social psychology which are torn from our sophisticated and conscious life" (*Prose* 1.114, 115). Both Tylor and Frazer use Darwin to buttress their theories of evolution: in Tylor, from savagery to barbarism to civilization, and in Frazer, from magic to religion to reason.

One of Tylor's contributions to the social sciences was his coinage of the term *survivals* to describe the "facts" of anthropology. "Survivals" refer to primitive beliefs and customs that have survived intact into the present. Tylor theorized that although these vestiges of thought and practice originally served some purpose, they now exist as irrational and nonfunctional floaters, which have lasted "by force of habit into a new state of society from that in which they had their original home" (116). Eliot knew the term from his graduate work and used it in book reviews during and after the war. In 1917, he reviewed Stanley A. Cook's analysis of the significance and meaning of survivals in *The Study of Religions*. Cook's working definition is similar to Tylor's: "Survivals in belief and custom are those curious phenomena which appear in the higher levels or in civilized lands, but take us away to the lower levels, to savage lands, and to bygone times" (149). The essential element, Cook says, is context: a *survival* is a fragment whose context has changed or disappeared (173).

Eliot's dissent from the conclusions of the social scientists is combined with praise for their practice of cataloging primitive customs. Of this sort of labor, he maintains, the "greatest master" is Frazer. "No one has done more to make manifest the similarities and identities underlying the customs of races very remote in every way from each other" (*Prose* 1.113). As shown by the references to *The Golden Bough* in his early criticism and in the headnote to *The Waste Land*, Eliot continued to admire Frazer's work. In 1924, he argued that Frazer's eminence, unlike that of Durkheim and Lévy-Bruhl, does not depend on "brilliant theories of human behavior" but on a "modest and steady" accumulation of facts. As his twelve-volume work progressed, Eliot notes, Frazer withdrew "in more and more cautious abstention from the attempt to explain." This "absence of speculation is a conscious and deliberate scrupulousness, a positive point of view." *The Golden Bough*, he concludes, is comparable in importance to the work of Freud in that it throws "its light on the obscurities of the soul from a different angle." In that it is "a statement of fact which is not involved in the maintenance or fall of any theory of the author's," *The Golden Bough* is "a work of perhaps greater permanence" (*Prose* 2.515). The work of Freud, like that of Durkheim, reveals the presence of a sophisticated theorist; that of Frazer reveals the presence of a cataloger of bits and pieces of primitive life. By refusing to squeeze his material to fit a preconception, Frazer was able to "extend the consciousness of the human mind into as dark a backward and abysm of time as has yet been explored" (*Prose* 2.515).

The distinction between facts and interpretations runs throughout Eliot's early prose, most clearly stated in "The Function of Criticism" (1923): "Interpretation . . . is only legitimate when it is not interpretation at all, but merely putting the reader in possession of facts he would otherwise have missed" (*Prose* 2.465). The significance of this contrast has been discussed by a number of critics, including Marc Manganaro, Richard Shusterman, Jeffrey Perl, and Piers Gray. As they have pointed out, this bias against theory is part and parcel of Eliot's literary criticism (Shusterman, 15-16, 45-49; Manganaro, 68-72). Gray shows the relation of this work in the social sciences to the work in idealism and applies both to a reading of the poetry (102-6, 111-14). Perl goes further, suggesting that the poet's work in the social sciences was part of his larger project in philosophy, a project that includes the turn from idealism to relativism, a turn that is reflected in major essays such as "Tradition and the Individual Talent" (66-68).

In the following pages, I discuss the relevance of the principles in the "Primitive Ritual" essay to the modernist form that emerged in *The Waste Land*. My contention is that, consistent with his distrust of deductive reasoning, Eliot adapted the inductive method for service in his writing. In order to begin with "facts," he had to formulate literary equivalents, a task in which he drew on Tylor's definition of the fact as a "survival" and Frazer's as a "description without explanation." In privileging such "facts," Eliot simultaneously discounted interpretation and generated a dialectic between internal and external interpretations to relativize and historicize the voices and cultures of *The Waste Land*. Like a number of other avant-garde artists, he experiments with arrangements of ostensibly unconnected fragments as a principle of form. His hallmark principle of parataxis—the juxtaposition of decontextualized fragments without transitions—is a literary relative of Frazer's methodology of cataloging fragments. The striking contrast between the psychological structure of "Prufrock" and the paratactic structure of *The Waste Land* is due in part to Eliot's intervening immersion in the social sciences.

"Facts" as Material in *The Waste Land*

> If literary critics . . . would study the content and criticize the methods of such books as *The Origin of Species* itself, and . . . *Primitive Culture*, they might learn the difference between . . . an interpretation and a fact.
>
> Eliot, "The Beating of a Drum" (1923)

Eliot began his work as a man of letters in 1915 with the conviction that the inductive method used in the physical sciences was superior to the deductive method used in philosophy and the social sciences. For the scientific method (beginning with objects or fragments thereof) to be useful in literary studies, however, he was forced to refine his definition of "facts." For use in poetry and criticism, "facts" should be considered as (1) words, and (2) objective correlatives, that is, feelings that have been objectified, "reduced to a state of fact . . . precise, tractable, under control." As part of an argument that "comparison and analysis are the chief tools of the critic," he maintains that it is not the ideas in a poem that are compared, but the words and images. "Comparison and analysis need only the cadavers on the table; but interpretation is always producing parts of the body from its pockets, and fixing them in place" (*Prose* 2.465).

Eliot's position on the relative importance of words and ideas in poetic composition is an echo of that held by Mallarmé. When Degas complained that in spite of being "full of ideas," he is unable "to get an inch further" in the composition of a sonnet, Mallarmé says, "But, Degas, you can't make a poem with ideas. You make it with words" (Valéry, 62). More specifically, for Mallarmé as for Eliot, poetry is not made of interpretations but of "facts," not as defined in biology but as defined in anthropology and adjusted for literary use. *The Waste Land* consists of "broken images" and "withered stumps of time," fragments that are analogous to the remains of belief, behavior, and culture that constitute "survivals," as formulated by Tylor in *Primitive Culture* and by Frazer in *The Golden Bough*. Eliot's verse is littered with uncontextualized fragments that no longer have the meanings with which they were formerly endowed: quotations and songs, ceremonies and rituals, actions and functions, sharply defined images and objectified feelings.

As a way of clarifying Eliot's use of materials borrowed from other writers, it is helpful to distinguish, first, between allusions and survivals, and second, between pure survivals and translations. Allusions are references to texts and events; survivals are rubble from the remote and recent past, including ruins from the Great War. In the language of his essays on the social sciences, allusions are interpretations, survivals are facts. "April is the cruellest month" is an allusion to *The Canterbury Tales*, but it is not a survival; it is an interpretation that reveals the state of mind of a modern speaker. "*Oed'und leer das Meer*," on the other hand, is a survival. Survivals can be mythic (Philomel, Tereu), religious (fertility rites), literary ("O swallow swallow"), material (buildings, sandwich papers), and, more complicated, psychological (revenge). Translated fragments represent another type of borrowing, for they fall in between an allusion and a survival, in between an interpretation and a fact. A translation, typically treated as a quotation from the original, is something less than that, for the process of translation requires interpretation. Eliot refers to this category in a comment on the opening line of *Ash-Wednesday*—"Because I do not hope to turn again"—which is a translation of a line from Guido Cavalcanti: "The line beginning Ash-Wednesday . . . is a straight borrowing and not an allusive borrowing. That is an important distinction."[4] Survivals emanate directly from the past, and although the context and original meaning may have vanished, the form and the voice have held. Translations, on the other hand, are mediated through a later, usually a modern, interpreter. Allusions, in contrast to both, issue from the mind of a poet who in the present remembers the past. The epigraphs of Eliot's early poems, including that of *The Waste Land*, are without exception survivals, decontextualized fragments that, as Tylor explained, take us back to "bygone times."

Failure to understand the function of survivals and translations led many of Eliot's early critics to accuse him of plagiarism. But the intactness of the fragment that belongs to a vanishing context and voice is essential to its usefulness as a window opening on the past, as a dialectical bridge both connecting and transcending history and myth. As a way of establishing a dialectical relationship between the past and present, Eliot often creates structural frames that include both survivals and allusions. In *The Waste Land*, the opening line of "A Game of Chess" contains an allusion to *Antony and Cleopatra*—"The Chair she sat in, like a burnished throne,/Glowed on the marble." The closing line consists of another reminder of Shakespeare, a far more powerful one, in part because it is a survival, a verbatim quotation of Ophelia's farewell in *Hamlet*—"Good night, ladies, good night, sweet ladies, good night, good night" (IV.v.72). The opening allusion notes an ironic parallel between a legendary queen and a modern woman; the closing survival is the pathetic voice of a girl about to commit suicide.

"A Game of Chess" also highlights the importance of distinguishing between internal and external interpretations. Internally, for the lady at her dressing table, the metamorphosis of Philomel is the focal point in a painting decorating her boudoir; for the narrator, it is a reminder of Ovid, one of several "withered stumps of time" in her room. Externally, the poet and his readers impose other interpretations, some pointing to issues of violence and gender. The internal interpretations in this minidrama include the thoughts of a male visitor to the lady's chamber, an intellectual and perhaps a veteran who is interpreting the behavior of the woman. He hums a "Shakespeherian Rag," its spelling modified to catch the beat. For him, the song is part of a chain of allusions, including not only fragments of Shakespeare's plays but also memories of friends lost in ships. The chain of allusions culminates in a survival, a line from *The Tempest*—"Those are pearls that were his eyes." Externally, for the poet (and his readers), the survival is a reminder of the poem's reflexivity. The poem itself is a "Shakespearean rag," which includes tatters from *Antony and Cleopatra*, *Hamlet*, *The Tempest*, and *Coriolanus*. In the larger context of the poem, the whole to which these and other ruins bear witness is Western civilization in various incarnations, including Europe before the guns of August 1914 began firing.

Eliot's epigraphs are the clearest examples of pure survivals. In "Sweeney among the Nightingales," written in the last year of the Great War, the epigraph is an unidentified seemingly unrelated line in ancient Greek—*ὤμοι, πέπληγμαι καιρίαν πληγὴν ἔσω*. It is the cry of Agamemnon, who is being murdered by his wife as he is taking his ritual bath at the end of the Trojan war. Taken from the *Agamemnon* of Aeschylus, this line is the same cry in the same language that was heard by Athenians twenty-five-hundred years ago. Changing the Greek original to "Alas, I have been struck with a deadly wound" would change the tenor of the poem. It would undercut the dialectic between the prehistoric king and the modern poet, between the ancient war hero and soldiers on the Western Front, between the wail of Agamemnon and the much older scream of Philomel in the bloody wood. The scream that sounds in the epigraph is the first part of a frame that enfolds complex layers of myth and history in the poem. The final lines, which conclude a vignette of a postwar scene in a bar in South America, allude to the murder of the king at Mycenae, the martyrdom of Christ on Golgotha, the mutilation of Philomel in the woods of Thrace, and the slaughter of soldiers in the trenches of France.

> The nightingales are singing near
> The Convent of the Sacred Heart,
>
> And sang within the bloody wood
> When Agamemnon cried aloud
> And let their liquid siftings fall
> To stain the stiff dishonoured shroud. (35–40)

Substituting a modern translation of the epigraph would weaken the stratification conveyed by the pairing of a pure survival in the epigraph and the complex allusion in the conclusion. Similarly, in *The Waste Land*, substituting a modern English translation of Petronius for the dual language (Latin and Greek) epigraph would generate a different poem. *The Waste Land* includes many examples of pure survivals. "Shantih" is a formal conclusion to an *Upanishad*, preserved for millennia in its original Sanskrit. "London Bridge is falling down falling down falling down" is a line preserved through time in nursery rhymes. The poem also includes evolved or impure survivals, changed in both form and import. Madame Sosostris, a fortune teller in postwar London, is an evolved survival, an unrecognized descendant of the Sibyl, Tiresias, and Ezekiel.

Relativism and the Limits of Interpretation in *The Waste Land*

> An interpretation as such is neither true nor false.
>
> Eliot, "The Interpretation of Primitive Ritual" (1913; Eliot's emphasis)

Eliot's relativism and his distrust of interpretation are underscored in part V of *The Waste Land*, "What the Thunder Said." The title of this section suggests that it will deal with interpretation, that is, with what the thunder meant. Eliot's note, in confirmation, says that the fable, which is from the *Upanishads*, concerns "the *meaning* of the Thunder" (italics added). The very concept of meaning, however, is undercut by a formal dialectic of internal and external interpretations and the relativism underscored by an interplay of survivals and allusions. The legend, in summary, is that the thunder god Prajapati says "Da! Da! Da!," and three groups of creatures—gods, men, and devils—hear the sounds as three ethical commands: control, give, and sympathize.[5] Eliot extends what is already a complicated web of interpretations by adding a modern gloss for each of the three "messages."

> Then spoke the thunder
> DA
> *Datta*: what have we given?
> My friend, blood shaking my heart
> The awful daring of a moment's surrender
> Which an age of prudence can never retract
> By this, and this only, we have existed
> Which is not to be found in our obituaries
> Or in memories draped by the beneficent spider
> Or under seals broken by the lean solicitor
> In our empty rooms (399–409)

The Indians who hear the sound of thunder are the first in a series of internal interpreters. They belong to a remote prescientific world, in which people believed that natural phenomena could convey transcendental meaning—in this case, that the thunderclap contains a message from the god of thunder. Their method of interpreting the divine message is simple. First, they "translate" the thunderclap into the onomatopoeic DA, which they consider to be the initial syllable of a divine imperative. Second, they expand DA into a command beginning with that syllable. The first group interprets it as "Datta" ("Give"), the second group as "Dayadhvam" ("Sympathize"), and the third as "Damyata" ("Control"). The Sanskrit sound for the thunder clap and the Sanskrit commands formulated by the Indians are survivals—remote in time and place, primitive in culture, objective facts. The Indian interpreters are overtaken by modern interpreters—subjective, desperate, with no connection to the transcendental. As indicated by the references to obituaries, solicitors, and seals, and by the allusion to *Coriolanus*, the secondary interpreters are contemporary English figures. In contrast to the Indians, they resemble those figures we hear in our offices and bedrooms. Their presence shifts the focus from ancient to modern and from meaning per se to the way meaning is constructed, from the desperation of a religious community longing for rain to the desperation of the secular self.[6]

The modern gloss on "*Datta*" is existentialist. Someone addresses a friend and declares that existence is authenticated by giving the self over to "the awful daring of a moment's surrender." In spite of evidence supplied by lawyers, obituaries, and wills, he believes that those who have never surrendered have never really existed. The gloss on the second command—"*Dayadhvam*"—is more intricate. Internally, someone who identifies with Shakespeare's Coriolanus says "I have heard the key / Turn in the door once and turn once only." Externally, in a note, Eliot reveals that the gloss is a double allusion—to passages in Bradley's *Appearance and Reality* and Dante's *Inferno*. The gloss on the third command—"*Damyata*"—contrasts the image of an expert seaman controlling a boat to a failed lover expressing regret—"Your heart would have responded / Gaily, when invited, beating obedient / To controlling hands."

The internal interpretations are followed by the superimposition of external interpretations, which end in a dialectical loop that demythologizes the sound of the thunder and cancels the messages of both ancient and modern interpreters. As explained by Brooker and Bentley:

> The most important point about the thunder is that it does not say anything at all, and further, it does not mean anything. It is like the birds who "say" twit, jug, and tereu, and the cock who "said" co co rico. As quotations, these words along with DA are onomatopoeic contrivances to simulate pure noise, pure insignificance. When such words reveal the presence of birds, cock, and thunder, they have those meanings, but when they are offered as quotations of what the birds, cock, and thunder said, they reveal that nothing whatsoever has been said. (180)

The survivals (the interpretations of the Indians) are often taken as Eliot's transmission of ancient wisdom, and the glosses by Europeans are seen as reflections on the modern self or as a veiled confession about his troubled marriage. But when the dialectic between internal and external interpretations is recognized, it becomes clear that the Indian legend is not a series of messages, but a chain of interpretations that originates in pure noise and ends by reverting to the same.

Parataxis and Modernist Form in *The Waste Land*

Poetic originality is largely an original way of assembling the most disparate and unlikely material to make a new whole.

Eliot, "Frontiers of Criticism" (1956)

One of the defining characteristics of literary modernism is the acceptance of parataxis—the juxtaposition without transitions of disparate and unlikely fragments—as a principle of form. Transitions, especially subordinating conjunctions, which connect a main clause to peripheral phrases, are interpretive by definition, for they point to temporal or logical relations. Generally speaking, the withdrawal from interpretation, which occurred at roughly the same time across the avant-garde, can be associated with the publicity given to the burgeoning social sciences, principally anthropology, and to the fascination du jour with *The Golden Bough*. In Eliot's case, the genealogy is unambiguous. His contrast of fact and interpretation was a direct result of his analysis of Durkheim's assumptions about the scientific method, and his preference for constructing poems out of disconnected survivals and objectified feelings was a conscious adaptation of the comparative methodology of the later volumes of *The Golden Bough*. The first two of Frazer's twelve volumes are propelled by a thesis, but the later volumes show little or no attempt to connect the facts to an originating theory; descriptions are simply collected and placed side by side. Frazer's comparative method worked for artists because it equipped them for what Eliot calls the "supreme difficulty of criticism—to make the facts generalize themselves" (*Prose* 2.244). The process, of which the "mythical method" described in Eliot's review of *Ulysses* is one version, is at bottom dialectical in that it compels the comparison and contrast that moves heterogeneous bits and pieces to transcend themselves in "new wholes."

In *The Waste Land*, the most concentrated collection of survivals, which is also the most striking instance of parataxis, appears in the last verse paragraph, which consists of a cascade of decontextualized, uninterpreted fragments.

London Bridge is falling down falling down falling down

Poi s'ascose nel foco che gli affina
Quando fiam uti chelidon—O swallow swallow
Le Prince d'Aquitaine à la tour abolie

> These fragments I have shored against my ruins
> Why then Ile fit you. Hieronymo's mad againe.
> Datta. Dayadhvam. Damyata.
> Shantih shantih shantih (426-33)

In this example of what Piers Gray refers to as the "poetry of incoherence" (211-44), there are survivals in five languages (English, Italian, Latin, French, and Sanskrit) from Eastern and Western culture, ranging from primitive to modern and from low to high, simply placed side by side. Although disparate, they share an interest in a cluster of themes, including suffering and metamorphosis, the nature of language, and transcendence through prayer and music. The intertextual threads are subtle enough to avoid undercutting the perception of parataxis, but strong enough to enable the facts to generalize themselves in the mind of the reader.

Parataxis also serves the impulse in modern literature to "make it new," by moving the temporal arts (literature) toward spatial form by facilitating simultaneity and stratification (Frank, 221-40). Eliot's best-known discussions of simultaneity are in "Tradition and the Individual Talent" and his review of *Ulysses* (*Prose* 2.105-14; 476-81). His discussions of the archeological concept of stratification occur primarily in his reviews of work by social scientists and fellow artists. In 1919, he argues that the artist "should be aware of all the metamorphoses of poetry that illustrate the stratifications of history that cover savagery" (*Prose* 2.138). In "Sweeney among the Nightingales," he creates a textbook example of stratification by seeing Tereus, Agamemnon, Christ, and Sweeney not only as part of a temporal sequence but also as a spatial construct, existing simultaneously in the mind of the artist and the reader. Such stratification is omnipresent in *The Waste Land*, culminating in the myth that is generated when all survivals are viewed at once, in a moment of time. The fragments of this master myth are found in every section of *The Waste Land*—in primitive rites, in historical events, in social and family relationships, and in institutions and cities, ancient and modern; to attend to its remains is to descend through layers of self and civilization into the vicinity of that "vanished mind of which our mind is a continuation" (*Prose* 2.370). By using the inductive method, eschewing interpretation per se, and arranging survivals as a spatiotemporal image, Eliot enables the reader to manipulate "a continuous parallel between contemporaneity and antiquity" (*Prose* 2.478).

Eliot's compositional procedure is echoed in the experience of reading the poem. The images and lines, first encountered as mere fragments, continuously and dialectically generate a larger whole, which "cracks and reforms and bursts" as reading and rereading occur. Eliot's experiments are similar to contemporaneous experiments in the visual arts, such as those in Cubist portraits and landscapes. His composite image of the "unreal city," for example, emerges from survivals (material, literary, mythic, religious) and from allusions found in four of the five sections of the poem (I, II, III, V). In "The Burial of the Dead," Eliot begins to create a space for the fleeting images of London, Paris, and Dante's Hell. The city image, which is even more extensive in the drafts, culminates in the Cubist projection of the "Unreal city" in "What the Thunder Said" (*WLF* 42-43).

> What is the city over the mountains
> Cracks and reforms and bursts in the violet air
> Falling towers
> Jerusalem Athens Alexandria
> Vienna London
> Unreal (371-76)

As a principle of literary form, the dialectical use of parataxis to compel comparative and intertextual reading confirms the continuity of Eliot's modernist masterpiece with his previous work, both as a student of the social sciences and as a literary critic.

5 Individual Works and Organic Wholes

The Idealist Foundation of Eliot's Criticism

> I think . . . of the literature of the world, of the literature of Europe, of the literature of a single country, not as a collection of the writings of individuals, but as "organic wholes," as systems in relation to which, and only in relation to which, individual works of literary art, and the works of individual artists, have their significance.
>
> Eliot, "The Function of Criticism" (1923)

The Two Eliots

> In one's prose reflexions one may be legitimately occupied with ideals, whereas in the writing of verse one can deal only with actuality.
>
> Eliot, *After Strange Gods* (1934)

In the mid-1930s, Eliot recalled that his decision in 1911 to study philosophy had been part of a "religious inclination"—by extension, part of an attempt to unify the elements of his divided self.[1] His decision to reverse course, as discussed in chapter 3, involved the recognition that philosophy offered only a more abstract version of the war within. In the early stages of his formal attempt to transcend self-division, he absorbed and largely accepted major principles from idealism, but by the end of 1914, he had turned to principles associated with relativism. His disenchantment reflected disillusionment with Bradleian idealism, which had seemed promising because it was anchored in experience but which, when pushed to its extreme in the Absolute, struck Eliot as wishful thinking, "like the prayers of childhood" (*Prose* 1.42). Most of his postwar poems, up to and including *The Waste Land*, and some of his postwar prose, including the reviews of his contemporaries, reflect the epistemological relativism that he expressed in correspondence and the ethical relativism expressed in his 1915 paper "The Relativity of the Moral Judgment" (*Prose* 1.197-215). The swing to relativism, with its emphasis on the limitations of points of view and the impossibility of knowing truth, is another manifestation of the "pendulum in the head," as he puts it in his 1921 pseudonymous "Song." But, and this is a crucial point in following Eliot's development as thinker and poet, nothing is abandoned "en route"; his relativism retains traces of both realism and idealism.

The composite nature of Eliot's thinking is nowhere more evident than in the coexistence of idealism and relativism in his postwar writings. His poetry, as discussed in chapter 4, clearly draws on the relativity of opposites such as primitive and modern, whereas his early criticism, including "Tradition and the Individual Talent," assumes principles central in idealism. His earliest critics noted this disjunction, and Eliot retrospectively confirmed their perception in his comment, quoted above, that prose and poetry proceed from different premises. The perception of contradictory strands in Eliot's life and work was buttressed by the about-face associated with his midlife conversion, and by the late 1920s, it was entrenched. In the 1930s, Paul Elmer More expressed frustration with the "cleft Eliot" (214), and Henry Hazlitt suggested that there were at least three Eliots—a poet, a critic, and a philosopher—and that it was inconceivable that these could be the same person (200). In the 1940s, W. H. Auden playfully made the same point in a *New Yorker* piece called "Port and Nuts with the Eliots," his plural referring to the notion that "T. S. Eliot is not a single figure, but a household" (506). There are many versions of the multiple Eliots, but all involve the perception of him as a critic preoccupied with dialectic and wholeness and a poet whose work is fragmented and paratactic.

Eliot's best critics dealt with the problem by using his prose, especially "Tradition" and the essays of the 1920s, to explain his poetry; thus they privileged wholeness over fragmentation and impersonality over personality. In the interwar years, Edmund Wilson and Cleanth Brooks used Eliot's comments on the "mythical method" to associate the fragments in *The Waste Land* with an all-inclusive monomyth (Wilson, 83-87; Brooks, 106-36). In 1945, Joseph Frank used the concept of "simultaneity" in the "Tradition" essay to argue that *The Waste Land* and *Ulysses* used "spatial form," meaning that all of the fragments are unified in a single moment in the mind of the reader (221-40). In the 1950s, Grover Smith used the Tiresias note to

The Waste Land to give the poem a unifying consciousness (74), and in 1978, Marianne Thormählen demonstrated Eliot's ability to convey wholeness while remaining faithful to fragments.

The publication in 1964 of Eliot's doctoral dissertation opened a new chapter in the discussion, and the advent of poststructuralism in the 1970s encouraged new perspectives on his disjunctive imagination. By taking into account both the idealist bias in his prose and contemporary developments in critical theory, critics such as Jeffrey Perl, J. P. Riquelme, and M. A. R. Habib not only tolerate Eliot's play of opposites but also make these oppositions part of their experience of reading his work. They see Eliot's fragments as interconnected, and they posit complex readings that have a place for both fragments and wholes and for both personality and impersonality. These and other analyses of the links between Eliot's divided self and the conflicting strands in his writing are helpful in understanding his view, discussed in the previous chapter, that poetry is made up of "facts," whereas prose consists of interpretations. In this chapter, I discuss Eliot's early criticism, including "Tradition and the Individual Talent," as a demonstration of the extent to which idealism remained central in his work.

The Durability of Idealism: Four Principles

Many of the ideas in Eliot's criticism, including the signature theories examined in this chapter, can be traced to principles he encountered in his graduate work in idealist philosophy. Four of those principles, only slightly modified, form the bedrock, not only of "Tradition and the Individual Talent" but of much of his subsequent criticism, as well. The first principle, one that contemporary emphasis on *différance* has obscured, is that the perception of likeness is more basic and more complex than the perception of difference. According to Jacob Bronowski, the ability to see likeness in nonidentical objects is the most fundamental principle in human thought. It is easy to see difference and even easier to see likeness in *identical* objects. But to see things as alike when they are not identical requires that the perceiver interject what is not obvious, not given. Bronowski argues that this ability has been of the essence in scientific breakthroughs. He remarks that Newton's "instant insight, as he himself told it, was precisely to see the likeness which no one else had seen, between the fall of an apple and the swing of the moon around the earth. The theory of gravitation rests upon this" (22). In philosophy, the focus on likeness in nonidentical objects is part of idealism. Realists focus on difference, on analysis; idealists on likeness, on synthesis. The focus on likeness is also important in art, the sine qua non of the analogical imagination. To think figuratively is to connect things that are not obviously alike; to construct similes and metaphors, one must have a mind that associates heterogeneous things. Mimesis, too, depends on perceiving and representing likeness.

The second principle, common to all idealists, is the realization that every object and every person is a part rather than a whole, and further, that parts imply a whole that includes other parts. It is this perception that drives idealists to the conclusion that reality is ideal and reality is one. The basic idea is that all fragments are by definition parts of wholes, which themselves are parts of larger wholes, which ultimately are parts of an all-encompassing organic whole (variously called the Idea, the Absolute, Experience, the Sensorium of God). The "whole" is always by necessity ideal, by necessity imagined. It is inseparable from memory and desire, from reasoned longing, from an appreciation of what is logically implied by difference.

The second principle leads inescapably to the third—the conviction that since everything is ultimately part of one thing, everything is connected to everything else within the system. All relations are internal, for all things are within systems, and given an ultimate perspective, within a single system. And since everything is connected, movement or change in any one part affects all other parts. As Edward Lorenz, a scientist working with similar assumptions, hypothesizes, the flap of a butterfly's wings in Brazil can eventually cause a tornado in Texas.[2] This sort of thinking accommodates opposites and insists on their interrelatedness: binaries are seen not simply as opposites but as interconnected terms dependent on each other for definition. Every idealist has his version of the notion that every knowable thing is a fragment, with fragments related in increasingly complex and comprehensive systems.

These three principles lead automatically to an emphasis on depersonalization because, in recognizing similarity, acknowledging that every knowable thing is a fragment, and accepting a comprehensive system that includes other (ultimately, all) parts, one is conceding that the autonomous self is a fiction. In philosophy, these three principles are associated with a static, timeless order. Yet there is also a fourth principle, one that introduces a temporal, dynamic dimension. This is crucial in understanding Eliot's notion of tradition, for his concept is not static (not merely spatial while also not merely temporal). It is a spatiotemporal construct that includes both categories. This fourth principle is that everything is constantly moving and changing in a roughly dialectical process. The first term is feeling; the second, intellect; and the third, a complex that includes and transcends both, a mind that can smell its thoughts as immediately as the odor of a rose (*Prose* 2.380). The idealist philosophers important to Eliot—Kant, Royce, Bradley, and Joachim—all possessed a dialectical imagination. Bradley, clearly the most important, understood reality in terms of an organic and dynamic triad: immediate experience/relational experience/transcendent experience. "Immediate experience" is associated with feeling, "relational experience" with intellect, and "transcendent experience" with a complex that includes both.[3]

An essential point in this triad is that the first and third terms, the terms involving unity, exist as abstractions or ideals. The middle term—the world of fragmentation, difference, relations, the world of language—is the concrete reality. But logically and psychologically, one deduces that there must have been a before and that there will be an after. It is only because one can imagine a before and an after that one can know a present, only because one can imagine unity that one can perceive fragmentation. Knowledge is preceded by feeling, by an immediate experience before self-consciousness, before the perception of subjects and objects; and knowledge will be superseded by an experience in which past and present are at once contained and transcended. One cannot go back to the state before the eruption of self-consciousness, and one cannot go beyond the relational realm except in imagination. In the time before and time after, there is only silence, or as Eliot phrases it in his dissertation, "annihilation and utter night" (*KE*, *Prose* 1.256).

From Philosophy to Criticism: "Tradition and the Individual Talent"

Reflection on these principles leads directly to "Tradition and the Individual Talent," the most important reference point for understanding Eliot's literary criticism. From 1919 until his death, Eliot remained committed to the main points of this groundbreaking essay. In 1923, he restated them in "The Function of Criticism"; in the 1930s, he reaffirmed them in *The Use of Poetry and the Use of Criticism* and extended them to culture and religion in *After Strange Gods*; in the 1940s, he repeated the literary version in his memorial lecture on Yeats and the cultural version in *Notes towards the Definition of Culture*. And less than two years before his death, in the introduction to the reprint of *The Use of Poetry*, he said once again "I do not repudiate

'Tradition and the Individual Talent'" (10). As suggested by the consistency of his comments over many years, his subsequent comments on the essay are extensions and clarifications rather than repudiations.

The four principles outlined above emerge in Eliot's concepts of tradition and impersonality. First, in regard to the importance of building on the perception of likeness, Eliot begins "Tradition" by rejecting criticism that focuses "upon those aspects of [a poet's] work in which he least resembles anyone else," that tries to find the "essence" of the poet in what is most "individual," in his "difference from his predecessors." At the same time, he embraces criticism that centers upon ways in which a poet resembles other poets, in which poems resemble other poems: "Not only the best, but the most individual parts of his work may be those in which the dead poets, his ancestors, assert their immortality most vigorously" (*Prose* 2.105). Similarly, in "The Function of Criticism," Eliot remarks that the chief task of the "second-rate artist . . . is the assertion of all the trifling differences which are his distinction" (*Prose* 2.459).

In an essay published in the same periodical (*The Egoist*) less than two months before the appearance of the "Tradition" piece, Eliot discussed the importance of the recognition of likeness in the life of a poet. He claims that there is a moment when a poet experiences:

> a feeling of profound kinship, . . . a peculiar personal intimacy, with another, probably a dead author. . . . When a young writer is seized with his first passion of this sort he may be changed, metamorphosed almost, within a few weeks even, from a bundle of second-hand sentiments into a person. . . . We do not imitate, we are changed; . . . and we become bearers of a tradition. (*Prose* 2.66–67)

In recognizing kinship, the poet moves from isolation to community, from the singular "I" to the plural "we"; he becomes, in Eliot's phrase, a "bearer of tradition." He moves dialectically, from being a bundle of confused and isolated personal feelings, to being part of a system (community), to being "a person."

Eliot maintains, moreover, that the ability to perceive likeness is a major qualification for poets. In 1921, he describes the metaphysical poets as having minds capable of a "rapid association . . . of heterogeneous images." One finds in their work a "heterogeneity of material compelled into unity by the operation of the poet's mind" (*Prose* 2.376). The poet's mind is dynamic, quickly perceiving likeness and moving on to form new wholes. The ordinary mind is static, perceiving difference and resting in fragments. In Eliot's words:

> When a poet's mind is perfectly equipped for its work, it is constantly amalgamating disparate experience; the ordinary man's experience is chaotic, irregular, fragmentary. The latter falls in love, or reads Spinoza, and these two experiences have nothing to do with each other, or with the noise of the typewriter or the smell of cooking; in the mind of the poet these experiences are always forming new wholes. (*Prose* 2.380)

Eliot further develops his basic assumption that genius is characterized by seeing likeness in nonidentical objects by adding the point that these objects can be radically different. One may be mental; the other physical; one associated with intellect, the other with feeling. In the mind of the poet, they are not two but two-in-one.

When applied to literature, the second principle (the perception of incompleteness) and the third (the realization that parts are systematically connected in larger wholes) constitute a precise formulation of what the "Tradition" essay refers to as the "historical sense." This involves, first, the acknowledgment that "no poet, no artist of any art, has his complete meaning alone"; second, a conscious and cultivated awareness of other artists to whom one can compare oneself and of other art to which one can liken one's own; and third, the awareness that the dead and the living, the past and the present, are systematically related in greater wholes. These wholes are organic and spatiotemporal, ensuring the realization of simultaneity within the tradition. The basic idea is given in miniature in a review Eliot published one month before the appearance of the "Tradition" essay: "When we assume that a literature exists . . . we suppose . . . writings and writers between whom there is a tradition . . . who are related as . . . *contemporaneous*, from a certain point of view, *cells in one body*" (*Prose* 2.92; italics added). In 1923, Eliot again describes "tradition" in terms of "systems in relation to which, and only in relation to which, individual works of literary art, and the works of individual artists, have their significance" (*Prose* 2.458). In the "Tradition" essay, he explains that being part of a system means that one is always conforming to and being judged by other parts of that system. This does not mean that the present must conform to the past or be judged by the past, but rather that there are continuous reciprocal adjustments within systems. The necessity to conform is "not one-sided; what happens when a new work of art is created is something that happens simultaneously to all the works of art which preceded it" (*Prose* 2.106). The principle holds in regard to judgment. Being judged "by the past" is an inevitable result of entering a system that includes past writers, and of course, it is reciprocal, for the old is judged by the new as much as the new is measured by the old.

The fourth principle—that within any system there is continuous dialectical movement in which opposites are both included and transcended—is discussed in Eliot's graduate papers on Kant and his dissertation on Bradley. In literary rather than philosophical terms, the principle is also evident in his criticism, beginning with "Tradition and the Individual Talent." For example, he posits a dialectical triad in which the primitive mind and the modern mind are at once included and transcended in a greater mind—the ever-changing mind of Europe, "a mind which changes . . . this change is a development which abandons nothing *en route*, which does not superannuate either Shakespeare, or Homer, or the rock drawing of the Magdalenian draughtsmen" (*Prose* 2.107). Similarly, he divides the self into a suffering self (associated with feeling) and an observing self (associated with thought) and sees these binaries as at once contained and intensified in a written self (associated with art): "The more perfect the artist, the more completely separate in him will be the man who suffers and the mind which creates" (*Prose* 2.109). The willingness to consider one's suffering self as material and as an object for criticism and re-creation is part of what Eliot means by "self-surrender" and "self-annihilation."

In a comment on Lucretius, Eliot offers a clear description of the dialectic of depersonalization, which occurs in the greatest art. "The marvel of Lucretius is the passionate act by which he annihilates himself in a system and unites himself with it, gaining something greater than himself" (*Prose* 2.563). The "self-annihilation," "self-sacrifice," and "self-surrender" mentioned here and in other essays are not isolated events, but part of a dynamic and continuous process. What is annihilated is the autonomous self, the self as an all-sufficient whole. This death of the self, moreover, is not an end in itself but a means to the greater end of realizing the self in writing. These images of annihilation refer to the middle term in a dialectical process that involves the experience of passion, the death of that passion (as an absolute, entire of itself), and the emergence of a stronger passion in art. This motif of a dialectical play between self-suppression and self-expression runs throughout Eliot's early criticism. The best art, he maintains, begins and ends in the personal. Valéry's poetry is "impersonal in the sense that personal emotion, personal experience, is extended and completed in something impersonal—not in the sense of something divorced from personal experience and passion" (*Prose* 2.563). In an essay on Shakespeare and Seneca, Eliot says that "what every poet starts from is his own emotions. . . . Shakespeare, too, was occupied with the struggle—which alone constitutes life for a poet—to transmute his personal and private agonies into . . . something universal and impersonal" (*Prose* 3.253).

Impersonality in Art: Four Variations

The relevance of the principles of idealism outlined above to Eliot's criticism can be substantiated by following his comments on impersonality in art. In 1935, he chided Stephen Spender for his treatment of Henry James in *The Destructive Element*, in the process giving a precise description of the three moments of the dialectical imagination in criticism. One should avoid criticizing "an author to whom you have never surrendered yourself. . . . You have to give yourself up, and then recover yourself, and the third movement is having something to say, before you have wholly forgotten both surrender and recovery. Of course, the self recovered is never the same as the self before it was given" (*L*7.617-18). This dialectical process—surrender, recovery, criticism—is at the heart of four variations of impersonality achieved in the writings of admired contemporaries—Pound, Joyce, Conrad, and Yeats. The first two variations are described in "Tradition and the Individual Talent"; the other two are briefly sketched in a number of early essays, but most clearly identified in his 1940 memorial lecture on Yeats.

The first variation requires the least comment, for it is an application of the idea of tradition to the issue of impersonality in art. The artist uses what Eliot calls a "method," which begins with the labor of consciously steeping oneself in the work of one's predecessors. This method depersonalizes by placing the artist and his work into a systematic relation with other artists and other works. Dante, for example, used a "philosophic method," built on shared ideas and beliefs. In entering into an intellectual community, he surrendered his personal ideas; at the same time, he expressed those ideas more intensely than would have been possible outside of the system. Joyce, on the other hand, used a "mythical method," enabling him to put his personal experience into a context that reached all the way back to the Trojan War. By using a two-thousand-year-old epic set in the Aegean, he was able to represent almost to perfection his own moment in a provincial capital on an island in the north Atlantic.

Ezra Pound, to take another example, used a "historical method." Pound's case is particularly enlightening, for in discussing it Eliot repeatedly makes the point that the end result is heightened self-expression. In "The Method of Mr. Pound," published in the brief interval between the two installments of "Tradition and the Individual Talent," Eliot described Pound's "method" in terms that replicate the description of the historical sense in the "Tradition" essay. Pound attempts to "acquire the entire past; and when the entire past is acquired, the constituents fall into place and the present is revealed." He then uses this understanding of history to construct "masks." This surrender of personality ends, paradoxically, in a poetry striking in its expression of Pound's own personality. He is more himself "behind the mask of . . . Propertius, than when he speaks in his own person. He must hide to reveal himself. But if we collate his disguises, we find not a mere collection of green-room properties, but Mr. Pound" (*Prose* 2.142). The "historical method," then, enables the writer to express himself by hiding himself, to express himself by putting himself into a situation in which the reader is forced to see him in a larger context. Eliot's own method in *The Waste Land* can easily be seen as a combination of the mythical method outlined in his review of *Ulysses* and the historical method as outlined in the essay on Pound.

The second variation of the process through which artists achieve impersonality is also introduced in the "Tradition" essay. The first part, published in September, ends with a teaser of the sort often used in serial publication—an invitation to consider a "suggestive analogy," in this case, between the action that takes place in the mind of a poet and "the action which takes place when a bit of finely filiated platinum is introduced into a chamber containing oxygen and sulphur dioxide" (*Prose* 2.108). The second part, published in December, begins by elaborating this analogy. In contrast to the "historical method" or the "mythical method," this process does not entail studying past monuments, nor does it involve donning a mask. Rather, it is associated with a sudden metamorphosis that occurs in the mind of the poet. Eliot explains the change in these terms: "When the two gases previously mentioned are mixed in the presence of a filament of platinum, they form sulphurous acid. This combination takes place only if the platinum is present; nevertheless the newly formed acid contains no trace of platinum, and the platinum itself is apparently unaffected. . . . The mind of the poet is the shred of platinum" (*Prose* 2.109; 113n16). In spite of admitting that this was a "doubtful analogy," Eliot later defended the central point (*Prose* 5.17). As elaborated in his essays of the 1920s and 1930s, this process may be summarized as follows: a fragment of experience enters the poet's mind and remains there—inert, dormant, sometimes for years. At a later time, an unrelated fragment enters his mind, and suddenly, something mysterious happens and something new emerges in the mind. This metamorphosis involves a flash of intuition in which unrelated things are seen as alike, and a dialectical process of self-surrender, which results in a rebirth of personality.

In an essay on Wordsworth and Coleridge, Eliot changes the metaphor from chemistry to magnetism:

> The mind of any poet would be magnetised in its own way, to select automatically . . . the material—an image, a phrase, a word—which may be of use to him later. . . . There might be the experience of a child of ten, a small boy peering through sea-water in a rock-pool, and finding a sea-anemone for the first time: the simple experience . . . might lie dormant in his mind for twenty years, and re-appear transformed in some verse-context charged with great imaginative pressure. (*Prose* 4.632)

Eliot claims that the recurrence of such images is mysterious and deeply personal.

> Why . . . out of all that we have heard, seen, felt, in a lifetime, do certain images recur, charged with emotion, rather than others? The song of one bird, . . . the scent of one flower, an old woman on a German mountain path, six ruffians seen through an open window playing cards at night at a small French railway junction where there was a water-mill: such memories . . . come to represent the depths of feeling into which we cannot peer. (*Prose* 4.688)

In a lecture at the University of Minnesota in 1933, Eliot described the origin of "La Figlia Che Piange" in similar terms—as the sudden recurrence of an image he had heard in conversation some six or seven months earlier (*Prose* 4.842). In "Tradition and the Individual Talent," he takes his examples from Dante, Shakespeare, and Aeschylus. In each case, there was an image "in suspension in the poet's mind, [waiting] until the proper combination arrived for it to add itself to" (*Prose* 2.109), and when the moment came, there was a sudden metamorphosis into something new, something at once personal and impersonal. A striking description of depersonalization followed by repersonalization is contained in the "Author's Note" to Conrad's *The Secret Agent*. In recalling the origin of the novel, Conrad uses language remarkably similar to Eliot's in the "Tradition" essay. The same chemical analogy is chosen to describe the process of transformation, and moreover, given that Eliot's essay and Conrad's "Note" are virtually contemporaneous, they are probably independent.

In February 1920, as part of a larger project to publish his collected works, Conrad wrote a brief "Author's Note" for *The Secret Agent* (1907), a novel about the 1894 attempt to blow up the Greenwich Observatory. Conrad's point of departure was his recollection that reviewers had focused on the personal element in the novel and had thus misunderstood both its origin and its meaning. To clarify his intention, he recounted the genesis of *The Secret Agent*. At the time of the Greenwich outrage, Conrad had remarked to Ford Madox Ford that it was inane for a man to be "blown to bits for nothing even remotely resembling an idea, anarchist or other." Ford replied, "Oh, that fellow was half an idiot. His sister committed suicide afterwards." Conrad made no response, and nothing more was said on the topic, but the sentence remained in his mind, "in a passive way" (*Secret Agent*, x).

A week or so later, Conrad read the memoir of the man who had been assistant commissioner of police during recent anarchist activities, and a small fragment of it remained suspended in his mind. Neither the comment by Ford nor the fragment from the memoir seemed remarkable, but a couple of years later, both suddenly surfaced in his imagination and he found himself writing *The Secret Agent*. His description of this imaginative train, like Eliot's description of the creative process in the "Tradition" essay, uses a chemical analogy.

> All of a sudden, I felt myself stimulated. And then ensued in my mind what a student of chemistry would best understand from the analogy of the addition of the tiniest little drop of the right kind, precipitating the process of crystallization in a test tube containing some colourless solution. It was at first for me a mental change, disturbing a quieted-down imagination, in which strange forms, sharp in outline but imperfectly apprehended, appeared and claimed attention as crystals will do by their bizarre and unexpected shapes. . . . Then the vision of an enormous town presented itself, of a monstrous town more populous than some continents. . . . Slowly the dawning conviction of Mrs. Verloc's maternal passion grew up to a flame between me and that background. . . . At last, the story of Winnie Verloc stood out complete from the days of her childhood to the end. (*Secret Agent*, xi–xii)

From start to finish, Conrad claims, this process took three days. *The Secret Agent* is "*that* story, reduced to manageable proportions." He maintains that after these three days, he never once doubted the reality of Mrs. Verloc's story, nor disputed her conviction that "life doesn't stand much looking into" (xii–xiii).[4] The Home Secretary, linked to her in the plot through her husband's role as a double agent, is also linked structurally by his motto—"Spare me the details"—which parallels her conviction about life. Writing the novel, Conrad says, was primarily a matter of separating foreground from background, Mrs. Verloc's story from "its obscurity in that immense town" (xiii).

Conrad makes an interesting distinction regarding the personal origins of art. The initial stimulation is personal, but often it is also insignificant and banal. In the process of writing, however, this stimulus is transformed into something that is simultaneously more personal and more universal. Conrad denied that he had any personal experience with anarchists, but added that there "were moments during the writing of the book when *I was an extreme revolutionist*" (italics added). In regard to his deep feeling for Winnie, he explained that in the process of "telling Winnie Verloc's story to its anarchistic end, of utter desolation, madness, and despair," he *became* Winnie. But this, he continues, was just part of his "business" as an artist: "In all my books, I have always attended to my business . . . with complete self-surrender. . . . I could not have done otherwise. It would have bored me too much to make-believe." Conrad says that his intention, which came *after* the crystallization of Winnie's story, was to apply "an ironic method . . . in the earnest belief that ironic treatment alone would enable me to say all I . . . wanted to say in scorn, as well as in pity" (xiii–xiv). Although it is true that Conrad *becomes* Mrs. Verloc, it is also true that he subjects her to criticism—by separating his empathizing self from his observing self. This separation is essential to the dialectical movement in which scorn and pity are both contained and transcended in the ironic self on display in this great novel.

In his 1940 memorial lecture on Yeats, Eliot identified two other variations of his understanding of impersonality in art. In the first, impersonality is achieved by perfection in craft, and in the second, by self-referential passion. He illustrates the first by reference to Yeats's early work and the second (and greatest) by reference to his late work. Eliot acknowledges that his preference for late Yeats will seem to contradict his position in the "Tradition" essay. "I have, in early essays, extolled what I called impersonality in art, and it may seem that, in giving as a reason for the superiority of Yeats's later work the greater expression of personality in it, I am contradicting myself." Denying that this is so, he clarifies his position:

> There are two forms of impersonality: that which is natural to the mere skilful craftsman, and that which is more and more achieved by the maturing artist. The first is that of . . . the "anthology piece," of a lyric by Lovelace or Suckling. . . . The second . . . is that of the poet who, out of intense and personal experience, is able to express a general truth; retaining all the particularity of his experience, to make of it a general symbol. (*Prose* 6.81)

Anthology pieces are lyrics that do perfectly what has been done perfectly before. Such poems "are as satisfactory in isolation, as 'anthology pieces,' as they are in the context of [the poet's] other poems" (*Prose* 6.80). Impersonality in these pieces is achieved by mastery of technique, and formal perfection is an end in itself, not a means to greater self-expression. With such poems, one is "hardly curious to know who wrote them, hardly wants to look further into the work of that poet." There are other poems "not necessarily so perfect or complete, which make you irresistibly curious to know more of that poet through his other work." In "anthology pieces" the dialectical process is short-circuited by technical perfection, a sense of completeness. The self is sacrificed, but no greater self emerges, for there is no dialectical loop back to a richer self. "Who Goes with Fergus" is "as perfect of [its] kind as anything in the language." But it does not contain "that sense of a unique personality which makes one sit up in excitement and eagerness to learn more about the author's mind and feelings. The intensity of Yeats's own emotional experience hardly appears" (*Prose* 6.80).

In the Yeats essay of 1940, Eliot illuminates both the consistency and the development of the notion of impersonality outlined over two decades earlier in the "Tradition" essay. In the earlier essays repudiating personality, he is referring to the second term in the dialectical process, the personality of the person caught in relations, in difference. In the later essays praising personality, he is referring to the third term in the process, the *achieved* personality, the written self, caught in works of art. Both early and late, however, he argues that impersonality is less a denial of personality than "the transformation of a personality into a personal work of art." Massinger, he maintains, was not a first-rate artist because "he did not, out of his own personality, build a world of art, as Shakespeare and Marlowe and Jonson built" (*Prose* 2.254).

Eliot claims that the fourth and greatest specimen of achieved impersonality can be seen in the later poems of Yeats, arguing that the older Yeats achieves self-transcendence not by self-surrender but by passionate *self-*

referentiality. Eliot singles out for admiration lines from the introductory rhymes to *Responsibilities* (1914):

> Pardon that for a barren passion's sake,
> Although I have come close on forty-nine,
> I have no child, I have nothing but a book,
> Nothing but that to prove your blood and mine.[5]

Addressing his ancestors, Yeats apologizes for having, in late middle age, nothing but poetry to show for his forty-eight years on earth. Eliot admires the reference to Yeats's barren love for Maud Gonne, and even more, the reference to his age. This is the opposite of the "anthology piece"; it is intense poetry, and the reader cannot but acknowledge the power of this voice, cannot but desire to know more of his work, and thus to put this voice into the context of a life passionately lived, placing this poem in the context of great lyric poetry.

Yeats's most personal poems, arguably, are those written about the experience of aging. It is strange but true that Yeats became more passionate as he aged, and as a seventy-year-old he was more fiercely personal than he had been at thirty. Like the old man in "Sailing to Byzantium," he was "sick with desire / And fastened to a dying animal." Yeats's later poetry is indelibly stamped with his personality. He expresses his personal feelings so intensely that his particularity becomes universality; in speaking for himself, he speaks for all old men. In illustration of this point, Eliot quotes "The Spur":

> You think it horrible that lust and rage
> Should dance attendance upon my old age;
> They were not such a plague when I was young:
> What else have I to spur me into song?

Eliot claims that these "not very pleasant" lines are "a personal confession," but not the confession of "a man who differed from other men, but of a man who was essentially the same as most other men; the only difference is in the greater clarity, honesty and vigour." And Eliot, mindful of his own aging, asks: "To what honest man, old enough, can these sentiments be entirely alien?" (*Prose* 6.83). In becoming more outspokenly himself, Yeats revealed not his essential difference, but his essential likeness with all men. Analogously, "in becoming more Irish, not in subject-matter but in expression, he became at the same time more universal" (*Prose* 6.82).

The dialectical pattern underlying Eliot's notion of impersonality owes much to philosophical idealism, but it is actually much older. In using terms such as *self-annihilation*, *self-surrender*, and *self-sacrifice*, terms carrying overtones of religion and violence, Eliot is associating his process not only with post-Hegelian dialectic but also with the most ancient commonplaces regarding the connection between life and death in nature, myth, and religion. This pattern is evident in Christ's words in the Gospel according to John (12:24): "Verily, I say unto you, 'Except a grain of wheat fall into the ground and die, it abideth alone; but if it die, it bringeth forth much fruit.'" Jesus is using an analogy from nature to suggest to his disciples the intimate connection between his rapidly approaching death and his promised resurrection. But the pattern is older even than Christianity, for it is based on the seasonal cycles of spring and fall, life and death, and as such, has been central in primitive religions all over the world, including those catalogued by Frazer in *The Golden Bough*. The single most important pattern in early Eliot is that of the dying God, which is based on the tension between death and new life. His concept of impersonality, and the four variations of depersonalization outlined in this chapter, can thus be seen, not only as consistent with, but also as an extension of, an immemorial pattern in nature and thought.

6 Poetry and Despair

The Hollow Men and the End of Philosophy

> I have written only one blasphemous poem, *The Hollow Men*: [it] is blasphemy because it is despair.
>
> Eliot to his brother, Henry (1936)

When writing about literary history, Eliot often projected a big picture view anchored in classic idealism. But when focused on his own situation, he tended to fall back on realism and relativism. In criticism, as discussed in chapter 5, he usually privileged wholeness; in poetry, fragments of thought and feeling. The latter is evident in the poems written after the war, including *The Waste Land* and verses excised therefrom. In *The Hollow Men*, his first major work after publication of *The Waste Land*, Eliot adjusts this pattern by using a bifocal structure, which frames fragments of despair with choral odes. Formally, the odes shape and restrain the despair; thematically, they reinforce it by undercutting the two philosophical positions that Eliot once found promising—idealism and relativism. This conjunction of anguish and critique represents a watershed in the poet's life, leading to his conversion, and in his art, inaugurating a style that is simpler, more ritualistic, and both more and less personal.

Although Eliot in the 1920s remained troubled by contradictions, the antitheses so important in his dissertation and philosophical essays were overwritten by personal counterparts, the idea by the reality. Of the several factors involved in this overtaking of abstract entities, two are preeminent. The first, his marriage, personalizes the polarity between thought and feeling as a conflict between men and women, as in "A Game of Chess."

> 'My nerves are bad to-night. Yes, bad. Stay with me.
> 'Speak to me. Why do you never speak. Speak.

'What are you thinking of? What thinking? What?
'I never know what you are thinking. Think.' (*WL* 111-14)

The silent male is clearly associated with intellect and the nervous female with emotion. Although this opposition is dramatized in early poems such as "Portrait of a Lady," it assumes dominance in the years following his marriage. The second factor, perennial illness, refashions the debate between body and soul as disjunction between body and mind. Illness is a reminder of psychophysical dualism, or as Yeats puts it in "Sailing to Byzantium," of being "fastened to a dying animal." Like Tiresias, the poet finds himself "throbbing between two lives" (*WL* 218), or in a phrase from one of *The Waste Land* excisions, "swinging from life to death" (*WLF* 99).

The Hollow Men is Eliot's *No Exit*, a portrait of his mind in what he described at the time as "*the blackest moment in my life*" (Eliot's italics; *L*2.592). The keynote of the whole, in his word, is despair. Eliot's despair, like that of the characters in Sartre's play, is intensified by the fact that he is not alone;[1] like Francesca da Rimini (*Inferno* V), he is chained to another damned soul. Chronically ill and on suicide watch during the 1920s, his wife, Vivien, wrote to John Middleton Murry: "I have been in despair. I mean real despair, which isolates and freezes one. . . . My despair is paralysing me" (*L*2.170). The nature and extent of Eliot's despair can be gleaned from two of his comments on *The Hollow Men*, neither of which has been explored by previous critics. One is from a talk he gave at Cambridge, unpublished before it appeared in volume 2 of the *Complete Prose*, and the other, a letter to his brother, is in a forthcoming volume of the *Letters*. The first, which dates from the period of the poem's incubation, points to what Eliot referred to as its informing principle; the second, written ten years later, emerged from his reflection on its significance as a watershed in his life and art.

Organic or Mechanical? Composition and Meaning in *The Hollow Men*

We do not know until the shell breaks what kind of egg we have been sitting on.

Eliot, *The Use of Poetry* (1933)

The history of the composition of *The Hollow Men* is important in understanding its structure and meaning. Like *The Waste Land* and *Ash-Wednesday*, it originated from independently composed lyrics that gradually or suddenly crystallized into a larger work.[2] In November 1924, Eliot perceived that a number of lyrics composed primarily in 1924 belonged together, and a year later, he added one more and an epigraph and arranged the five into the final poem, published in November 1925. The four poems from 1924 were published in various overlapping arrangements: "Doris's Dream Songs" (*Chapbook*, November 1924), "Three Poems" (*Criterion*, January 1925), and "The Hollow Men" (*Dial*, March 1925). The *Criterion* group—"Eyes I dare not meet in dreams," "Eyes that last I saw in tears," and "The eyes are not here"—projects intense psychological pain through a brilliant combination of synecdoche ("eyes") and metonymy ("tears"). The chronology of the publication of the first four parts of the final sequence, outlined by Ricks and McCue (*Poems* 1.711), is as follows:

I "We are the hollow men"—November 1924
III "This is the dead land"—November 1924
II "Eyes I dare not meet in dreams"—6 January 1925
IV "The eyes are not here"—6 January 1925

Eliot described these four lyrics to Scofield Thayer as "scraps . . . drops of blood out of an exhausted stone," adding, "There is yet another in the series which is not yet written" (*L*2.566-67). The lyrical scraps incubated for almost a year waiting for the sequel that Eliot knew was coming. Late in 1925, the shell broke. With the addition of the title page, the epigraph from *Heart of Darkness*, and the final ode, the scraps were transformed into a single poem with a lyrical center framed by choral odes. The lyrical core preserves the despair of the incubation period, and the framing odes and epigraph contain and contextualize it, philosophically and theologically.

As several critics have noted, this history of the composition as occurring in two stages is a key to understanding *The Hollow Men*. Ronald Bush, for example, argues that Eliot was "recapitulating the last stages of composing *The Waste Land*, [in which] the title and . . . controlling myth were added to frame and unify his fragments. . . . In the process, he introduced a spurious plot [that sent] readers hunting through history and literature to reconstruct the skeletons of stories that at best suggestively mirror the action that is there on the page" (96). Noting that Eliot's "very last act" was "to append the epigraph from *Heart of Darkness*," Bush claims that this was a last-ditch effort to unify his lyrical bits and pieces (96). But the late addition of the epigraph does not mean that it was an afterthought; generally speaking, the framing elements and epigraphs in Eliot arise from epiphanic moments, sudden recognitions of what had been incubating all along.[3]

My counterargument, based on Eliot's account of the way a poet's mind works, is that the two stages of composing *The Hollow Men* are organically related. As he claims in "Tradition," there is often an image suspended "in the poet's mind until the proper combination arrive[s] for it to add itself to" (*Prose* 2.109). The late additions to *The Hollow Men* point to passages that had haunted Eliot for years. They suggest a structure in which despair is framed and deepened by an awareness of the inadequacy of philosophical solutions. Three of the parts composed in 1924 (II, III, and IV) constitute a core of personal lyrics, the cri de coeur of a poet in extremis, or as Eliot described them, "drops of blood from an exhausted stone." The 1925 additions complete the sequence by generating the frame and clarifying the theme. The frame seals the despair by exposing the insufficiency of idealism and relativism to cope with it. In adding an allusion in part V to Shakespeare's Brutus and in the epigraph to Conrad's Kurtz, Eliot reveals that the hollowness at issue is the hollowness of an attenuated idealism. Both characters point to the emptiness of high-minded speech, the frailty of eloquence when confronted with brute reality. The late addition of references to these two intellectuals results in the surfacing of submerged allusions suggesting that *Julius Caesar* and *Heart of Darkness* had been in the back of Eliot's mind from the beginning. For example:

> In this last of meeting places
> We grope together
> And avoid speech
> Gathered on this beach of the tumid river. (*HM* IV.6–9)

This reference to the "last of meeting places" beside the "tumid river" points to the damned souls on the banks of the river Acheron in *Inferno* III, but with the addition of the epigraph, it is evident that it is also as an allusion to the natives beside the Congo in *Heart of Darkness*.

My analysis focuses on the transformative late additions (title, epigraph, part V) and on two of Eliot's comments about *The Hollow Men*. The first occurred in 1924, during the poem's incubation; the second in 1936, in a moment of crisis that inspired a pithy assessment of the poem's significance. These two comments highlight both the lyrical core and the ritualistic frame and support the position that the late additions are organically related to the 1924 lyrics.

The retrospective remark was written a decade after the publication of the poem. In response to an accusation by his brother that the satiric poems ("The Hippopotamus," "Mr. Eliot's Sunday Morning Service") were blasphemous, Eliot protested that he had "written only one blasphemous poem, *The Hollow Men*: [it] is blasphemy because it is despair, it stands for the lowest point I ever reached in my sordid domestic affairs."[4] This comment illuminates the meaning of the sequence in both personal and theological terms—as an expression of the hopelessness that Eliot felt in 1924 and as his later interpretation of that despair. During the intervening years, his understanding of both despair and blasphemy evolved, honed by continuing reflections on Dostoevski and Baudelaire.[5] In reading *The Brothers Karamazov* and *Les Fleurs du mal*, he came to see that despair could be a spiritual cul-de-sac or, conversely, a stage in the progress of the soul. "Genuine blasphemy," he said in 1930, "is the product of partial belief, and is as impossible to the complete atheist as to the perfect Christian" (*Prose* 4.157). To curse God is to acknowledge his existence. This concept of blasphemy is not only an explanation of Baudelaire's Satanism, but also of the larger spiritual movement in which *The Hollow Men* was succeeded by *Ash-Wednesday*.

The second comment was contemporaneous with the composition of the lyrics that ended as parts I-IV of *The Hollow Men*. The first arrangement of the lyrics appeared as "Doris's Dream Songs" in November 1924. On 30 November, in response to a note from Ottoline Morrell, Eliot explained that they were part of "a longer sequence. . . . I laid down the principles of it in a paper I read at Cambridge, on Chapman, Dostoevski and Dante" (*L*2.546). The paper, which he read to the Cambridge Literary Society on 8 November, focused on a phenomenon that he had noticed in "*The Brothers Karamazoff*." In Dostoevski, Eliot observes, one is aware that

> there are everywhere two planes of reality, and that the scene before our eyes is only the screen and veil of another action which is taking place behind it. The characters themselves are partially aware of this division, aware of the grotesque futility of their visible lives, and seem always to be listening for other voices and to be conducting a conversation with specters. Hence their distraction, their inability to attend to the business at hand in a practical way. (*Prose* 2.553)

For Dostoevski's characters, the pervasive consciousness of the thin line separating the visible and the invisible worlds includes a hunch that the invisible realm is the real world and an inclination to listen for voices that are trying to engage us in conversation. This phenomenon, which causes his characters to feel alienated and to behave in ways that others interpret as off-key, is at the heart of Harry's disquiet in *The Family Reunion*. Like the characters in Dostoevski, he sees the Furies and hears remote voices.

To clarify the context of Dostoevski's marriage of sensuality and mysticism, Eliot contrasts him with Dante, who "knew as well as . . . Dostoevski that man belongs to two worlds" (*Prose* 2.554). But for Dante, this was not a problem. Because he was at ease with the Christian explanation for the uncanny, he was able to imagine himself as a tourist in the world beyond the screen. Dostoevski, on the other hand, sensed the reality of the other world, but lacked Dante's map for negotiating the dangerous terrain. Dostoevski was forced to struggle against "that movement which culminated in Goethe—the movement which accepted the divorce of human and divine, denied the divine, and asserted the perfection of the human to be the divine" (*Prose* 2.555). The felt reality of the uncanny drives one, in Eliot's words, to either "theology or glands." Dante accepted the theological explanation; Freud pushed the materialistic and glandular. Dostoevski's characters, and Eliot himself, were caught in the middle. Eliot's critique of the folly of trying to collapse the two worlds into one was to continue, and it is most fully developed in his analysis of humanism.

Eliot's identification with characters in Dostoevski was foreshadowed in a 1917 letter to his cousin Eleanor: "I have been living in one of Dostoevski's novels, you see, not in one of Jane Austen's" (*L*1.210). The connection with Dostoevski was noted by the ever-observant Bertrand Russell, who told Ottoline Morrell that the Eliots reminded him of characters in Dostoevski. Eliot "has a profound and unselfish devotion to his wife, . . . but she has impulses of cruelty to him . . . a Dostojevsky type of cruelty, not a straightforward everyday kind" (*Autobiography*, 2.64). By 1924, Eliot's thoughts on Dostoevski's characters were centered on their spiritual preoccupations and the disorientation created thereby.

In order to highlight Eliot's convictions regarding the existence of two worlds and his disenchantment with idealism and relativism as central in *The Hollow Men*, I now turn to the transformation of the text by the late additions. The emptiness of idealism is shown in the addition of Kurtz and Brutus, and the peril of living in the in-between, associated with relativism, is exposed in part V—"Between the idea / And the reality . . . / Falls the Shadow." The existence of two worlds, one visible and one spectral, is dramatized in preoccupations with the kingdoms of death—"death's other kingdom" (I), "death's dream kingdom" and the "twilight kingdom" (II), "death's other kingdom" (III), "death's twilight kingdom" (IV), and finally, in the fifth lyric, added as the shell broke, the all-inclusive Kingdom of God.

Kurtz, Brutus, and the Critique of Idealism

Metaphysical systems are condemned to go up like a rocket and come down like a stick.

Eliot, *Knowledge and Experience* (1916)

Eliot's critique is not aimed at classical philosophical idealism or at the empirical idealism of Bradley, but rather, at a less technical version often adopted by intellectuals as a primary guide to life. He focuses on two idealists —Conrad's Kurtz and Shakespeare's Brutus—one a representation of egoism, the other of self-deception, both of a link between high-mindedness and violence. Both are driven by an idée fixe: Kurtz by white supremacy, Brutus by honor. Eliot's addition of these two characters is one of many indications that his late additions are culminations of an organic process; epiphanic moments that bring to birth what had been incubating all along. Generally speaking, these moments suggest an underlying continuity in his intellectual life; in his poetry, they often become part of a frame that contains and defines a major theme.

The epigraph from *Heart of Darkness*—"Mistah Kurtz—he dead"—was not plucked from a sourcebook to unify Eliot's lyrical scraps. As shown by *The Waste Land* drafts, he had been brooding for years on the scene in *Heart of Darkness* in which this snippet appears. His first choice for the epigraph to *The Waste Land* was a passage from this scene.[6] "Did he live his life again in every detail of desire, temptation, and surrender during that supreme moment of complete knowledge? He cried in a whisper at some image, at some vision,—he cried out twice, a cry that was no more than a breath—'The horror! The horror!'" (*Heart*, 68). This description of the "supreme moment" of the dying Kurtz encapsulates what Eliot identified in the Cambridge lecture as the theme of his developing poem: "The scene before our eyes is only the screen and veil of another action which is taking place behind it" (*Prose* 2.553). In the scene that had been haunting Eliot, Conrad's Marlow is reminiscing about his trip to the Congo to retrieve an ivory trader who had fallen ill. As he sails away with the dying agent, Marlow witnesses and attempts to interpret the death throes of Mistah Kurtz. "I saw on that ivory face the expression of sombre pride, of ruthless power, of craven terror—of an intense and hopeless despair" (*Heart*, 68). As the old sailor rejoins his colleagues, an African boy enters to announce "Mistah Kurtz—he dead" (*Heart*, 69). Kurtz is characterized as an educated European who epitomizes a marriage of intelligence and evil, an identity inseparable from the vision that elicits his grimace and his cry. In affixing this epigraph to his title page, Eliot links the two worlds—the visible world of Kurtz and the invisible world that he perceives as he crosses the frontier.

Eliot's epigraph calls to mind not only the dying of Kurtz, but his death as a fait accompli. In this Eliot underscores another major theme: Kurtz's death is more than the death of a character; it represents the end of a hollowed-out version of idealism. He is known first and from afar for high-minded ideas and artistic gifts. The comments of the brick maker at the Central Station are typical: Kurtz is "a prodigy . . . an emissary of pity, and science, and progress. . . . [a man] of higher intelligence, wide sympathies, singleness of purpose" (*Heart*, 28). One of his allegorical paintings—"a small sketch in oils, . . . representing a woman draped and blindfolded carrying a lighted torch"—projects Justice and Enlightenment emerging out of a "somber—almost black" background (*Heart*, 27). As Marlow approaches Kurtz's compound, however, he discovers that this idealist is a genocidal egoist who decorates his fence posts with human heads. Marlow speculates:

> They [the heads] only showed that Mr. Kurtz lacked restraint . . . that there was something wanting in him—some small matter which . . . could not be found under his magnificent eloquence. . . . The wilderness . . . had whispered to him things about himself which he did not know . . . and the whisper had proved irresistibly fascinating. It echoed loudly within him because he was hollow at the core. (*Heart*, 57–58)

Marlow later learns from Kurtz himself that his ideas had been formed in Europe. His mother was half-English, his father was half-French, and his education occurred primarily in England. "All Europe contributed to the making of Kurtz" (*Heart*, 50).

The European idea that Kurtz brought to Africa is outlined in the pamphlet that he wrote for the guidance of the "International Society for the Suppression of Savage Customs." He began with the argument that "we whites, from the point of development we had arrived at, must necessarily appear to [savages] in the nature of supernatural beings—we approach them with the might as of a deity. . . . By the simple exercise of our will we can exert a power for good practically unbounded" (*Heart*, 50). This is the nineteenth-century rationalization for colonialism, an example of the inherent doubleness of civilization itself, explored by Kipling in *The Man Who Would Be King*. Kurtz's "moving appeal to every altruistic sentiment," written at the beginning of his work in the Congo, contained a postscript written much later in an unsteady hand: "Exterminate the brutes!" (*Heart*, 51). This postscript is the dark twin of Kurtz's idealism.

Shakespeare's *Julius Caesar* was also in Eliot's mind as he composed *The Hollow Men*. In his 1924 introduction to Valéry's *Le Serpent*, written while he was working on the poem, Eliot compared a line from Valéry—"*Entre le vide et l'événement pur*" (Between the emptiness and the pure event)—to lines in which a sleepless Brutus, having agreed to participate in the assassination of Caesar, reflects on the psychological and moral quagmire in which he is now trapped (*Prose* 2.561). And in his contemporaneous dramatic experiment, *The Superior Landlord* (later published as *Sweeney Agonistes*), Eliot used the first three lines of the Shakespearean passage as an epigraph.

> Between the acting of a dreadful thing
> And the first motion, all the interim is
> Like a phantasma, or a hideous dream:
> The Genius and the mortal instruments
> Are then in council; and the state of man,
> Like to a little kingdom, suffers then
> The nature of an insurrection. (*Julius Caesar* II.i.63–69)

Brutus enters *The Hollow Men* through the strong echo of this passage in the series of "betweens" in part V, all dealing with the interim between the idea (the first motion) and the reality (the action). In his edition of Shakespeare, Hardin Craig says that these lines are "one of the most perfect expressions in Shakespeare of the psychology of warring emotions, hesitation, and inward conflict" (778n). This passage, like that from *Heart of Darkness*, is an expression of the double vision that Eliot refers to in the Chapman lecture.

The backdrop to Brutus's distress is the civil war that broke out in 49 BC. Both Brutus and Cassius joined the opposition and fought against Caesar. When their side lost, both were forgiven and elevated by Caesar. The Machiavellian Cassius repays this generosity by forming a conspiracy to assassinate him, and to give the plot legitimacy, he recruits Brutus to lead it. This situation generates the conflict in Brutus, who says that he is "with himself at war" (I.ii.46), torn between his love for Caesar and his love of the "general good."

> If it [Cassius's plan] be aught toward the general good,
> Set honour in one eye and death i' the other,
> And I will look on both indifferently:

For let the gods so speed me as I love
The name of honour more than I fear death. (I.ii.85-89)

This clash between "the idea and the reality" is the crux of the play. Like Kurtz, Brutus is an idealist, but unlike Kurtz, he is taken in by his own rhetoric. Believing that absolute power corrupts absolutely, he concludes that "Caesar must bleed" (II.i.171), not for what he has done, but for what he might do.

Since the quarrel
Will bear no colour for the thing he is,
Fashion it thus; that what he is, augmented,
Would run to these and these extremities;
And therefore think him as a serpent's egg
Which, hatch'd, would, as his kind, grow mischievous,
And kill him in the shell. (II.i.28-34)

Brutus rationalizes the murder as a religious duty: "Let us be sacrificers, but not butchers. . . . Let's carve him as a dish fit for the gods" (II.i.166, 173). He predicts that in the eyes of the common people, "We shall be called purgers and not murderers" (II.i.180). Blinded by his idea of honor, Brutus fails to see that the murder will lead to a new civil war.

Eliot claimed that his title echoes several sources, primarily Kipling's poem "The Broken Men" and William Morris's romance *The Hollow Land* (*Prose* 5.158). The exact phrase, however, is taken from Brutus's description of his fellow conspirator Cassius.

When love begins to sicken and decay
It useth an enforced ceremony.
There are no tricks in plain and simple faith;
But hollow men, like horses hot at hand,
Make gallant show and promise of their mettle;
But when they should endure the bloody spur,
They fall their crests, and, like deceitful jades,
Sink in the trial. (IV.ii.20-27)

Brutus defines the term by reference to its opposite, men of "plain and simple faith." "Hollow men" are like horses that retain the beauty of the thoroughbred but lack its essence. As Brutus discovers too late, Cassius is like one of these show horses.

Although Shakespeare's Brutus is self-deceived, he is not evil. He is no Kurtz and no Cassius, but in his own way, he too is a hollow man. He combines idealism with Stoicism, and like his mentor and father-in-law, Cato of Utica, when faced with the collapse of his ideas, he calmly takes his own life. His antagonist, Marc Antony, acknowledges that he was a model of civic virtue.

> This was the noblest Roman of them all:
> All the conspirators save only he
> Did that they did in envy of great Caesar;
> He only, in a general honest thought
> And common good to all, made one of them. (V.v.68–72)

Although Eliot clearly has Shakespeare's tormented idealist in mind, it is important to note the undertow generated by the prominence of Dante in *The Hollow Men*. Dante's Brutus is not judged by his high thoughts but by his base actions. His Brutus is a butcher, not a sacrificer; he is a traitor, and as such, he is in Judecca, the lowest part of Hell. As Dante and Virgil complete their journey through Hell, they see Satan devouring the shades of Judas, betrayer of Christ, and Cassius and Brutus, betrayers of the state.

The Shadow Falls: *The Hollow Men* and the End of Philosophy

In his early poetry, Eliot dramatizes the painful conflicts of the human condition and struggles to find ways of reconciling them. In subsequent years, he migrates from the weak idealism of Bergson to the dialectical idealism of Bradley to relativism. All three positions suggest ways of dealing with contradictions and all lean toward resolution of contraries. But for Eliot, all proved to be inadequate. As discussed in previous chapters, he was unable to accept either idealism or realism (including materialism); he rejected Bergson's displacement of reality to a bridge between mind and object,[7] and he remained unconvinced by the relativist's displacement of reality from opposing poles to the relation between them.[8] As revealed in his lecture on Chapman, he came to accept as "principle" the impossibility of overcoming dualism, now conceived of primarily in terms of the natural and the supernatural. His move toward the position that the human condition is one of innate duality had been anticipated in his approval of T. E. Hulme's position "that neither human nor divine will be denied, that they are inseparable and eternally in conflict, this recognition of duality is the Doctrine of Original Sin" (*Prose* 2.555).

The closing ode of *The Hollow Men* encapsulates this intellectual odyssey by arranging a series of abstractions that are separated by an intervening and blocking shadow. Eliot's emphasis is on the weakness of positions that suggest dissolving oppositions by focusing on the "in-between." The theme of "in-betweenness" is evident on the page in part V of *The Hollow Men*, caught in typography and supported by poetics and syntax. First, the preposition "between" is the linchpin that controls the mood and structure of the ode. It is the first word in the three primary stanzas and the first in almost every other line. Second, the preposition and its appositional "Shadow" are underscored by syntactical variations. The normal syntax would be "The Shadow falls between X and Y." By beginning each segment with "Between" and ending each with the capitalized "Shadow," Eliot effects a displacement that suggests that philosophical entities are less important than relations between them.

> Between the idea
> And the reality
> Between the motion
> And the act
> Falls the Shadow
> *For Thine is the Kingdom*
> Between the conception
> And the creation
> Between the emotion
> And the response
> Falls the Shadow
> *Life is very long*
> Between the desire
> And the spasm
> Between the potency
> And the existence
> Between the essence
> And the descent
> Falls the Shadow
> *For Thine is the Kingdom* (V.1-24)

In the theme and variations pattern Eliot here uses, all of the prepositional phrases are variations of the first—"Between the idea and the reality." In each variation, the first abstraction is associated with idealism (idea, motion, conception, emotion, desire, potency, and essence), and the second with realism or materialism (reality, response, existence, matter, action). Most philosophers have a version of this binary, and as discussed in earlier chapters, Eliot spent years thinking about it. In Bergson, it is memory and matter; in Bradley, appearance and reality; in Aristotle, potency and existence; in Plato, essence and descent; and in the social sciences, interpretations and facts. In Eliot's lecture on Chapman, which he says contains the informing principle of *The Hollow Men*, the binary is divine and human, and the principle is that the two can be distinguished but cannot be reconciled. Between the "idea" and the "reality," there is a descent in the meaning of the concept (intangible to tangible, higher to lower, mind to matter) and a drop in the musical pitch (from "e" to "ah"). The last line of each stanza uses meter to complete the downward movement. Having firmly established a rising beat by beginning each unit with iambs, Eliot in the last line reverses course, substituting falling for rising meter, trochees for iambs (from "Be-*tween* the i-*de*a" to "*Falls* the *Sha*-dow)."

The relativism suggested by the reiterated preposition, however, is as unsatisfactory as idealism. The multivalent "Shadow" is at best a chimera. It points to the endless literal and moral shadows in *Heart of Darkness*, *Julius Caesar*, and the *Inferno*, as well, perhaps, as to the shadow in Ernest Dowson's "Cynara" (*Prose* 5.158).[9] Southam's reasonable surmise is that the Shadow is "whatever it is in human affairs or within human beings that prevents fulfillment and success" (203). In keeping with the principle outlined in the Chapman lecture, the Shadow seems to be the insurmountable ambivalence separating the idea and the reality. In each occurrence, "Falls the Shadow" is followed by an italicized fragment that suggests a potential bridge across the divide. The first, from Conrad's *Outcast of the Islands*, is literary, and the other two, from the Lord's Prayer, are religious. The fragment of prayer—"*For Thine is the Kingdom*"—is followed by a coda in which the prayer disintegrates not into the bluster of lost violent souls, but into the whimper of lost listless ones. The chant of philosophical parallels is framed by universalizing quatrains—the first associated with childhood ("Here we go around the mulberry bush"), the second with apocalypse ("This is the way the world ends").

Unanswerable or Meaningless: "A penny for the Old Guy"

Soon after finishing *The Hollow Men*, Eliot mentioned his disillusionment with philosophy to his mother. "After my first enthusiasm, I found modern philosophy to be nothing more than a logomachy, believed in by its professors, chiefly because they had to make their living out of it" (*L* 4.411). The larger meaning of the dark beauty of *The Hollow Men* is caught in the Guy Fawkes epigraph of part I. By substituting "A penny for the Old Guy" for the children's cry "A penny for the Guy," Eliot layers a theological pun on the historical allusion. The "old man" is Paul's term for the unredeemed self: "our old man is crucified with Christ" that "henceforth we should not serve sin" (Rom. 6:6). For Eliot, the "old man" would have included the self at war with itself, the man who could not let go of "matters that with myself I too much discuss / Too much explain" (*AW* I.28–29). Section I of *The Hollow Men* is an acknowledgment that the "old guy" is filled with straw, and Section V records his dying whimper.

The critique of idealism and relativism in *The Hollow Men* is part of Eliot's rejection of the autonomous intellect, the distrust of which is evident in his earliest work. In "The Love Song of J. Alfred Prufrock," it is associated less with the content of specific ideas than with the capacity of thinking to deaden sensibility and inhibit action. In "Gerontion," Eliot creates a modern Socrates, who sits on a porch and thinks himself to death. In his philosophical prose and early literary criticism, Eliot praises "philosophy without prejudice"—that is, philosophy that "accepts the data" and follows "the argument to the end." "If it ends . . . in zero, well, we have at least the satisfaction of . . . having ascertained that certain questions which occur to men to ask, are unanswerable or are meaningless" (*Prose* 2.516). This inductive process is evident in his poetry, both in his use of fragments and in his preference for synecdoche over metonymy.

In 1918, in a memorial piece on Henry James, Eliot argues that, unlike his father and brother, both distinguished philosophers, Henry had the ability "not to think." "James's critical genius comes out most tellingly in his mastery over, his baffling escape from, Ideas; a mastery and an escape which are perhaps the last test of a superior intelligence. He had a mind so fine that no idea could violate it." Eliot's paradoxical claim is that James, "the most intelligent man of his generation," maintains in his fiction a point of view "untouched by the parasite idea" (*Prose* 1.650). In 1919, Eliot makes a similar claim about Conrad. Unlike Kipling, who is associated with the idea of Empire, Conrad "has no ideas." He is the "antithesis of Empire." At the same time, like James, he does have an unmistakable and all-pervasive "point of view" (*Prose* 2.35). In Eliot's eyes, even minor writers can distinguish themselves by prioritizing experience (feelings and objects) over theories. In his preface to a new edition (1932) of Charles-Louis Philippe's *Bubu de Montparnasse* (1901), he remarked that Philippe possessed a rare gift: "the ability not to think, not to generalise, . . . not to corrupt [personal experience] by afterthoughts" (*Prose* 4.418).[10] This acknowledgment of the insufficiency of the intellect is part of the hopelessness that Eliot represents in *The Hollow Men*, one of the reasons that he later confided to his brother that it represented the blackest moment before the break of dawn.

Love and Ecstasy in Donne, Dante, and Andrewes

The progress of Eliot's spirit through the slough of despond is captured in three sequentially composed writings in the mid-1920s. The first is the iconic modernist poem *The Hollow Men*; the second, a series of lectures on metaphysical poetry delivered at Cambridge University; and the third, an essay on Lancelot Andrewes appearing in the *Times Literary Supplement*.[1] The poem, an evocation of despair, was largely composed and partially published in the fall of 1924; it was completed and published as *The Hollow Men* in November 1925. The underlying idea of the poem, outlined in Eliot's 1924 lecture on Chapman, is the inevitability of dualism (subject and object, mind and body, human and divine). The second, an analysis of what happens to love in the absence of dualism, was composed in December 1925 and delivered as the Clark Lectures at Cambridge between January and March 1926. The third, a tribute to a preacher whose sermons on the Incarnation suggested a way forward, was composed in the summer of 1926 and published in September. These works, which overlapped in time, constitute stops and steps of the mind as Eliot moved from despair to analysis to clarity in the blackest moments of his life.

A World without Objects: Donne and Descartes

> The real abyss between the classic scholastic philosophy and all philosophy since . . . was impressed upon the world by Descartes, . . . when he clearly stated that what we know is not the world of objects, but our own ideas of these objects. The revolution was immense. Instead of ideas as meanings, as references to an outside world, you have suddenly a new world coming into existence, inside your own mind and therefore . . . inside your own head.
>
> Eliot, Clark Lectures (1926)

The psychophysical dualism that had troubled Eliot from the beginning of his career is addressed directly and at length in his 1926 Clark Lectures at Cambridge. The overall topic of the lectures is the history of love poetry from Dante to Donne, with a promise to write later of Donne's successors, especially Laforgue. The thesis is that European poetry between the thirteenth and twentieth centuries was characterized by a "disintegration of intellect," essentially a separation of the thinker from the object of thought, and that this development was part of a broader breakdown in the history of ideas. The chasm separating Dante and Donne, Eliot maintains, is a corollary of that between Aquinas and Descartes. Having argued that objects have no existence outside the mind, Descartes claims that since the body is an object like any other, it may well be simply a phantom conjured up by the imagination. As Descartes says in a passage of *Meditation* VI quoted by Eliot:

> Because I can discover no other convenient mode of explaining it [the body], I conjecture with probability that the body does exist; but this is only with probability, and although I examine all things with care, I nevertheless do not find that from this distinct idea of corporeal nature, which I have in my imagination, I can derive any argument from which there will necessarily be deduced the existence of the body. (Qtd. in *Prose* 2.635; trans. 2.645n7)[2]

The question that Eliot asks in the eight Clark Lectures is what happens to love poetry, and to love itself, in a world without objects. What happens when the subject is self-contained and self-sufficient, when ideas refer not to meanings outside the self, but to a world inside one's head? Eliot explores this question by comparing the poetry and philosophy of the seventeenth century with that of the thirteenth, with emphasis on Donne and Dante. In his essay on Andrewes, to be discussed later in this chapter, he raises a parallel question in regard to religion.

Eliot's epigraph to the series of lectures constitutes a miniature of the overall topic by juxtaposing lines of love poetry from the periods before and after Descartes. The first is from Dante's *Vita Nuova* (XVIII), composed at the end of the thirteenth century, and the second is from an anonymous popular song, composed in the twentieth century.

> *Madonne, lo fine del mio amore fu già il saluto di questa donna, di cui voi forse intendete; ed in quello dimorava la mia beatitudine, chè era fine di tutti i miei desiderii.* (*Prose* 2.609; 2.623n1)[3]

> (Ladies, the end and aim of my love formerly lay in the greeting of this lady to whom you are perhaps referring, and in this greeting dwelt my bliss.)

> I want someone to treat me rough.
> Give me a cabman.

The "end and aim" of the *Vita Nuova* is to achieve happiness by contemplating "the beauty and dignity of the object contemplated by stating the effect of that beauty and dignity upon the lover in contemplation" (*Prose* 2.655). In contrast, the aim of "treat me rough" is to achieve transient ecstasy through the exploitation of the senses. The first balances the subject (the lover) and the object (a beautiful woman who exists outside the lover). The second focuses entirely on the self.

Eliot's methodology in this analysis is consistent with that in his previous work. In a version of the scientific method that he adapted for use in literary criticism, he moves inductively from particulars to generalizations (facts to interpretations). In the opening lecture, he chides those who "evolve from [their] insides" a theory and then search for works that embody it. Far better, he says, is beginning with the "material in hand" (*Prose* 2.612). He says that he will begin not "with Poetry as an abstraction, but with particular poems" (623), chosen to illuminate the connection of poetry and philosophy suggested by the term *metaphysical poetry*. Eliot focuses on poems of love and ecstasy, because love by definition deals with subjects and objects and ecstasy refers to a euphoric state in which lovers (subjects and objects) are transcended. For the Cartesian moment, he uses Donne's "The Extasie" (ca. 1602), and for the pre-Cartesian, Dante's *Vita Nuova* (1292–94).

Donne, Eliot suggests in "Donne in our Time," was a major harbinger of Descartes (*Prose* 4.373). The poet anticipates the philosopher in two important ways—first, by emphasizing the primacy of intellect, and second, by assuming the disjunction between soul and body. In support of the first, Eliot maintains that exhibit number one is Donne's language. His conceits are farfetched and intellectual (which is why Johnson refers to them as "metaphysical"). In "The Extasie," Donne announces his topic in the title and plays on its literal meaning (literally: standing outside of) in a conceit as the fusion of souls that have exited from their bodies. The opening stanza of "The Extasie" begins with such a conceit.[4]

> Where, like a pillow on a bed,
> A pregnant bank swel'd up, to rest
> The violets reclining head,
> Sat we two, one another's best. (Qtd. in *Prose* 2.656)

The mise-en-scène is clear enough—two lovers sitting on a riverbank. Eliot strenuously objects to this stanza, claiming that it "begins with one of the most hideous mixed figures of speech in the language." The simile comparing the bank to a pillow (and why, he asks "on a bed"?) "does neither dignify nor elucidate," and moreover, "the simile comes into sharp collision with a metaphor—the bank is pregnant" (*Prose* 2.655-56). "The pregnant bank swells, which is just what it should not do, for the whole scene that follows is represented as static; otherwise it would not be an 'ecstasy' at all. We learn why the bank swelled up; it did this in order to provide a pillow for the drooping head of the violet" (*Prose* 2.656). Eliot objects to conceit after conceit, claiming that such bizarre figures obscure what Donne is trying to say about ecstasy. Regarding the famous image—"Our eye-beames twisted, and did thred/Our eyes, upon one double string"—Eliot says: "As for the threading of the eyes like buttons on a double thread, one thread proceeding from each eye to the other, it not only fails to render the sense of losing oneself in an ecstasy of gazing into the eyes of a loved person, it actually aggravates the difficulty of finding out what it is all about" (*Prose* 2.656). Pointing to "that over-emphasis, that strain to impress more than to state," Eliot adds a further point about Donne's conceits, one he was to repeat a few years later—"he was more interested in *ideas* themselves as objects than in the *truth* of ideas" (Eliot's emphasis; *Prose* 4.373). Donne entertains ideas, without any indication that he believes them. His method involves "playing upon an idea, arresting it and turning it about for examination" (*Prose* 2.656-57). In the love poems, even when focused on sex, he shows more interest in the ingenuity of his thoughts than in the beloved other.

The second way in which Donne anticipates Descartes is his insistence on "a distinction, a disjunction, between soul and body" (*Prose* 2.658). Our bodies, Donne says, "are ours, though they are not wee. We are/The intelligences, they the spheare" (ll. 51-52). The main "idea" in "The Extasie"—"the union, the fusion and identification of *souls* in sexual love" (Eliot's emphasis; *Prose* 2.616)—requires this separation. The poem is divided into three movements. In the first (ll. 1-28), the scene is set, and although there are two bodies sitting by the river, there is only one soul. In the second (ll. 29-48), the effect of this fusion is revealed. The "new soule"—"interinanimated" by love—is stronger, "abler" than separate, embodied, souls; in a particularly sentimental touch, Donne suggests that the fusion mitigates loneliness.

> When love, with one another so
> Interinanimates two soules,
> That abler soule, which thence doth flow,
> Defects of lonelinesse controules. (Qtd. in *Prose* 2.657)

In the third movement, the lovers reanimate their bodies so that their love can be perceived by others.

> So must pure lovers soules descend
> T' affections, and to faculties,
> Which sense may reach and apprehend,
> Else a great Prince in prison lies.
> To our bodies turne wee then, that so
> Weake men on love reveal'd may looke;
> Loves mysteries in soules doe grow,
> But yet the body is his booke. (Qtd. in *Prose* 2.658)

The body in this drama is a prop that exists only as a means to an end. Eliot concludes that Donne's "conception of the ecstasy of union between two souls is not only philosophically crude but emotionally limiting" (*Prose* 2.659). Donne's "deliberate overstimulation, exploitation of the nerves . . . has in it, to me, something unscrupulous. It is the work of a man of profound and subtle intellect, for whom thought has lost its primary value" (*Prose* 2.699). Dante, in contrast, understood the "good of the intellect" and placed those who had lost that good in the vestibule of Hell (*Inferno* III.16–18). This poem by Donne, Eliot argues, represents a defining moment in the "disintegration of the intellect." Some have associated Donne's ideas in "The Extasie" with Plato, but Eliot counters that "the separation of soul and body in this way is a modern conception." Neither Plato nor Aquinas would have accepted the idea that "two souls of separate bodies could form one" (*Prose* 2.659).

Eliot extends his argument about the deleterious effect of Cartesian dualism by looking at Richard Crashaw, whose poems were published in the same decade as the *Meditations*. He argues that Donne and Crashaw represent two different ways in which Descartes's attitude toward the object was realized in poetry. In Donne, the object disappears into the mind; in Crashaw, it disappears into the body. As "Donne is a voluptuary of thought"; Crashaw is a "voluptuary of religious emotion." "As with Donne the thought is split up into thoughts, each inspected and tasted, so with Crashaw the emotion is split up into emotions; instead of one emotion, . . . you have emotion piled on emotion, as a man drinks when he is afraid of becoming sober" (*Prose* 2.709). Eliot illustrates Crashaw's approach to the object by looking at "The Tear," a poem about the Virgin Mary. In a vivid example of the displacement of intellect by feeling, Crashaw addresses the tear falling from Mary's eye.

> Faire drop, why quak'st thou so?
> Cause thou streight must lay thy head
> In the dust? O no,
> The dust shall never be thy bed;
> A pillow for thee will I bring,
> Stuft with down of Angels wing. (Qtd. in *Prose* 2.711)

Eliot says that Crashaw's apostrophe to the Virgin's tear represents a break between sense and thought. Donne "supplied a bank as a pillow for the drooping head of a violet; but Crashaw supplies a pillow, stuffed with . . . down from moulting angels . . . for the head—of a tear. One cannot conceive the state of mind of a writer who could pen such monstrosities" (Eliot's emphasis; *Prose* 2.711). With this comparison, Eliot returns to Donne. Both his intellectual ecstasy and Crashaw's emotional high are specious. Each in its own way represents the Cartesian moment in the history of poetry, a moment marked by an attitude toward the object that disfigures the poems in which it appears.

A World of Subjects and Objects: Dante and Beatrice

Using Donne's "Extasie" as a reference point, Eliot moves to a reading of Dante's *Vita Nuova*, an autobiographical work in which love poems are connected by prose commentaries that give them shape and meaning. The poems were composed in late adolescence; the prose was added a decade or so later. Instead of dividing himself into a soul and body, as Donne does, Dante doubles himself, as in the *Divine Comedy*, into a "then" and "now." Using the poems composed in his youth and what he finds in his "Book of Memory," he resurrects the young lover who is living through the experiences captured in the poems (the "then") and who does not understand them or know how they will turn out in the end. Using the prose composed in the present (the "now"), he presents himself as a mature man looking back and making sense of his experience. This break in time by which the self is doubled is crucial to understanding the *Vita Nuova* and it is also the main point in Eliot's reading, that is, that Dante succeeds in holding together the subject and the object of thought. The poems composed in adolescence are subjective; the prose added in maturity encloses that subjectivity within a frame that is essentially objective. The ensuing dialectic binds the poetry and prose into a single unified work of art.

The background for the passage quoted by Eliot is that Dante, at age nine, saw Beatrice and was smitten by her beauty; at age eighteen, he saw her again and she greeted him. This greeting, which has the quality of a miracle, leads to a vivid dream and states of ecstasy. To conceal his obsession with Beatrice, he uses a "screen" lady, and is so fervent in this charade that his behavior generates a scandal. When he sees Beatrice again, she refuses to greet him. Devastated by this rebuke, he attempts to regain her recognition, but as revealed in a sonnet in XVI, he collapses, finding that the mere sight of her is unbearable.

> Hoping to help myself, I gather courage
> and pale and drawn and lacking all defense,
> I come to see you hoping to be healed;
> but if I raise my eyes to look at you
> a trembling starts at once within my heart
> and drives out and stops my pulses' beat.[5]

This is followed by the passage that Eliot quotes, which addresses a question that is as relevant to Donne as to Dante: What is the end and aim of love? The lover is being mocked by ladies who ask about his bizarre behavior with Beatrice. He explains that henceforth his happiness will not be contingent on her salutation, but rather on the poems that he plans to write in praise of her.

> There came a day when certain ladies . . . were met together for the pleasure of gentle company. . . . One of them . . . addressed me by my name, saying, "To what end lovest thou this lady, seeing that thou canst not support her presence? Now tell us this thing, that we may know it: for certainly the end of such a love must be worthy of knowledge." Whereupon, I said thus unto them: "Ladies, the end and aim of my Love was but the salutation of that lady of whom I conceive that ye are speaking: wherein alone I found that beatitude which is the goal of desire. And now that it hath pleased her to deny me this, Love, my Master, . . . hath placed all my beatitude there where my hope will not fail me." Then those ladies began to talk closely together; and . . . after a little while, that lady who had been

> the first to address me, addressed me again in these words: "We pray thee that thou wilt tell us wherein abideth this thy beatitude." And answering, I said but thus much: "In those words that do praise my lady."[6]

Eliot's argument regarding the love poetry of the fourteenth and the seventeenth centuries includes two main points, both of which highlight the contrast between Dante and his successors, namely, Donne and Crashaw. The first is that both the subject and the object are real in Dante's love poetry; the second is that both subject and object are essential in the progress of the soul toward God. The early twentieth-century critic Remy de Gourmont had argued that Beatrice was not a real woman, but an ideal, essentially a figment of Dante's imagination. Eliot rejects this argument as part of the post-Cartesian tendency to deny the reality of the object (*Prose* 2.650). He insists that Beatrice was a young Florentine woman who was adored by Dante. Moreover, he maintains that Dante's memory of his childhood experience rings true. "The *Vita Nuova* is to my thinking a record of actual experiences reshaped into a particular form. . . . The emotions . . . which Dante records as experienced at the age of nine, are not at all incredible; they are possible at an even earlier age, though I do not assert that a young person of nine would be able to formulate them consciously in those words" (*Prose* 2.650). Eliot claims that the *Vita Nuova* is an objective work, comparable to "a scientific monograph, the record of experiments upon sentiment" (*Prose* 2.669). The objectivity, as suggested above, is achieved by doubling the self through the dialectic of the "then" and the "now." One of many passages that emphasize this dialectic occurs in *Vita Nuova* III. Dante writes a sonnet about the dream precipitated by Beatrice's greeting and sends it to his poet friends, including Guido Cavalcanti, for commentary. They are bewildered, leading Dante to say: "The true interpretation of the dream I described was not perceived by anyone, *then*, but *now* it is very clear to even the least sophisticated" (italics added).[7]

Dante's greatness, however, does not derive from his objectivity alone but also from his ability to maintain an equilibrium between the subject and the object. In Dante, one finds

> a system of thought and feeling; every part of the system felt and thought in its place, and the whole system felt and thought; and you cannot say that it is primarily "intellectual" or primarily "emotional," for the thought and the emotion are reverse sides of the same thing. In Donne you get a sequence of thoughts

> which are felt; in Crashaw . . . a sequence of feelings which are thought. In neither do you find a perfect balance. (*Prose* 2.718)

Dante was not only the most objective of poets; he was also the most subjective. In Eliot's reading, "the inner life of Dante was not only more extensive, but had heights of feeling unknown to the later poet [Donne]" (*Prose* 2.655). His view that Dante's account of his youth is largely true does not prevent him from concurring in the common view that Beatrice, in addition, is an ideal figure in an allegory of love, both the love of Dante, for whom she represents beauty and beatitude, and the love of God. As Charles Singleton has shown by close attention to Dante's figurative language and to his Trinitarian numerology in the *Vita Nuova*, Beatrice is not only a Florentine lady; she is also a figure for Christ (20).

Eliot's analysis of seventeenth-century poetry and philosophy led to a reformulation of one of his signature concepts, the "dissociation of sensibility." The problem of the unification of thought and feeling, as previously discussed, had been on his mind for years. In a 1921 review of Grierson's anthology of metaphysical poetry, he claimed that in the seventeenth century "a dissociation of sensibility set in from which we have never recovered." In a comparison of seventeenth- and nineteenth-century poets, he argued that the earlier poets had a "unified sensibility," which enabled them to balance the subjective and objective aspects of human experience. His highest praise was reserved for Donne, to whom "a thought . . . was an experience; it modified his sensibility." Nineteenth-century poets, by contrast, failed to integrate thought and feeling. Tennyson and Browning thought and felt, but unlike Donne, they did not "feel their thoughts as immediately as the odour of a rose" (*Prose* 2.380). In the Clark Lectures, Eliot reconsiders this position; instead of comparing Donne to Tennyson and Browning, he compares him to Dante. This shift of perspective results in a reversal of his evaluation of the seventeenth-century poets, who are now seen as representing the breakdown in the mind of Europe. Dante is the poet of the "unified sensibility," Donne the poet of dissociation, and Laforgue the poet of disintegration.

Lancelot Andrewes and the Ecstasy of Assent

In March 1926, Eliot gave his final lecture at Cambridge on Dante and Donne, after which he turned to an essay on Lancelot Andrewes for the *TLS*.

On 6 July, he told the editor that he was trying to come to terms with Andrewes, a process he described as "a pretty serious matter for me, as I shall have to clear up my mind and try to come to conclusions, . . . affecting my whole position" (*L*3.209). This article is the third of three works completed during the 1925-26 watershed in Eliot's intellectual and spiritual life. In "The Hollow Men," he enlarges the immediate experience of despair; in the Clark Lectures, he analyzes modern despair as the culmination of the disappearance of the object that began in the seventeenth century with Descartes; in the essay on Bishop Andrewes, he ponders the possible transcendence of despair in a world without objects. These documents have many connecting threads. All three deal with the psychological and spiritual implications of dualism, and all explore extreme states of despair and ecstasy. The essay on Andrewes, one of Eliot's most important, extends his discussion of the dissociation of sensibility, reformulates his notion of ecstasy, and deepens his understanding of the Incarnation.

In his 1926 *TLS* essay, Eliot associates Andrewes (1555-1626), who was a generation older than Donne (1572-1631), with the late medieval synthesis of Dante and links Donne with its early modern breakdown. In a comparison of their sermons, he argues that Andrewes, like Dante but unlike Donne, successfully harmonized subject and object, emotion and intellect. "Andrewes's emotion is purely contemplative; it is not personal, it is wholly evoked by the object of contemplation, to which it is adequate; his emotion is wholly contained in and explained by its object. But with Donne, there is always something else. . . . Donne is constantly finding an object which shall be adequate to his feelings" (*Prose* 2.825). Andrewes's sermons are impersonal, because he begins with the object; Donne's are "a means of self-expression" because he begins with the subject (his ideas) (*Prose* 2.825).

The comparison of Donne and Andrewes had been percolating in Eliot's mind for several years, during which he had modified his position on Donne. In a 1921 essay on the metaphysical poets, he argued that Donne had a unified sensibility, and in the 1926 lectures at Cambridge, he maintained that Donne represented a dissociation of sensibility. This reversal is anticipated in "The Preacher as Artist," a 1919 review in which Eliot contrasts the ease of detaching passages from Donne's sermons with the difficulty of detaching them from Andrewes's. "The fact . . . that you can extract from the sermons of Donne is indicative. It is possible to select sermons of . . . Bishop Andrewes, but it would probably be futile to attempt to select passages out of the sermons" (*Prose* 2.165). Donne's artistry is in the creation of "purple paragraphs" (*Prose* 2.168), which can be separated from his argument and used or misused. This point is carried over to the 1926 essay. "Donne will certainly always have more readers than Andrewes, for the reason that his sermons can be read in detached passages and for the reason that they can be read by those who have no interest in the subject" (*Prose* 2.826). In the 1926 essay on Andrewes, Eliot uses this very point to show that Donne, in contrast to Andrewes, failed to integrate emotion and intellect. Andrewes's sermons must be taken as a whole because his thoughts and emotions are so tightly interwoven that they cannot be separated. In Andrewes, "intellect and sensibility were in harmony" (*Prose* 2.820). In Donne, the purple passages are moving, but moving to no end.

The contrast between Donne and Andrewes is reflected in their respective realizations of ecstasy.

> When we have saturated ourselves in [Andrewes's] prose, followed the movement of his thought, . . . we find his examination of words terminating in the ecstasy of assent. Andrewes takes a word and derives the world from it: squeezing and squeezing . . . until it yields a full juice of meaning which we should never have supposed any word to possess. (*Prose* 2.822)

In Donne, ecstasy is an intellectual state achieved by playing with words and logic. In Andrewes, it is a complex of passion and precision achieved by moving an audience word by word into a state that Eliot refers to as an "ecstasy of assent." Andrewes was the heir of Dante, who secured ecstatic stasis by devoting himself to the contemplation of a beloved object. Donne was the father of the modern lyricist (singer of "I want someone to treat me rough"), who secured ecstasy by adding violence to the process.

The paradoxical phrase "ecstasy of assent" points, on the one hand, to the unification of sensibility and intelligence, which is the goal of Eliot's quest for wholeness. On the other hand, it raises a question: assent to what? The answer, unmistakable in his writings on Andrewes and confirmed in all his subsequent work, is the Incarnation. But why is assent, usually associated with reason, here associated with ecstasy? The answer has to do with the meaning of Incarnation—both the word and the Christian dogma—and with the joy it effects in the life of the genuine believer. The literal meaning of the word is a state of being that combines spirit and flesh, and the Christian dogma refers to the union of deity and humanity in Christ. The Incarnation, then, would not be viable in a world without objects, a world in which transcendence is nullified. To be credible, the Incarnation requires two planes, the human and the divine; to work as a model of wholeness, it requires both subjects and objects. As a theological response to the psychophysical dualism that had troubled Eliot from the beginning of his life as a poet, the doctrine of the Incarnation validated some of his deepest longings.

The Incarnation was an "essential dogma" for Andrewes, who preached on it every Christmas for decades. Eliot owned his collection, *Seventeen Sermons on the Nativity*, and referred to it often over the years. In 1919, he quoted from it in "The Preacher as Artist" and alluded to one of the sermons in "Gerontion"; in the 1926 *TLS* essay on Andrewes, he quotes several passages. The occasion for these sermons (Christmas) dictated the subject (Incarnation), and because the audience was the same from year to year (King James I), the presentation and argument had to seem new. It was particularly valuable, Eliot remarked, to "be able to compare seventeen developments of the same idea" (*Prose* 2.821). The doctrine is principally supported by three biblical texts, and in the Christmas sermons, Andrewes returns to them again and again, always with a slightly different twist. The first two are the nativity narratives in the opening chapters of Matthew and Luke. These record the Annunciation, the angels' appearance to the shepherds, the Nativity, the visit of the Magi, the slaughter of the innocents, and Simeon's song when the infant is consecrated in the temple. The third text, indispensable for the theological underpinning of the doctrine, is in the first chapter of John: "In the beginning was the Word (*Logos*), and the Word was with God and the Word was God. . . . And the Word was made flesh, and dwelt among us" (1:1, 14). As shown by allusions in "Gerontion" and "Mr. Eliot's Sunday Morning Service," by 1926 this text had been in Eliot's mind for nearly a decade. Moreover, for years to come, it would inform his poetry, especially *Ash-Wednesday* V, "Journey of the Magi," "A Song for Simeon," choruses from *The Rock*, and *The Dry Salvages*.

In the Clark Lectures, as part of the contrast between Dante and Donne, Eliot argues that the highest form of poetry is incarnational. In the *Vita Nuova*, "what is ordinarily apprehensible as an intellectual statement, is translated in sensible form." In "The Extasie," Donne fails to "clothe the abstract, for a moment, with all the painful delight of flesh" (*Prose* 2.617). In the earlier essays and poems, Eliot had entertained the idea of the Incarnation; in the 1926 essay on Andrewes, he discusses it as an essential doctrine in Christianity; and in 1927, as is discussed in the following chapter, he embraced it as a belief.

8 Eliot's Second Conversion

Dogma without Dogmatism

> I do believe . . . that the chief distinction of man is to glorify God and enjoy Him forever.
>
> Eliot, "Literature, Science, and Dogma" (1927)

In a private move that shocked his admirers and surprised his intimates, including his wife, Eliot was baptized at Holy Trinity Church in Finstock near Oxford on 29 June 1927. The following year, in a preface to *For Lancelot Andrewes*, he went public, describing his new position "as classicist in literature, royalist in politics, and anglo-catholic in religion" (*Prose* 3.513). Most critics see this event as a bright line dividing the "two Eliots": Romantic/classic; American/British; and agnostic/Christian. There is considerable support for understanding his life and work in this way. The symbolism of baptism, after all, is death and rebirth. In the words of St. Paul, "we are buried with him by baptism into death, that as Christ was raised up from the dead, . . . so we also should walk in newness of life" (Rom. 6:4). The two major poems bracketing Eliot's baptism conform to this symbolism. His epigraph for the opening lyric in *The Hollow Men* is a Pauline pun, "The old guy is dead," and his description of *Ash-Wednesday* suggests that it is a rebirth, "a deliberate modern *Vita Nuova*" (*L*5.171).

Eliot himself was clearly mindful of a break with his past. "I do believe," he said three months before his baptism, "that the chief distinction of man is to glorify God and enjoy Him forever" (*Prose* 3.46). In the context of the review of Richards's *Science and Poetry*, Eliot's personal and emphatic "I do believe" seems gratuitous, but as the formal response to the first question of the *Westminster Shorter Catechism* (1647), it is telling.

> Question: What is the chief end of man?
>
> Answer: Man's chief end is to glorify God and enjoy Him forever.

This articulation of his credo without a touch of irony indicates that Eliot was anticipating his baptism. That he experienced it as a turning point is explicit in his letters. On the eve of his first Ash Wednesday service as a convert, he told William Force Stead: "I have made my first confession, and feel as if I had crossed a very wide and deep river: whether I get much farther or not, I feel very certain that I shall not cross back, and that in itself gives one a very extraordinary sense of surrender and gain" (*L4*.96). Pascal referred to crossing this deep river as a "second conversion," the first being the nominal acceptance of the religion of one's family or friends. Eliot, who had his own first conversion with Bergson, refers to the second as "conversion simply" (*Prose* 4.340).

Some critics, including Lyndall Gordon, Ronald Schuchard, and me in earlier chapters of this study, have made the case that Eliot was deeply religious from the beginning. This position, like the case for discontinuity, is also supported in Eliot's writings. On more than one occasion in the 1930s, he referred to the continuity between his earliest inclinations and his mature commitments. On New Year's Day 1936, for example, he told his brother that his early academic choices had foreshadowed a religious turn. "My previous interests—my interest in Sanskrit and Pali literature . . . and in the philosophy of Bergson; and . . . my abortive attempt to make myself into a professor of philosophy [were] due to a religious preoccupation."[1] The religious preoccupation can be seen as an underground stream pulsing through his early poems, beginning with the debates between body and soul of 1910.

What Eliot refers to as "conversion simply" should not be taken as a statement that conversion is simple. As discussed in chapter 4, he distinguished between internal and external interpretation and maintained that, in religion, internal values, although irretrievable, are of the essence. While any description of Eliot's conversion is bound to be reductive, several elements can be identified. First, there is the ingrained and evolving conflict between feeling and intellect, intertwined with personal suffering from which there seems to be no honorable exit. Second, there is the pragmatism evident in his attempt to find the "one scheme . . . which would work" (*Prose* 4.427). Third, there is the influence of others who seemed to be searching for truth—negative models such as I. A. Richards and Bertrand Russell, and positive models, chiefly Lancelot Andrewes and Blaise Pascal. Of these, the case of Pascal is paramount, for as Eliot indicated and others have noted, it is strikingly similar to his own.

Eliot's psychological and philosophical pivot in the 1920s was real, but because it was so dramatic, it tends to mask the underlying continuity in his intellectual development. In his 1924 lecture on Chapman and Dostoevski, he reformulates his contraries as the recognition of two worlds. Instead of focusing on body and soul, he emphasizes human and divine as part of an ongoing dialectic, which he will soon see as a validation of the Incarnation. In earlier writings, Eliot had attempted to settle the quarrel between soul and body, subject and object, and mind and world. In later work, he accepts dualism and embraces a theology of paradox. The backdrop to this theology, documented in his letters, includes continuous physical and psychological pain, and as argued in my chapter on *The Hollow Men*, the black hole of despair. Two years after his conversion, he referred to this despair in existentialist terms as a sense of the void.

> There seem to be certain persons for whom religion is wholly unnecessary. . . . They may be very good, or very happy; they simply seem to miss nothing, to be unconscious of any void—the void that I find in the middle of all human happiness and all human relations, and which there is only one thing to fill. I am one whom this sense of the void tends to drive towards asceticism or sensuality, and only Christianity helps to reconcile me to life. (*L*4.432–33)

In 1937, the erstwhile student of philosophy again suggested that conversion involved the elimination of alternatives: "Conversion to Christianity is apt to be due, I think, to a latent dissatisfaction with all secular philosophy" (*Prose* 5.478). Having rejected Bradley's push of idealism to its limit, he associated his conversion, according to Robert Sencourt, with disapproval of Russell's push of agnosticism to its limit (132). In reviews of Russell's *Why I Am Not a Christian* and of Richards's *Science and Poetry*, Eliot argued that both were boxed in by dogma, and that Richards, like Russell, was a "dupe of his own skepticism." Richards's commitment to psychological theories blinded him to the moral dimension in human behavior, and Russell's to materialism led him "to fortify his faith with the appearance of reason" (*Prose* 3.160). Eliot's larger argument is that all thinking persons, including agnostics, believe in something beyond "the 'hows' of science." He claims to be "amazed at Mr. Russell's capacity for believing. . . . St. Augustine did not believe more" (*Prose* 3.46). What Eliot himself hoped to achieve was dogma without dogmatism; he wanted his mind to reflect what Keats called "negative capability," the ability to be at home with ambivalence, to be able to say yes without being sure.

Eliot's Triadic Imagination: Epistemology, Poetry, Theology

Eliot's progress toward a theological resolution was facilitated by his tendency to think in triads. The dialectical imagination is by definition triadic, a structure that in itself nudges the mind to move beyond contradictions. In the decade following his graduate work in philosophy, Eliot adjusted his epistemological triads (Bradley's feeling/thought/felt thought) for use in poetry and theology. In his prose, there is no better example of triadic structures than "classicist in literature, royalist in politics, and anglo-catholic in religion" (*Prose* 3.513), a formula in which the first two commitments, previously perceived as opposed, are contained and transcended in the third. In poetry, there are numerous examples, many of which, as in *The Waste Land*, use triads to secure closure.

> Datta. Dayadhvam. Damyata.
>   Shantih   shantih   shantih   (*WL* 432–33)

Similarly, in *The Hollow Men*:

> *This is the way the world ends*
> *This is the way the world ends*
> *This is the way the world ends*
> *Not with a bang but a whimper.*   (*HM* V.28–31)

By using exact repetition, as in the eerie triads of "Fragment of an Agon," he imitates the rhythm of both primitive religion and avant-garde modernism.

> Hoo
> Hoo
> Hoo
> KNOCK KNOCK KNOCK
> KNOCK KNOCK KNOCK
> KNOCK
> KNOCK
> KNOCK   (166–73)

As is evident in these examples, the first iteration is not the same in weight or affect as the last, which gives even exact repetition both a dialectical and a liturgical feel.

Eliot's triadic inclination is consistent with his theological imagination. The Incarnation, for example, is triadic (God/man/Christ), as is the Trinity

(Father / Son / Holy Spirit). His attention to the triadic nature of these doctrines puts him in sync with Christian writers whom he greatly admired—St. Augustine, Dante, Julian of Norwich, and Jacques Maritain. In "Marina," the conclusion is not overtly theological, but it is a new love song, with a note of recognition that cleanses the yellow feline fog of yesteryear.

What seas what shores what granite islands towards my timbers
And woodthrush calling through the fog
My daughter. (33-35)

In "Difficulties of a Statesman," he updates "Shantih."

RESIGN RESIGN RESIGN (53)

Eliot's most striking examples of postconversion triads are in *The Rock* and *Murder in the Cathedral*, both of which use fragments of the liturgy. In *Murder*, Thomas concludes his sermon with "In the Name of the Father, and of the Son, and of the Holy Ghost. Amen." This is what in earlier work Eliot referred to as a "survival"—that is, an intact fragment that is out of context in place and time. In Eliot's plays, the Chorus naturally thinks and speaks in triads. While Thomas is under the sword, the Women of Canterbury chant "Clear the air! clean the sky! wash the wind!" (*CPP* 213) and they end the play with a prayer:

Lord, have mercy upon us.
Christ, have mercy upon us.
Lord, have mercy upon us.
Blessed Thomas, pray for us. (*CPP* 221)

Even without the sacred setting, the later triads are theologically resonant. The closing lines of *The Family Reunion*, Eliot's first full-length secular play, point not only to the curse on the house of Wishwood but also to Adam's curse and to the redemption available through Christ, the second Adam.

And the curse be ended
By intercession
By pilgrimage
By those who depart
In several directions
For their own redemption
And that of the departed—
May they rest in peace. (II.iii; *CPP* 293)

As suggested by this example, Eliot's later work utilizes the music of the triad and the logic of transcendence to extend the rhetoric and concerns of his early work and, simultaneously, to move beyond them in the construction of a dialectical theology and a *vita nuova* in life and in art.

Model Christians: Bishop Andrewes and Pascal

What I should like to see is the creation of a new type of intellectual, combining the intellectual and the devotional—a new species which cannot be created hurriedly. I don't like the purely intellectual Christian or the purely emotional Christian, both forms of snobbism. . . . The co-ordination of thought and feeling—without either debauchery or repression—seems to me what is needed.

Eliot to Paul Elmer More (1929)

In describing the sort of Christian he aspired to be, Eliot adapted his old antithesis between intellect and emotion to move dialectically to "a new species." In 1926, as discussed in chapter 7, he had represented Lancelot Andrewes as a model for this sort of balanced Christian. Not only did Eliot admire the intellectual mastery in the *Sermons*, but as indicated in a letter to his mother written soon after his conversion, he was also moved by the bishop's devotional life. "I am also sending you a tiny book which has been of great value to me: Lancelot Andrewes's *Private Devotions*. . . . Anything the great Andrewes wrote is beautifully written. These are the prayers which he wrote for his own use . . . I like to turn to them during the night whenever I cannot sleep" (*L*3.736). The fact that Eliot murmured these prayers in the night supports the idea that, in matters of faith, Andrewes was his Virgil. Not only did the bishop convince him of the truth of the Incarnation, he also provided comfort and nurture. The first lines to appear in Eliot's poetry after his baptism—the opening lines of "Journey of the Magi"—are not his own, but Andrewes's, the significance of which will be discussed later in this chapter.

Eliot identified another model for his "new type of Christian"—the seventeenth-century French mathematician Blaise Pascal. In 1931, in an introduction to the *Penseés*, Eliot praised him in terms that represent another variation of the pairing of intellect and emotion, this time echoing the mind and body of the earlier poems. "No Christian writer [is] . . . more to be commended than Pascal to those who doubt, but who have the mind to conceive, and the sensitivity to feel, the disorder, the futility, the meaninglessness, the mystery of life and suffering, and who can only find peace through satisfaction of the whole being" (*Prose* 4.349). The dialectic is suggested by the fact that, grammatically, thinking and feeling share a single object. In order for a person to transcend the meaninglessness of life, he must have the capacity to accept its mystery, and that requires thinking and feeling at once. Eliot continues to explain the progress of the "intelligent believer."

> The man who is trying consciously and conscientiously to explain to himself the sequence which culminated in faith . . . proceeds by rejection and elimination. He finds the world to be so and so; he finds its character inexplicable by any non-religious theory; among religious he finds Christianity . . . to account most satisfactorily for the world and especially for the moral world within; and thus, by what Newman calls "powerful and concurrent" reasons, he finds himself inexorably committed to the dogma of the Incarnation. (*Prose* 4.342)

Pascal's method, Eliot shows, was dialectical, moving from doubt to despair to commitment, from facts to dogma to faith. For the intellectual, the process invariably involves skepticism. "*Every* man who thinks and lives by thought must have his own scepticism, that which stops at the question, that which ends in denial, or that which leads to faith and which is somehow integrated into the faith which transcends it" (*Prose* 4.344-45). Physically, Pascal's facts included serious ongoing illness, and spiritually, "the demon of doubt which is inseparable from the spirit of belief." His doubt was severe, like that which Hopkins in his "terrible sonnet" on Despair calls "carrion comfort." Pascal's "despair, his disillusion, are . . . no illustration of personal weakness; they are perfectly objective, because they are essential moments in the progress of the intellectual soul; and for the type of [soul represented by] Pascal, they are the analogue of the drought, the dark night, which is an essential stage in the progress of the Christian mystic" (*Prose* 4.345). Eliot contrasts Pascal to Voltaire, who "start[ed] from the other end," beginning not with facts but with theory. Beginning with materialism, he had to reject the virgin birth because his theory posited the impossibility of parthenogenesis (*Prose* 4.343).

"In my own case"

Having described Pascal's conversion, Eliot indicates that he is recalling his own trek through illness, doubt, and despair. His description of Pascal turns out to be a self-portrait.

> In my own case . . . one of the reasons [for conversion] was that the Christian scheme seemed to me the only one which would work. . . . [It] was simply the removal of any reason for believing in anything else, the erasure of a prejudice, the arrival at the skepticism which is the preface to conversion. . . . The Christian scheme seemed the only possible scheme which found a place for values which I must maintain or perish, . . . the belief, for instance, in holy living and holy dying, in sanctity, chastity, humility, austerity. (*Prose* 4.427–28)

Eliot's Christian experience can best be understood in developmental terms. As he noted in 1963, "I joined the Church of England in 1927, but only became interested in Anglo-Catholic practices and opinions later" (*L*3.573). His experience included three overlapping stages, all emphasizing both thinking and feeling, with the emotional elements more pronounced in the first stage and the intellectual in the last. The man who in April 1926 suddenly prostrated himself before the *Pietà* in St. Peter's Cathedral in Rome was overcome by feelings too complex to describe (*L*3.xvii). He both is and is not the man who in April 1936 offered to write for the *Catholic Herald* from the perspective of a convert to English Catholicism: "Assuming that Anglican and Roman Orders and Sacraments are equally valid, on what grounds did a person brought up altogether outside the Christian Faith elect to become a member of the former community rather than the latter?"[2] Nor is he the public intellectual who, in November 1955, told the Ecumenical Club: "For the person who can both think and feel, . . . Christian faith is something that has to be won individually, with serious reading, with hard thinking, with discipline and much study of one's own emotions."[3] All three responses are authentic, but the first is the private response of a drowning man, the second the public response of an apologist, and the last the confident statement of a churchman. The first stage begins in 1926 with his rereading of Andrewes and lasts two or three years; the second begins around 1929 and lasts into the mid-1930s; the third begins in the mid-1930s and continues for the rest of his life. The first stage, inseparable from the need to cope with his private life, especially with the crosscurrents of his marriage and health, is the most personal. The second, in which he attempts to justify his conversion to himself and to his family and friends, is the most defensive and dogmatic. The third, in which he relaxes into his position as a voice for English Catholicism, is the most impersonal and intellectual.

Discussions of Eliot's religion are often based more on retrospective remarks by the apologist or the church warden than on the initiating currents of the convert. This inevitably leads to a bias in favor of the former. In *Anglo-Catholic in Religion*, to take a recent example, Barry Spurr provides a valuable picture of the ecclesiastical context of Eliot's commitment, but in an attempt to distinguish between the poet's experience and that of evangelicals, he protests against using the term *conversion*. "In relation to . . . Eliot's poetry and plays, 'conversion' is a term best avoided, having practically no relevance . . . to the understanding and appreciation of his verse" (113). The word, Spurr argues, is tainted by its association with Protestantism, especially with the powerful role played by "the emotional element" in fundamentalist churches. It suggests "an instantaneous event, as a result of which the convert is changed utterly," and further, it obscures Eliot's emphasis on "the difficulties of faith and the elusiveness of transcendental experience" (112–13).

Eliot, however, uses *conversion* as it is traditionally understood, to indicate a change in religious orientation accompanied by a change in belief (Merriam-Webster). In the essay on Pascal, he repeatedly uses the term, and in the prose of the 1930s, he often discusses the intellectual clarification that accompanies "conversion to Christianity" (*Prose* 5.478). Moreover, he describes his experience in terms that stress both its suddenness and its emotional import. Having "a passionate conviction about anything is like falling in love: it is not merely to risk being ridiculous . . . ; it is to surrender oneself to something, to surrender liberty, the liberty of thinking responsibly" (*Prose* 4.427).

One of the most moving of Eliot's early statements on his religious faith is contained in a letter to his mother in August 1927, less than two months after his baptism. She was in her final illness, and he was hoping to see her before she died. He assures her that although he plans to visit her next winter in America, he is confident that he will also meet and know her in a future life. He continues: "Any ideas that we can have of the future life can only be right in that such ideas may be more nearly right than any other ideas that we could have. That is what I always feel about the truths of religion; it is not a question of something absolutely true (or false) in so many words; but they are more nearly true than is the contradiction of them" (*L*3.647–48). Of course, as he sometimes told his brother, Henry, he always tried to be upbeat when writing to their mother, and it may be that he was simply trying to comfort her. But these words have the ring of truth, and it is equally plausible to take them at face value. It may be that the convergence of her illness and his faith induced him to be even more open with her than with his brother. If so, the letter reveals a couple of things about his state of mind at the time of his baptism. First, his convictions about religious truth originated not in ideas about absolute truth but in a feeling about truth, a best guess. Second, his description here of religious truth, and his faith that he and his mother will meet in a future life and know as they are known, suggests a more tolerant and open theology than that which he will embrace in the 1930s.

Charlotte's Dream: "Journey of the Magi"

As the first poem to have been composed after Eliot's baptism, "Journey of the Magi" is considered to be a line of demarcation in both his life and his art. The poet's comment to Conrad Aiken that his "Christmas poem" was written "in three quarters of an hour after church time and before lunch one Sunday morning, with the assistance of half a bottle of Booth's gin" (*L*3.700) sounds tongue-in-cheek, but like so many of Eliot's quips, it may also be true. Because of its pivotal place in his oeuvre, the poem has attracted much commentary, and because of its accessibility and relation to a major holiday, it is one of his most anthologized. As critics have duly noted, Eliot is here indebted to the gospel of Matthew, to Andrewes's nativity sermons, and to his own contemporaneous translation of St-John Perse's *Anabase*. The fullest account of these matters is in Timmerman and in the commentary in Ricks and McCue (*Poems* 1).

In "Journey of the Magi," as Bush observes, Eliot refers simultaneously to three symbolic areas—"the fictional frame, the correspondences of Christian typology, and his own deepest and most troublesome feelings" (128). These fields of reference correspond roughly to his three major sources, and respectively, to three eras—mythic, historical, and ever-present. Most commentators posit their own versions of these triads. For Timmerman, there are three journeys: that of the pre-Christian Magi, that of the Christian bishop Andrewes, and that of the questing Eliot (and reader) (65). The poem does not begin at the beginning with a reprise of the Gospel, with its traditional accoutrements. When a reviewer lamented that "there is no star, there are no gifts, there is actually no birth and no worship" and then suggested an alternative rendering with an uplifting conclusion, Eliot responded: "We start with different fantasies of what such an occurrence would have been like" (*L*3.861). His fantasy begins in medias res, by pointing to the Christmas sermons that Andrewes preached for King James I, himself a biblical scholar. In keeping with the occasion, Andrewes interprets the myth as part of a cluster related to the coming *of* Christ and, by extension, the coming *to* Christ. His larger theme is the Word made flesh, the Incarnation, and the relation of that event to the death and resurrection of Christ. The theme is inherently dialectical, in that it involves both the preservation and transcendence of opposites (God and man, Logos and flesh, Word and word) in Christ, who, in biblical terms, is fully God and fully man in one person.

Eliot highlights his indebtedness to Andrewes by beginning with an adaptation of the description of the journey in the 1622 Christmas sermon. Using telltale quotation marks, he signals the presence of the Anglican bishop.

> 'A cold coming we had of it,
> Just the worst time of the year
> For a journey, and such a long journey:
> The ways deep and the weather sharp,
> The very dead of winter.' (1-5)

Because the poem is a dramatic monologue in which one of the Magi, now old and back in his kingdom, tries to recall what happened to the three of them "a long time ago," Eliot changes Andrewes's third-person plural ("A cold coming *they* had of it") to first-person plural in the reconstruction of the journey and arrival, and to a mixture of plural and singular in the old man's struggle to understand his situation. This pronominal modification embeds the standpoint of the first-century participant into that of the seventeenth-century preacher. In each case, the point of view is retrospective. For the Magus, the story is mediated through decades of reflection on a personal experience; for Andrewes, it is mediated through centuries of interpretation. The change of pronouns generates a marriage of opposites connecting a restless traveler who is no longer at home in the "old dispensation" and a sophisticated bishop who is very much "at ease" in the "new." The mind that both contains and transcends these opposites is that of the modern reader.

The narrative structure is also dialectical in that it consists of leaving home, traveling to a strange country, and returning home. In the first of three stanzas, the Magus recalls a winter journey across mountains; in the second, he remembers his arrival in Bethlehem amid conflicting signs of life and death; and in the third, back in his palace, he reflects on the meaning of his experience—"were we led all that way for / Birth or Death?"—and tells a scribe that despite his disorientation, he "would do it again." The conclusion of his reflection is ambiguous.

> I had seen birth and death,
> But had thought they were different; this Birth was
> Hard and bitter agony for us, like Death, our death.
> We returned to our places, these Kingdoms,
> But no longer at ease here, in the old dispensation,
> With an alien people clutching their gods.
> I should be glad of another death. (37-44)

In Timmerman's view, the Magus confronts "the paradoxical mystery of the still point—the concomitant birth and death of the Christ" and arrives at a "personal understanding" of his own death and rebirth (79-80). But does he? In the Western Church, the story of the Magi is associated with Epiphany (6 January, the revelation of Christ to the Gentiles), but there is no epiphany for this man. He has no way of understanding the significance of hands "dicing for pieces of silver," "vine-leaves over the lintel," and "three trees on the low sky." For him, "three trees" are "three trees," not portents of the death of the child, nor of his own death and rebirth. He has experienced something that has altered his consciousness, but it has not brought peace; *au contraire*, it has rendered him homeless, an orphan in history and a stranger in his own country. He is estranged from his people and their gods, and like his predecessors in Eliot's poetry, Gerontion and the Sybil, he is longing for death.

Eliot rarely commented on the interpretation of his poems, but in correspondence with a critic whose reading of "Journey of the Magi" he considered farfetched, he wrote: "I certainly do not accept the interpretation. . . . I meant that the Magi were drawn by a power which they did not understand, and I used them as types of a kind of person who may be found at almost any period of history. I meant them to be pathetic as Dante's Virgil is pathetic" (*L*3.861). At this moment in his own journey, Eliot was tuned in to the distant music of his American childhood. Soon after his baptism, he wrote two letters to his family: the first, to his mother, a world away and dying, has been lost; the second, to his brother, mentions the lost letter: "I enclose a copy of a letter which I have just written to mother. I hope it will do." In a postscript, he adds: "I gather that Mother is likely to live about six months or a year? Is this your opinion?" (*L*3.598). Three weeks later, on 22 August, he wrote to both again, expressing to her his desire to visit and to Henry the complications of getting away from a suicidal Vivien. He had recently sent his mother, once an aspiring poet, a copy of "Journey of the Magi,"[4] and had told her: "Whenever I have done anything that the world has thought good, or that the world is likely to think good for a generation or two after I am dead, I have always felt that it was something that you and I did together, or even something that you had dreamt of and projected before I was born" (*L*3.648).

This poignant tribute rings true because his poem seems to echo hers on the same topic. "The Three Kings," published in the 1877 issue of the *Christian Register*, had been part of his childhood holiday festivities.

> We are three kings who have traveled far,
>   O'er desert waste and sandy plain.
> Before us moved a radiant star,
>   Its light along our path has lain.
> Faint and weary, our journey's end
>   We seek; but the star moves onward still.
> We know not whither our footsteps tend,
>   Obedient to a higher will. (Qtd. in *Poems* 1.759)

Her three kings, like his Magi, were "drawn by a power which they did not understand." The congruity between her last two lines and his explanation of what he meant is one of many clues that Eliot's conversion was inseparable from Edenic memories of a happy childhood in St. Louis, a topic to be explored in the following chapter.

9 An Exilic Triptych

The Waste Land, *Ash-Wednesday*, "Marina"

The longest way round is the shortest way home.

Alexander Maclaren, *The Wearied Christ*

In the broadest sense, Eliot's awareness of himself as an exile was framed by his childhood and his second marriage, the only periods, he told Pound in 1961, in which he felt truly at home.[1] His most intense feelings of exile occurred during the 1920s, roughly between the death of his father in 1919 and his mother in 1929. In a letter to his brother in America, written soon after their father had died, he referred to the humiliations of life as a resident alien in London. "Don't think I find it easy to live over here. It is damned hard work to live with a foreign nation and cope with them—one is always coming up against differences of feeling that make one feel humiliated and lonely. One remains always a foreigner" (*L*1.370). The exilic imagination is triadic and dialectical, moving from expatriation to wandering to homecoming. The first two can be seen in Eliot's jeremiad, but not even a glimmer of the third, which is dissolved by his "always." He sees Londoners only as objects, chiefly as eyes through which to see himself, and he is too absorbed with his private nightmare to be dreaming of home. This sense of dislocation is reflected in most of his work over the decade. *The Waste Land* in 1922, *Ash-Wednesday* in 1927–30, and "Marina" in 1930 constitute a triptych of the exilic imagination, with *Ash-Wednesday* as the central panel. Together they represent the pain of separation, the longing to reconnect, and the return to a lost world. In *The Waste Land*, the motif is primarily embedded in allusions to Ezekiel, the prophet of exile; in *Ash-Wednesday*, to Ezekiel and to the expulsion from Eden; in both, to Dante, the poet of exile. In "Marina," the theme of return is conveyed in parallels to Shakespeare's *Pericles*. In all three panels, but especially in *Ash-Wednesday* and "Marina," the return is associated with America.

Triptych I: By the Waters of Leman

The river sweats
Oil and tar
The barges drift
With the turning tide

Eliot, *The Waste Land* V

The exilic motif in *The Waste Land* can be seen in references to the *Aeneid*, the *Commedia*, and *The Tempest*, but is most evident in allusions to the Psalms and the book of Ezekiel. Dante's primary paradigm of exile and return, as explained in his letter to Can Grande della Scala, was the sojourn in Egypt and the Exodus;[2] Eliot's primary paradigm was the captivity of the Israelites in Babylon. In 587 BC, Nebuchadnezzar swooped down on Jerusalem and carried away the king and his court; shortly thereafter, he leveled the city and moved the survivors to Babylon. The lament of the captives is preserved in Psalm 137.[3]

> By the rivers of Babylon, there we sat down, yea, we wept, when we remembered Zion. We hanged our harps upon the willows in the midst thereof. For there they that carried us away captive required of us a song; and they that wasted us required of us mirth, saying, Sing us one of the songs of Zion. How shall we sing the LORD's song in a strange land? If I forget thee, O Jerusalem, let my right hand forget her cunning. If I do not remember thee, let my tongue cleave to the roof of my mouth; if I prefer not Jerusalem above my chief joy.

This beautiful dejection ode is in the mind of the singer on the banks of the Thames in *The Waste Land*.

> By the waters of Leman I sat down and wept . . .
> Sweet Thames, run softly till I end my song,
> Sweet Thames, run softly, for I speak not loud or long.
> But at my back in a cold blast I hear
> The rattle of the bones, and chuckle spread from ear to ear. (*WL* 182–86; Eliot's ellipsis)

Eliot's identification with the exiles is underscored by his having written part of *The Waste Land* on the shores of Lake Leman (Lake Geneva), where he had gone for medical treatment. The geographical displacements and overlays, from the "rivers of Babylon" to the "waters of Leman" to the

Thames of London, suggest several kinds of exile—geographical, cultural, and moral. The point of view, as revealed in the "straight borrowing" (as Eliot refers to exact quotes integrated into his poems) from Spenser's *Prothalamion*, is that of a lyric poet. In the Psalm, the exiles refuse to sing because they are "in a strange land"; in Spenser, and also in Eliot, the poet sings "to ease [his] pain." The Hebrew children remember Jerusalem and weep for her; Eliot's singer, homeless beside a polluted river, weeps for himself.

The poet by the river Thames hearing "the rattle of the bones" points to the prophet Ezekiel, whose vision of dry bones is important both here and in *Ash-Wednesday*. Ezekiel was one of the Hebrew captives in Babylon, sitting with his compatriots beside the river: "I came to them of the captivity . . . that dwelt by the river . . . , and I sat where they sat, and remained there astonished among them for seven days" (Ezek. 3:15). Between 593 and 571 BC, Ezekiel had seven visions, all recorded in his book.[4] The first predicts the exile, and the last foretells the return. Ezekiel, who is addressed by the Lord as "Son of man," enters *The Waste Land* in the second paragraph with the first sketch of the poem's central image—a waste land.

> What are the roots that clutch, what branches grow
> Out of this stony rubbish? Son of man,
> You cannot say, or guess, for you know only
> A heap of broken images, where the sun beats,
> And the dead tree gives no shelter, the cricket no relief,
> And the dry stone no sound of water. (*WL* 19–24)

Eliot's note to these lines references Ezekiel 2:1, in which God commissions the "Son of man" to warn the inhabitants of Jerusalem that their holy places will be shattered—"your altars will be waste and ruined, your idols broken and destroyed"—and to assure them that they will return and rebuild (Ezek. 2:1ff; 6:6).

In Ezekiel, as in *The Waste Land*, exile is related to war, and the prophet's vision of broken altars, a shattered city, and a valley of bones bears an eerie resemblance to photographs in the London *Times* of collapsing churches and human remains on the Western Front. Eliot's readers would have caught the pathos in the question that his narrator first poses and then declares unanswerable. But the "Son of man" that he faces is no prophet. Unlike Ezekiel, he cannot remember his Jerusalem; the only thing that he knows is "a heap of broken images." Imprisoned in subjectivity, he refuses to speculate on whether roots will sprout in the dead land. He cannot say if the displaced peoples will be able to go home. He is himself an exile, and like Gerontion, the Sibyl, and Madame Sosostris, he cannot see beyond the desolate scene.

In the mid-1920s, Eliot attempted to move beyond the rubble of postwar Europe in part by reflecting on love and exile. As previously discussed, he abandoned his attempt to resolve life's antinomies through philosophy and accepted dualism as part of being human. In the Clark Lectures, he discusses what happens to love in the absence of epistemological dualism. *Without* objects, *eros* becomes an expression, as in Donne, of one's own ingenuity, or as in Crashaw, of one's feelings. *With* objects, as in Dante, love can rise to contemplation of the beloved. In his discussion of Lancelot Andrewes, Eliot extends this analysis to spiritual love. What happens to *agape* in the absence of metaphysical dualism? Without the supernatural, religion becomes, as in Goethe, a divinization of the natural; without the divine, as in George Bernard Shaw, it becomes perfection of the human. Without dualism, transcendence of any kind, including religious transcendence, is precluded, and *agape* is unimaginable. In this chapter, I consider a parallel question in the context of exile: What happens to "home" in a world without objects?

Exilic Triptych II: In the Valley of Dry Bones

Sister, mother
And spirit of the river, spirit of the sea,
Suffer me not to be separated

Eliot, *Ash-Wednesday* VI

The central poem associated with Eliot's exilic imagination is *Ash-Wednesday*, a sequence of six lyrics composed between 1927 and 1930. The pathos of exile reverberates throughout, In allusions to the river and the sea, to St. Louis and Gloucester, and to the prophet of exile, Ezekiel, and the poets of exile, Dante and Guido Cavalcanti. In language and style, it is one of Eliot's most complex works, with symbols—such as "jeweled unicorns"—that are at once beautiful and baffling. Most readings are grounded in the poet's biography or, given his testimony that he was attempting a modern *Vita Nuova* (*L*5.209), in his use of Dante. Drawing on Eliot's description of the poem as an attempt to explain himself to himself (*L*5.287), Ron Bush interprets it as "a struggle between secular and religious ways" of doing so (131). In keeping with the poet's claims that it registers "the experience of a man in search of God" (*L*5.288), John Timmerman reads it as a conversion poem, of which "Salutation" (*AW* II) "dramatizes the first stage" (92). Lyndall Gordon, attentive to Eliot's statement that it is an exposition of love (*L*7.618), reads it as a tribute to Emily Hale (234). Ronald Schuchard concurs, but focuses equally on Eliot's awareness of himself as an exile (149–50).

The motif of exile, as Schuchard demonstrates, is inseparable from Eliot's resurgent appreciation for his American roots. The working title on his draft is "All aboard for Natchez, Cairo, and St. Louis," the call of the conductor announcing the train from Boston to Union Station in St. Louis, the train Eliot took to go home during his years at Harvard.[5] The first line—"Because I do not hope to turn again"—is a translation of the opening of Cavalcanti's "Ballata, written in exile at Saranza," composed in 1300 as the poet, far from home, lay dying. The line not only introduces the exilic theme but also constitutes the opening part of the frame that holds the sequence together. The closing section includes an image of the Eliot summerhouse at Gloucester, with its "wide windows," its "granite shore" surrounded by goldenrod, and its view of "white sails" and whirling seabirds (*AW* VI.192–200). These images of home are followed by *Ash-Wednesday*'s concluding prayer, recalling his family, his nursery by the Mississippi, and his seaside summers on Cape Ann. "Sister, mother / And spirit of the river, spirit of the sea, / Suffer me not to be separated" (*AW* VI.32–34).

My reading, which accepts as a given the relevance of the biographical materials and the parallels to Dante, is focused on two elements that have received much less attention. The first is the continuing influence of Eliot's philosophical studies on the structure of his thought, and the second, basic in understanding the theme of exile, is the long shadow cast by the Old Testament on his imagination.

Three principles from Eliot's work in philosophy are evident in *Ash-Wednesday*. The first, as discussed in previous chapters, is a recognition of the intractability of dualism. In the Chapman lecture of 1924, the binary is human and divine; in *The Hollow Men* of 1925, it is the idea and the reality; and in the Clark Lectures of 1926, it is *eros* and *agape*, a binary further explored in *Ash-Wednesday*, which he describes as is "an exposition . . . of the relation of *eros* and *agape*, based on my own experience" (*L*7.618; Eliot's italics). The second principle is relativism. Knowing involves an awareness of relations, a perception of the "in-between." In *The Hollow Men*, the in-between is associated with a Shadow; in *Ash-Wednesday*, it is imagined as an echelon, a rung in a ladder connecting *eros* and *agape*; in *Four Quartets*, it is represented as the intersection between history and timeless moments. The third principle is dialectical thinking, an element that permeates Eliot's mind and art at every level. Knowing, he suggests, requires returning to one's starting place (to innocence, to ignorance), an idea articulated in his 1914 philosophical essays and repeated in the 1942 conclusion to *Little Gidding*. The meaning of the starting place, of home, is revealed dialectically in a narrative of leaving/wandering/returning. And so is the meaning of human love, as indicated in a letter written less than three months after his baptism and contemporaneous with the beginning of *Ash-Wednesday*. "If two people (say, a man and a woman in the greatest intimacy) love God still more than they love each other, then they enjoy greater love of each other than if they did not love God at all" (*L*3.711). Following this remark on the movement from *eros* to *agape*, with a loop back to a richer *eros*, Eliot turns to another example, the enjoyment of French food. Recalling dinners in Bordeaux and Paris, he recounts an experience he has had "only in flashes."

> It is the sudden realization of being separated from all enjoyment, from all things of this earth, even from Hope; . . . and at that moment of illumination, a recognition . . . that one can do without all these things, a joyful recognition of what John of the Cross means when he says that the soul cannot be possessed of the divine union until it has divested itself of the craving for all created beings. And after this one returns (I do anyway) to the *canard aux oranges* . . . with a keener pleasure. (*L*3.712-13)

Having described this sudden movement from the mundane to the ethereal followed by a return to his roast duck, Eliot quips, "If we are rightly directed, a good dinner can lead us towards God, and God can help us to enjoy a good dinner."

The relevance of both the philosophical principles and the Old Testament are evident in "Salutation," published in 1927 and included in the *Ash-Wednesday* sequence as number II.[6] In this, the earliest of the lyrics to have been composed, Eliot resumes his meditation on exile, and as in *The Waste Land*, the theme is mediated through the prophet Ezekiel. The exilic theme is strengthened by allusions to the flight of Elijah in I Kings 19 and, of utmost importance, to the archetypal scene of exile in Genesis 3, the expulsion from the Garden of Eden. More obliquely, the exile from Eden is recalled in an allusion to Ecclesiastes 12.

The exilic theme is clearer in "Salutation" as a stand-alone piece than as part of the sequence. In the latter, titles of individual poems are replaced with numbers, I-VI, and epigraphs are deleted or replaced. In *Ash-Wednesday* II, the loss is substantial. The deleted title and epigraphs establish the connection between Dante and Ezekiel, which is central in the poem. The title refers primarily to the scene in the *Vita Nuova* in which Dante explains the reordering of his loves after Beatrice withholds her salutation. There are two epigraphs, one from Ezekiel—"The Hand of the Lord was Upon Me"—and the other from the *Purgatorio*—"*e vo significando*" ("giving utterance"). In the first, Ezekiel introduces his vision of dry bones by saying that it was given to him by the God of Israel; in the second, Dante claims that his poetry is dictated by the God of Love. "I am one who, when Love/inspires me, takes note and/go setting it forth after the fashion which he dictates within me (I'mi son un che, quando/Amor mi spira, noto, e a quell modo/ch'e' ditta dentro vo significando) (*Purgatorio* 24.52-54). Both poet and prophet authenticate their visions by claiming that they are secretaries of a higher power.

Eliot's account of the genesis of *Ash-Wednesday* hints that he, too, was at least in part the vehicle of a higher power. In a letter to Bishop George Bell, he said that a number of the images originated from "recurrent dreams" and were intended to be understood "on the same plane of hallucination" as the *Vita Nuova* (*L*5.257). The opening stanza does indeed seem to be the transcription of a dream.

> Lady, three white leopards sat under a juniper-tree
> In the cool of the day, having fed to satiety
> On my legs my heart my liver and that which had been contained
> In the hollow round of my skull. And God said
> Shall these bones live? shall these
> Bones live? (*AW* II.1-6)

This surreal scene contains three biblical fragments, all exact quotations and all related to exile—Elijah's flight from Jezebel, Adam's expulsion from Eden, and Ezekiel's vision in Babylon. As previously discussed, Eliot stressed the importance of distinguishing between exact quotations and allusions in poetry.[7] Exact quotations, which he calls "straight borrowings," emanate directly from the past, whereas allusions emanate from the mind of a poet who is interpreting the past. The former establishes direct and intimate communication with the dead; the latter is indirect, more psychological than historical. The biblical fragments in this paragraph are "straight borrowings" giving voice to the dead. The first—"under a juniper tree"—is from

I Kings 19:1-8, in which the prophet Elijah is forced into exile by political shenanigans in King Ahab's court.[8] Exhausted and hungry, he rests beneath a desert shrub known as a juniper tree and, like the Sibyl, prays for permission to die. Falling asleep, he dreams of an angel, who instructs him to arise and eat. He awakes to find cakes and water, which sustain him for forty days in the wilderness. It is a story of the unexpected deliverance of a fugitive, especially relevant to the journey of forty days that begins on Ash Wednesday.

The second biblical fragment—"in the cool of the day"—is from the primal scene of exile in the Garden of Eden (Gen. 3). After the fall, newly conscious of their nakedness and guilt, Adam and Eve encounter God walking in the garden "in the cool of the day." They try to hide but are unable to escape the divine interrogation, which leads immediately to exile and eventually to death (3:8-11). These two phrases return in the coda:

> Under a juniper tree the bones sang, scattered and shining
> We are glad to be scattered, we did little good to each other,
> Under a tree in the cool of the day, with the blessing of sand (II.48-50)

But of course, as with all meaningful returns, this one is no replica. In the first stanza, it is the first-person narrator who laments the desiccation of "my legs my heart my liver and that which had been contained / In the hollow round of my skull" (3-4). In the last stanza, it is the bones, the happy "we" that sings, and via the reference to "the cool of the day" the juniper tree morphs in the third line into the tree of the knowledge of good and evil in Eden.

The third biblical borrowing in the opening lines of "Salutation" is from Ezekiel's vision of dry bones in chapter 37, one of the most vivid representations of exile in all of literature. Eliot's poem contains four verbatim quotations from the prophet, two of which form a frame around the entire lyric. The epigraph (later deleted) is the first verse of chapter 37, and the coda is a "straight borrowing" from chapter 48. The other two quotations are in the first stanza: "And God said / Shall these bones live?" in lines 4-5; "And God said / Prophesy to the wind" in lines 21-22. As in *The Waste Land*, the prophet, who is sitting with his fellow exiles by the rivers of Babylon, is transported "in spirit" to a valley of death. The depth of relevance of his vision to "Salutation" and to the theme of exile makes it worth quoting at length.

> The hand of the LORD was upon me, and carried me out in the spirit of the LORD, and set me down in the midst of the valley, which was full of bones. / And caused

> me to pass by them round about; and behold, there were very many in the open valley; and lo, they were very dry. / And he said unto me, Son of man, can these bones live? And I answered, O LORD GOD, thou knowest. / Again he said to me, Prophesy upon these bones, and say unto them, O ye dry bones, hear the word of the LORD. / Thus saith the LORD GOD to these bones; Behold, I will cause breath to enter into you, and ye shall live. / And I will lay sinews upon you, and will bring up flesh upon you, and cover you with skin, and put breath in you, and ye shall live; and ye shall know that I am the LORD. / So I prophesied as I was commanded; and as I prophesied, there was a noise, and behold a shaking; and the bones came together, bone to his bone. / And when I beheld, lo, the sinews and the flesh came up upon them, and skin covered them above; but there was no breath in them. / Then said he unto me, Prophesy unto the wind, prophesy, Son of man, and say to the wind, Thus saith the LORD GOD; Come from the four winds, O breath, and breathe upon these slain, that they may live. / So I prophesied as he commanded me, and the breath came into them, and they lived, and stood upon their feet, an exceeding great army. (Ezek. 37:1–10)

As the scene vanishes, the Lord God interprets the amazing dream.

> Son of man, these bones are the whole house of Israel: behold, they say, Our bones are dried, and our hope is lost; we are cut off . . . Thus said the LORD GOD: Behold, O my people, I will open your graves . . . and bring you into the land of Israel. (Ezek. 37:11–12)

The bones are not simply remains; they are exiles, the living dead, cut off from home. Ezekiel's vision permeates "Salutation," beginning with the opening lines. Eliot divides the speaker into spiritual and material components (spirit and bones; soul and body), into an "I" who talks (describes, worries, summarizes) and a "We" who chirps and sings. As the "I" describes his situation, God intervenes with a question, the very posing of which insinuates a glimmer of hope—"Shall these bones live?" The stanza ends by directing the reader back to Ezekiel, quoting the passage in which God answers his own question.

> In Ezekiel: "Prophesy unto the wind, . . . saith the Lord GOD . . . and breathe upon these slain, that they may live" (37:9).
>
> In *Ash-Wednesday*: And God said
> Prophesy to the wind, to the wind only for only
> The wind will listen. (*AW* II.21–23)

In previous poems, Eliot had ironized this ancient symbol of presence by using it to suggest absence. In "Preludes," for example, the wind is a random gust that "wraps / The grimy scraps / Of withered leaves about your feet" (ll. 5-7), but here, in *Ash-Wednesday*, he redeems the symbolism; the wind is the divine breath that reanimates the bones, enabling them to sing.

And the bones sang chirping
With the burden of the grasshopper. (*AW* II.23-24)

In the language of a beautiful biblical poem about old age, the bones sing of the time in which "the grasshopper shall be a burden and desire shall fail, because man goeth to his long home. . . . Then shall the dust return to the earth as it was, and the spirit shall return unto God, who gave it" (Eccles. 12:5, 7). The reference to the primeval exile is part of the larger Ash Wednesday theme (dust to dust), but it also suggests that the restoration will not give immunity from aging, that the revived bones will reenter natural cycles. Like Ezekiel by the Babylonian waters and Elijah under the juniper tree, the narrator will be revived, but like all mortals, he will return to dust.

In the opening vision of "Salutation," the question "Shall these bones live?" is raised and answered in the affirmative. As the section ends, the wind begins to revivify the bones and they begin to sing. Their song integrates the references to Dante and the Bible with the themes of love, conversion, and exile. Addressed to a Dantean "Lady of silences," it is a prayer focused on the complications of *eros* and *agape*.

The single Rose
Is now the Garden
Where all loves end
Terminate torment
Of love unsatisfied
The greater torment
Of love satisfied
. . . . . .
Grace to the Mother
For the Garden
Where all love ends. (*AW* II.32-38, 45-47)

That this is a litany of the bones in a poem grounded in Ezekiel's vision connects it to the theme of exile; that it is addressed to the Lady connects it to love, both human and divine. Given the borrowings from Genesis 3 in the opening stanza and the coda, the references to the Garden point not only to the contentious postlapsarian scene but also, via the theme of Grace and the presence of the Lady, to the Edenic dream of reentering paradise.

The coda of "Salutation" includes a reprise of the opening lines, bringing together the scriptural accounts of exile, from the encounter with God "in the cool of the day," to the shelter of Elijah "under a juniper tree," to the promise of return in Ezekiel.

> This is the land which ye
> Shall divide by lot. And neither division nor unity
> Matters. This is the land. We have our inheritance. (*AW* II.52–54)

This conclusion, which shows the exiles back at home, completes the dialectic of exile: expatriation/exile/repatriation. The promise given in the valley of dry bones—"ye shall live"—has been fulfilled. Eliot's lines are an exact quotation from chapter 48, the last chapter in the book of Ezekiel: "This is the land which ye shall divide by lot unto the tribes of Israel for inheritance, and these are their portions, saith the LORD GOD" (48:29).

Eliot's realization that "Salutation" would be at home in a sequence related to Ash Wednesday is not surprising. In the Christian calendar, Ash Wednesday is the day that commemorates the primeval exile. Eliot's understanding of this milestone in the Christian year was informed by the sermons of Bishop Andrewes, who repeatedly associated it with returning from exile. The defining text for the ceremony is taken from the archetypal scene in which Adam and Eve, newly fallen, are expelled from Eden and told that reentry will be blocked by flaming swords. In the service outlined in *The Book of Common Prayer*, the priest marks the penitent's forehead with ashes and intones God's words to Adam: "Remember, O man, that dust thou art, and unto dust shalt thou return" (Gen. 3:19).

Exilic Triptych III: From the Waters of Leman to the Shores of Casco Bay

> What seas what shores what granite islands towards my timbers
> And woodthrush calling through the fog
> My daughter.
> Eliot, "Marina"

As a meditation on exile, *Ash-Wednesday* is framed on one side by *The Waste Land* and on the other by "Marina." This triad is part of the dialectic of exile, in which the last term involves a return to the first, which has been transformed by the intervening journey. At the beginning of the 1920s, Eliot was separated from his first world and acutely conscious of himself as a stranger in war-ravaged Europe; at the end, he was contemplating his return to America following a long absence. In *The Waste Land*, the protagonist is weeping beside a polluted river in London, and in "Marina," a weary sailor is listening to a wood thrush calling him through the fog in Casco Bay, Maine, not far from the Eliot summer home on the New England coast. The first panel in this triptych projects a cursed land, and the last a blessed one. The central panel, as discussed in the previous section, depicts a desert containing dry bones on the verge of revivification, a vision shaped by Eliot's engagement with Dante and Ezekiel. When related to Eliot's life, this sequence suggests, on one level, an end to his long exile, and on another, a journey through despair to hope.

Moving from *Ash-Wednesday* to "Marina" is like moving from Ash Wednesday to Easter. Gone are the Old Testament figures of *Ash-Wednesday*, "Journey of the Magi" and "A Song of Simeon"; their successor is a beautiful girl named Marina. But to understand her importance to Eliot, one must return to her nursery in Shakespeare. The immediate background of the poem is Eliot's rereading of the late plays in conjunction with their interpretation in G. Wilson Knight's *Myth and Miracle*. Earlier critics had argued that these plays were evidence of Shakespeare's decline; Knight maintained, conversely, that they constituted a spiritual breakthrough. In an interpretation that resonated with Eliot, Knight argues that the overall trajectory of Shakespeare's plays is dialectical, moving from the "mental division" of the problem plays to a partial resolution in the great tragedies, and finally, to the mysticism of the final plays (23). The joy that runs through *Pericles*, *The Winter's Tale*, *Cymbeline*, and *The Tempest*, Knight suggests, is "the inevitable development of the questioning, the pain, the profundity and grandeur of the plays they succeed" (9). He supports his thesis on the mystical plays with an analysis of remarkably similar recognition scenes in which a daughter or wife lost in a tempest is miraculously restored through music. The conjunction of miracle and music in these epiphanic scenes points beyond tragedy to "the awakening light of some religious or metaphysical truth" in their author (14).

The concept of "recognition" (Greek: *anagnorisis*) comes from Aristotle's discussion of plot in the *Poetics*. It refers to the sudden apprehension of a previously unknown or veiled truth that issues in a reversal of fortune

(Greek: *peripety*). The greatest example is the recognition by Oedipus that he has killed his father and married his mother. In tragedy, the recognition leads to horror; in comedy, to joy. Whether horrific or joyous, the recognition is the culmination of a triadic and dialectical structure—knowing/not knowing/knowing again or, in Plato's formulation, knowing back—and in Eliot's view, the "knowing back" is knowing "for the first time" (*LG* 242). Although "Marina" is above all a recognition poem, it is also one of Eliot's postconversion epiphany poems. The two concepts are cousins. Recognition is related to knowing, epiphany to seeing. *Epiphaneia* refers to an unveiling or showing, a "seeing back" that makes a difference in how and what one sees. In Western Christianity, Epiphany commemorates the visit of the Magi to the infant Christ, an event reimagined in Eliot's first epiphany poem, "Journey of the Magi."[9]

The first readers of "Marina" were puzzled by the incongruity between the Latin epigraph, which is from Seneca's *Hercules Furens*, and the text, which is a retelling of Shakespeare's *Pericles*.[10] The intent, as Eliot explained in letters to friends, was to juxtapose the comic and tragic in a way that deepened his overall meaning. He repeatedly referred to this conjunction of opposites as a "crisscross." To G. Wilson Knight, to whom he had sent a copy of the poem, he wrote: "The quotation is from Seneca's *Hercules Furens*; . . . I wanted a crisscross between Hercules waking up to find that he had slain his children, and Pericles waking up to find his child alive" (*L*5.368). To his illustrator McKnight Kauffer, he explained that the "crisscross between the text and the epigraph" was essential for his theme.

> The theme is a comment on the Recognition Motive in Shakespeare's later plays, and particularly . . . the recognition of *Pericles*. The quotation is from *Hercules Furens*, where Hercules, having killed his children in a fit of madness induced by an angry god, comes to without remembering what he has done. . . . The exact point [is] the contrast of death and life in Hercules and Pericles. (*L*5.270)

In a later letter, Eliot explained that the epigraph from Seneca—Quis hic locus, quae regio, quae mundi plaga? (What place is this, what land, what quarter of the globe?)—was "merely an antithetical form of recognition," in which Hercules "comes to his senses to see his children dead in front of him, before he realized that they were dead by his own hand."[11] Eliot discusses the plot in his 1927 introduction to *Seneca his Tenne Tragedies*, published as "Seneca in Elizabethan Translation" (*Prose* 3.195-234). At the end of his labors, Hercules returns home and learns that his wife and children are being threatened by the tyrant Lycus. In order to save them, he rushes off to kill the villain. As he returns, Juno strikes him with madness, and in his insanity, he kills his wife and children.

The epigraph serves two major functions. The first is that it increases the immediacy of the horrific. It is another of Eliot's "straight borrowings," an unaltered unmediated voice speaking in its own language across two millennia. The second is that it is essential for the crisscross effect that defines the architecture of the poem. By juxtaposing "the two extremes of the recognition scene" (*L*5.166), Eliot suggests a dialectical move from joy to horror to a higher joy that is both tempered and intensified by the inclusion of the horrific. The crisscross is replicated within the two plays in that the moment of recognition includes and transcends its opposite. Thus Hercules' horror is intensified by the joy he has known with his family, and Pericles' happiness is heightened by the anguish he has endured for more than a decade. Analogues of the chiasmic crossing of positives and negatives appear in Eliot's prose, as when he praises Baudelaire's aphorism "La volupté unique et suprême de l'amour gît dans la certitude de faire le mal" (*Prose* 4.162).[12] Thematically and structurally, this crossing of opposites suggests that the pain of exile secures the joy of homecoming.

Most of Eliot's comments on the recognition theme appear, appropriately, in his essays on drama. "In Shakespeare's plays this is primarily the recognition of a long-lost daughter, secondarily of a wife" (*Prose* 4.475). In *Pericles*, the exiled Prince loses his wife, Thaisa, and newborn daughter, Marina, in a tempest. The wife, who has given birth and is assumed dead, is placed in a casket and buried at sea, and the infant is left in the care of the King of Tarsus. In the labyrinthine plot, the wife washes ashore, is resuscitated, and becomes a priestess of Diana: the infant develops into a beautiful girl who is kidnapped by pirates and sold to a brothel. Once established in his kingdom, Pericles embarks on a journey to find the long-lost daughter and is told that she is dead. Crazed by grief, he returns to sea, and in yet another twist of the plot, he is tossed up near the place inhabited by his daughter. In an attempt to calm the confused old sailor, the governor calls on Marina, who is known for her beatific presence and her music. As she sings, Pericles' mind begins to clear: "My dearest wife was like this maid, and such a one/My daughter might have been" (V.i.107-8). When her name is revealed, he perceives that this is a miracle. "But are you flesh and blood?/Have you a working pulse? And are no fairy?" (V.i.153-54). Eliot's poem is a monologue by the father at the moment of recognition, the moment when his nightmare melts into the sweetest of dreams. The plot then moves to the recovery of his wife, a recovery symbolizing a resurrection.

Both in Shakespeare and in Eliot, the "recognition" marks a mystical moment in which the fog clears and one recognizes a face that enables him to pass through an "unknown, remembered gate" and know not only the place but also the face "for the first time" (*LG* V.242-43). Eliot's speaker, echoing his Shakespearean namesake, says

> What is this face, less clear and clearer
> The pulse in the arm, less strong and stronger—
> Given or lent? (17-18)

"Marina" ends, dialectically, with a return to the beginning, one of the most beautiful in English poetry, comparable to that in Coleridge's "Frost at Midnight."

> What seas what shores what granite islands towards my timbers
> And woodthrush calling through the fog
> My daughter. (33-35)

The old sailor again hears the wood thrush, but as in all great returns, its music is more profound, both for him and for the reader. The perfection of this return owes much to the poet's variations. In the opening lines, as in the epigraph, there is uncertainty, confusion, a "where am I," "why am I here?" moment. In the last lines, confusion has melted into recognition, into the *nostos* of a weary sailor who sees the shores of home. The ship is given a direction, now moving "towards my timbers"; the sailor is "knowing back" to the woodlands of his childhood. The wood thrush that in the opening lines is "singing" is now "calling," calling his name. Finally, the overture ends with "O my daughter," and in that interjection—that "O"—there is a mixture of strong emotions—pain, grief, desire, surprise. The coda drops the "O" and in the father's simple "My daughter," we sense his recognition and the peace that passeth understanding.

Eliot's comments on "Marina" leave little doubt that what impressed him most in Knight's interpretation was the dialectical movement from suffering through tragedy to joy, a process in which the spiritual breakthrough is symbolized by the recognition of a long-lost daughter. "We can hardly read the later plays attentively without admitting that the father-and-daughter theme was one of very deep symbolic value to [Shakespeare] in his last productive years" (*Prose* 4.475). In "The Development of Shakespeare's Verse," Eliot maintained that Perdita (*The Winter's Tale*), Miranda (*The Tempest*), Imogene (*Cymbeline*), and Marina have a special beauty that cannot be found in his earlier heroines. "They belong in a world from which some emotions have been purified away, so that others, ordinarily invisible, may be made apparent. To my mind, the finest of all the 'recognition scenes' is [in] . . . *Pericles*. It is a perfect example of the 'ultra-dramatic,' a dramatic action of beings who are more than human . . . or rather, seen in a light more than that of day" (*Prose* 5.555). Eliot continued to ponder the redemptive value of the father-daughter relationship in conjunction with the knowing back of recognition and the seeing through of epiphany. He returned to the symbolism of this archetypal motif in his late play, *The Elder Statesman*, and while writing that play, he experienced its power in his May-December marriage to a woman who was both daughter and wife and whose presence led to the recognition (a true "knowing back") that a little boy still lived within the septuagenarian poet.

In 1958, in response to an inquiry about the recognition motif in "Marina," Eliot remarked: "I had no daughter, but the relationship interested me, and recognition in my experience is something that comes repeatedly in life."[13] Eliot's longing for a daughter, inseparable from his feeling for America, is perhaps behind a curious entry in the St. Louis section of the *1928 Summer Social Register*, a work that gives the summer addresses of prominent Americans, "where it differs from the Winter Address." The Eliot entry, which misspells Vivien's last name, lists three daughters.

> Eliot Mr. & Mrs. Thomas S (Vivien H Haight-Wood)
> Juniors: Misses Betty, Verona & Aurelian

The summer address for the Eliots and their daughters is given as "Castle Eliot" in "East Coker, Somerset Eng." The form for this parodic entry was submitted, presumably by Eliot himself, in the watershed year of 1927.[14] It is both a joke and a serious fantasy in which he is seeing back to what might have been.

The mystical moment represented in "Marina" is accompanied by a new music, caught in images and in sounds and rhythms. The cry of the mangled nightingale—"Twit twit twit / Jug jug jug jug jug jug"—in *The Waste Land* and the Song of the Bones in *Ash-Wednesday* are succeeded by the song of the wood thrush singing through the mist of the New England coast. The new music is more sensuous, more responsive to nature, and more evocative of memories that point to recognition. "Marina" represents the high point in his idealization of his youth, of America, and of his family and Emily Hale, an idealization born of desire but as is discussed in the next chapter, unsustainable as a touchstone for happiness.

10 "Into our first world"

Return and Recognition in *Burnt Norton* and *Little Gidding*

Home is where one starts from.

Eliot, *East Coker* V

Eliot's First World: St. Louis and Gloucester

I have spent many years out of America altogether; but Missouri and the Mississippi have made a deeper impression on me than any other part of the world.

Eliot to M. W. Childs, Missouri Historical Society (1930)

The last poem that Eliot wrote before his long-anticipated return to America, "Marina," is a paean to the landscape of coastal New England. In the opening lines, the persona sees the gray rocks on the Atlantic shore and hears the music of the wood thrush "singing through the fog" near the Eliot summer home; in the closing lines, he hears the same bird "calling through the fog." The thrush is calling him home, to his first world. "I find that as one gets on in middle life the strength of early associations, and the intensity of early impressions, becomes more evident; and many little things, long forgotten, recur" (*L*5.282). In 1932, Eliot finally ended his long exile in England and attempted to reclaim the world of his American childhood and youth—St. Louis and Gloucester. Over the next nine months, he visited the graves of his parents and spent time with his surviving siblings and old friends, including Emily Hale. In 1933, he returned to London, and in his first major poem, *Burnt Norton*, he again hears the thrush calling him to return to his first world, but in this scene, he realizes that the thrush is a tempter and the first world a chimera. In juxtaposition to this fanciful first world, he presents another, which consists of timeless moments and which gradually, over the course of *Four Quartets*, evolves into the Edenic moments of *Little Gidding*.

The desire to return to one's first world is part of the larger theme of exile. It is inextricably connected to the attempt to regain what has been lost by completing a "loop in time" (*CPP* 229), and it inevitably involves self-deception and an idealization of the past. Eliot describes the mindset in "Shakespeare and Stoicism of Seneca," published in the watershed year of 1927, as "the human will to see things as they are not." He names this oxymoronic quality "*bovarysme*" and illustrates it by pointing to Emma Bovary's romantic illusions (*Prose* 3.248). In Eliot's poetry, the most memorable representation of such willful self-deception is the "water-dripping song" in part V of *The Waste Land* (331–58). He told Ford Madox Ford that these were the only "*good* lines in *The Waste Land*. . . . The rest is ephemeral" (Eliot's italics; *L*2.188). The first half of this passage describes the absence of water. "Here is no water but only rock/Rock and no water." The jagged rocks are seen as "carious teeth that cannot spit," and the thunder is dry and sterile. The second half responds to this desperate desire with two conditionals: "If there were water"; and "If there were the sound of water only." But as the narrator knows, "there is no water." In spite of this, he longs to hear what he knows is a counterfeit: "the hermit-thrush sing[ing] in the pine trees/Drip drop drip drop drop drop drop," a song that mimics the sound of water falling on rocks. Although the imaginary water does not assuage his thirst, it generates a smidgen of joy, in part by establishing a dialectic between desire and deceit.

The "water-dripping song" also introduces one of Eliot's major symbols for the complications of desire—the hermit-thrush, a small, shy bird that sings from hiding places. Eliot associated its seductive, ostensibly disembodied music with his early childhood summers in Gloucester and Quebec Province, where his uncle kept a family camp (*L*1.2n2). In a note in *The Waste Land*, he mentions hearing the bird in Quebec and quotes Chapman's *Handbook of Birds of Eastern North America* on its habitat and song. It lives in "secluded woodland and thickety retreats" and sings in notes that are unequalled "in purity and sweetness of tone and exquisite modulation" (*WL* n357).[1] At the end of the 1920s, the thrush reappears in "Marina," and in the early 1930s in *Burnt Norton*. In both, the bird is associated with the tension between desire and various forms of self-deception. The birds that Eliot loved in childhood are related to the theme of exile, which pervades the work of his middle and late poetry: *The Waste Land*, *Ash-Wednesday*, and "Marina"; the American landscapes of "New Hampshire" and "Cape Ann"; and *Burnt Norton* and *Little Gidding*.

In a cameo appearance in *Ash-Wednesday*, the bird is associated with the idealization of Emily Hale and with the speaker's desire to reclaim the possibilities of youth. The lyric is a tribute to a lady who is part Mary and part Beatrice and whose presence restores the years by "restoring . . . the ancient rhyme. Redeem the time" (*AW* IV.17–19).

> The silent sister . . .
> . . . .
>   bent her head and signed but spoke no word
> But the fountain sprang up and the bird sang down
> Redeem the time, redeem the dream
> The token of the word unheard, unspoken (IV.22, 24–27)

The grammar of these lines suggests that the bird who sings "redeem the time" does so at a signal from the silent woman and that his song is accepted as a token for her unspoken word. Although assigned to external messengers, the imperative originates from within the speaker, who longs to move forward by looping back and retrieving possibility. The biblical phase, "redeem the time," literally means to "buy back the time"—in this context, to reclaim the years between the poet's departure for England and his return; "redeem the dream," similarly, means to recover the lost dreams of childhood and youth.

In 1919, as previously noted, Eliot confided to his brother that he would always be a foreigner in England (*L*1.370). In 1927, he attempted to resolve this issue by changing his citizenship and joining the English church. These gestures, however sincere, are another reminder of the cleft Eliot, for at the same time that he was pledging allegiance to England, he was working to arrange his return to America, pushed by the misery of his life with Vivien, drawn by his reconnection with Emily Hale, and more urgently, by his desire to see his mother, Charlotte, the most intimate link to his personal paradise lost. Seriously ill from the mid-1920s, she died in September 1929, before he could complete his travel arrangements. Grief-stricken, he wrote to his brother that now, more than ever, he wanted to return to St. Louis. In 1932, having received an invitation to give the Norton Lectures at Harvard, he was finally able to set sail for Boston. Three areas of his life in America are relevant to understanding the tension between knowledge and desire as it relates to a reformulation of his exilic imagination. The first is his relationship with his family, especially his only brother, Henry; the second is his relationship with Emily Hale; and the third, intersecting the other two, is his critique of Unitarianism.

Eliot in America: Between the Idea and the Reality

Whatever I hoped for
Now that I am here I know I shall never find it.
The instinct to return to the point of departure
And start again as if nothing had happened,
Isn't that all folly? It's like the hollow tree.

Eliot, *The Family Reunion*

Eliot arrived in America on 25 September 1932, the day before his forty-fourth birthday. The nine months that he spent in America constitute a turning point in his life and in his poetry. His primary activities were related to work—the Norton Lectures at Harvard, the Page-Barbour Lectures at the University of Virginia, the Turnbull Lectures at Johns Hopkins, and various engagements requiring him to cross the country from Boston to Los Angeles and Buffalo to Charlottesville. He lectured at Scripps College in California, where Emily Hale was teaching, and at Washington University in St. Louis, where he visited the graves of his parents. Generally speaking, the reunion with family was satisfying. He spent time with his siblings in Cambridge and visited his Aunt Rose in St. Louis. Between 29 December and mid-January, he visited Emily Hale in California, and they remained in touch throughout the spring. When she arrived in Boston at the end of the semester, he called on her at the home of her aunt and uncle. In June, she was with the Eliot family for a vacation in New Hampshire, and on 17 June, she joined them for his lecture at Milton Academy. As his time in America drew to a close, he wrote to Paul Elmer More, "There is something I want here (domestic affection), and something I want in England, and I can't have both. . . . One side suffers from dullness, the other from nightmare" (*L6*.584).

It was inevitable, however, that there would have been a gap between Eliot's expectations and his experience. Of the elements contributing to the de-idealization of America, one was paramount, and it had to do with religion. Because of his family's eminence in Unitarianism, the clergy invited him to address them in King's College Chapel in Boston. Reluctantly, he agreed, and on 3 April 1933, he spoke to the Boston Association of Unitarian Ministers. The audience included not only distinguished Unitarians but also his brother and sisters and presumably the surrogate parents of Emily Hale, Dr. and Mrs. John Perkins. The title of Eliot's lecture, "Two Masters," is taken from the Sermon on the Mount, in which Christ says, "No man can serve two masters: for either he will hate the one, and love the other; or else he will hold to the one and despise the other. Ye cannot serve God and mammon" (Matt. 6:24).[2]

Eliot's argument deals with the importance of choosing between polar opposites—good and evil, black and white—and with the moral peril of trying to avoid saying yes or no. This was not a new issue for Eliot. The inability to choose is behind Prufrock's paralysis, and moral neutrality characterizes the inhabitants of *The Waste Land*. The moral significance of choosing pervades Eliot's criticism, evident in his fascination with *Inferno* III (the region of the undecided)[3] and, more explicitly, in his discussion of morality in the 1930 essay on Baudelaire: "So far as we are human, what we do must be either evil or good; so far as we do evil or good, we are human; and it is better . . . to do evil than to do nothing: at least, we exist" (*Prose* 4.162). In the Boston lecture, Eliot applied this logic to religion, maintaining that a faith based on fence-straddling is doomed to collapse. He predicted that a Christianity anchored in humanitarianism would wither and be succeeded by more robust alternatives, namely, orthodoxy or atheism. When the audience received his talk as an attack on liberal Protestants and Unitarians, Eliot seemed surprised, and he complained that the Unitarians "attacked me for not being a Papist" (*L*6.582). Their criticism points to an underlying problem with Eliot's argument. Given his logic, he should have espoused Calvinism or Catholicism; instead he embraced Anglo-Catholicism, the position of which epitomizes the via media between religious extremes.

Eliot's brother was among those who were shocked by the lecture. After Eliot returned to England, Henry wrote to ask why he had chosen "to address to the clergy of Boston, a city saturated with associations of your ancestors . . . a fanatically intolerant and shocking tirade" (*L*7.754). He accused Tom of insulting his Unitarian hosts and dishonoring his Unitarian parents. Particularly upset by the tone of the lecture, Henry comments at length on Eliot's religious conversion.

> The step toward the Church was . . . in line with the best hagiological traditions that the monstrous sinner, the author of "The 'Potamus" and "Mr. Eliot's Sunday Morning Service" should, passing through the travail of the soul . . . of *The Waste Land*, arrive, barefoot, in sackcloth, and penitent at the foot of the Cross. The tableau is, I must say, perfect. (*L*7.755)

Henry suggests that the authenticity of Tom's faith is belied by the inclusion in his collected work of "blasphemous poems (and they certainly are blasphemous, despite your fallacious . . . reasoning that one cannot blaspheme unless one believes)" (*L*7.757). Pierced to the core, Eliot was especially distressed by the suggestion that he had joined the church for show. "If it is not an accusation of . . . humbug in the most serious matter of all—what is?" He insisted that he would never knowingly dishonor his parents and denied that his poems were blasphemous.[4]

The American interlude, culminating in the devastating analysis in Henry's letter, highlights two factors that were to be reflected in Eliot's poetry. First, it completed the de-idealization of his memories of his first world, including those of his relationship with his brother and Miss Hale. Second, it underscored the importance of religious convictions. Eliot was an uncompromising Trinitarian, for whom the Incarnation was the central doctrine. His siblings, Emily Hale, and his hosts in King's College Chapel were Unitarians, who believed that the Incarnation was a myth among other myths. In several papers written at this time, Eliot insists that "*religious* differences are at least as important as racial, linguistic or geographical" differences (*Prose* 4.321; Eliot's italics). A central point of his Boston speech was that taking religion seriously means choosing between two masters; a central notion of his audience was that it means tolerance for a wide spectrum of views. In retrospect, these factors explain why he would never marry Emily Hale, and why he had to reimagine the motif of return that was to permeate the *Quartets*.

The turn in Eliot's imagination that occurred between April and June 1933 in Boston was sealed when he received Henry's postmortem on the visit. The change can be traced in his poetry, beginning in "New Hampshire" (1933), written after a farewell vacation with his family and Emily Hale. He juxtaposes images of childhood and seasonal cycles, not to idealize his lost years, but to acknowledge that they are unredeemable. The most telling lines are addressed to a dark bird: "Black wing, brown wing, hover over; / Twenty years and the spring is over" (ll. 5-6).

Burnt Norton: Reimagining the "first world"

Into our first world, shall we follow
The deception of the thrush? Into our first world

Eliot, *Burnt Norton* I

In *Burnt Norton*, written after his disillusionment in America, Eliot reimagined the concept of "redeeming the time" by creating in poetry a new "first world," which is represented in two versions. In the first, he dramatizes entering a world generated by memory and desire, and in the second, a world made possible by immediate experience and freedom from desire.[5] The first version imagines returning to the past, to a moment *in time* before the future was fixed, in order to redeem a might-have-been present; the other concentrates on a present moment, in which there is an intersection of movement and stillness that opens a window on ultimate reality. The overall structure of *Burnt Norton*, in keeping with the predominant tendency of Eliot's thought, is dialectical, progressing from one first world to the other and ending in a return to the beginning that includes and transcends both in a more comprehensive form. This pattern is substantiated and deepened when Eliot adds the three wartime *Quartets*. The two worlds have the same goal (redeeming the time) and both involve a meditation on time's puzzles. The common features lead most critics to conflate the rose-garden moment and subsequent mystical moments in the poem. Steve Ellis, for example, one of Eliot's most astute readers, sees the intersection of time and timelessness in the Incarnation as "once more recapitulat[ing] the rose-garden experience of *Burnt Norton*" (106).[6]

Eliot returned to London in 1933, and in 1934, Emily Hale spent the summer in England. In September, they visited the gardens of Burnt Norton together. Within a year, the memories of that visit would be represented in the poem that would later become the first of *Four Quartets*. The opening lines originated as part of the second temptation scene in *Murder in the Cathedral*. In the play, a tempter tells Thomas, "The Chancellorship that you resigned / When you were made Archbishop—that was a mistake / On your part—still may be regained" (*CPP* 185). The desire to return to the past and create a different present is precisely the temptation that Eliot faced in the rose garden at Burnt Norton. In the draft of the play, Thomas rebukes his tempter, declaring "What might have been is a conjecture/Remaining a permanent possibility/Only in a world of speculation" (Gardner, 82). The visitor to the garden, similarly tempted, repeats Thomas's answer, with one substitution. Instead of "conjecture" (possibly true and thus a genuine temptation), the visitor in the garden says "abstraction" (knowingly unreal). In its new context, the meditation introduces a major theme of the garden scene and of the poem as a whole—redeeming the time.

> Time present and time past
> Are both perhaps present in time future,
> And time future contained in time past.
> If all time is eternally present
> All time is unredeemable. (*BN* I.1-5)

These lines are a reflection on the imperative presented by the bird of *Ash-Wednesday*—"redeem the time" (IV.26-27), recontextualizing the directive by putting it at the center of a temptation scene.

The opening lines of *Burnt Norton* are impersonal, but in an abrupt shift, they become deeply personal. In remembering a recent moment in a rose garden in Gloucestershire, the speaker recovers the memory of a lost moment two decades earlier in America. Given the presence of the poet's former fiancée and the emphasis on the "might-have-been," the reactivated memory points to a Prufrockian moment in which not choosing was actually choosing, in which indecisiveness had determined the course of a lifetime. The mise-en-scène of the remote memory is the Massachusetts of Eliot's youth, and of the more recent, the rose garden of Burnt Norton. The scene in the rose garden is one of temptation in which two might-have-been lovers attempt to redeem a lost world.

> Footfalls echo in the memory
> Down the passage which we did not take
> Towards the door we never opened
> Into the rose-garden. My words echo
> Thus, in your mind.
>
> . . . .
>
> Other echoes
> Inhabit the garden. Shall we follow?
> Quick, said the bird, find them, find them,
> Round the corner. Through the first gate,

> Into our first world, shall we follow
> The deception of the thrush? Into our first world. (*BN* I.11-15, 17-22)

The visitor to the garden not only acknowledges self-deception; he desires it. The key line is "shall we follow the deception of the thrush?" This is different from "shall we follow the thrush?" or even the "song of the thrush." The emphasis falls on the word "deception" ("of the thrush" is a modifier, an adjective). The answer, given in the same line, is yes, in spite of the guilty knowledge that is attached to it. Here, as in other passages, the bird has a tag line—"quick, quick"—and speaks in imperatives—"go, go"; "follow, follow"; "redeem the dream"; "find them, find them." The protagonist and his companion gladly follow the bird into an imaginary world in which they dance with flowers, and the thrush sings along with "unheard music in the shrubbery." Their minuet is cut short by a change in the weather that cancels the luminous might-have-been. A passing cloud drains the pools, and the bird that had urged them to enter demands that they leave. "Go, go, go, said the bird: human kind/Cannot bear very much reality" (*BN* I.43-44). The expulsion is justified, ironically, in words that Thomas uses to console the grieving women of Canterbury, "Human kind/Cannot bear very much reality" (*CPP* 271). The return to *Murder in the Cathedral* as the coda to this part of *Burnt Norton* frames the experience of the visitors with the greater temptations of Becket in the cathedral and Jesus in the Garden of Gethsemane. Even Christ, who prayed that he would be spared the cup of suffering, could not return to the past and alter the present.

The framing of the garden vignette with passages used in *Murder in the Cathedral* identifies the scene as one of temptation. The motif is bolstered by the reference to dust on roses, which brings to mind the conclusion in the primeval garden of temptation: "Thou art dust and unto dust shalt thou return" (Gen. 3:19). In Eden, the tempter comes in the form of a serpent, but in Eliot's poetry, he appears in the guise of the thrush first met in the water-dripping song. Here, in the garden of Burnt Norton, the tempter returns, and as in *The Waste Land*, he appears by invitation. The temptation in *The Waste Land*, however, is to see things as they *are* not; here it is to see things as they *were* not. The first is generated by the desire for water; the second by a mixture of memory and desire, mingled with regret.

Eliot's experience in the rose garden did not cause him to abandon his attempt to redeem the time, but to reimagine it in spiritual terms. In part II of *Burnt Norton*, he goes beyond the fanciful garden scene by describing an alternative first world, one different in kind from that associated with the rose-garden. The new rendition includes the past, but faces forward, with no suggestion of returning to a moment in time past. The rose-garden sketch is drenched in desire and guilty knowledge; the subsequent experience is free of desire and can be experienced only by negating the will. The first is a shared experience ("My thoughts echo/Thus, in your mind" I.14); the second is solitary. The preface to the presentation of the alternative first world situates it "at the still point of the turning world" and describes it in terms of freedom and also of *kenosis*, the term used in Philippians 2:7 to describe the process by which Christ emptied himself and assumed the form of a servant.

> The inner freedom from the practical desire,
> The release from action and suffering, release from the inner
> And the outer compulsion, yet surrounded
> By a grace of sense . . .
> . . . concentration
> Without elimination, both a new world
> And the old made explicit, understood
> In the completion of its partial ecstasy,
> The resolution of its partial horror. (II.24–32)

The "new world" is revealed by the purging of desire and the negation of will. Existing in the present moment at the crossroads of history and eternity, it is described in sensuous images linked to memories of yesterday and yesteryear, memories not canceled but transcended and understood for the first time.

> Time past and time future
> Allow but a little consciousness.
> To be conscious is not to be in time
> But only in time can the moment in the rose-garden,
> The moment in the arbour where the rain beat,
> The moment in the draughty church at smokefall
> Be remembered; involved with past and future.
> Only through time time is conquered. (II.37–43)

In the rose-garden scene, the characters yield to temptation; they are duped and thus unable to redeem the time. Here, in this pregnant moment, the protagonist is called rather than tempted, and in accepting this calling, he is able to redeem the time. As in the rose-garden episode, everything hinges on memory. Without memory, the experience in America as a young man and in the rose garden as a pensive exile would have been irredeemably lost. The solitary experience had a beginning and an end, which means that it was "in time," but given that it was a form of immediate experience, time was not in it. The memory in time of a moment outside of time grounds the possibility that time, and with it the Adamic exile, can be overcome.

Burnt Norton ends with a return to the beginning. In both form and theme, the last paragraph mimics the opening section—a philosophical meditation followed by references to a garden world. The subject of the meditation is the interdependence of three parallel antitheticals—movement and stillness, desire and love, and time and timelessness.

Desire itself is movement
Not in itself desirable;
Love is itself unmoving,
Only the cause and end of movement,
Timeless and undesiring
Except in the aspect of time
Caught in the form of limitation
Between un-being and being. (V.25-32)

As in the first section of *Burnt Norton*, the abstract musing is succeeded by concrete and sensuous images of a rose garden ringing with the laughter of hidden children, and the deceptive thrush returns for a curtain call.

Sudden in a shaft of sunlight
Even while the dust moves
There rises the hidden laughter
Of children in the foliage
Quick now, here, now, always—
Ridiculous the waste sad time
Stretching before and after. (V.33-39)

This return is not a loop back to a replica of the rose garden but to a more comprehensive vision, which incorporates both models of the first world in the poem: (1) the moment in the rose garden and (2) the memory of the moment that grounds the quasi-mystical experience described in part II. As in all dialectical returns, the final place cannot be identical to the starting place because it is in time and includes intermediary contradictory experience. It is, is Eliot's words, "both a new world / And the old made explicit, understood / In the completion of its partial ecstasy, / The resolution of its partial horror" (II.29-33). This phenomenon is beautifully represented in various poems by Wordsworth, including the *Prelude* and, with special clarity, "Tintern Abbey," in which the narrator returns after five years to the same place and finds that it is and is not the same.

The key to understanding the conclusion of *Burnt Norton* as a higher stage, which includes and transcends opposing models of a first world (also the oppositions of desire and love, movement and stillness), is the line "Sudden in a shaft of sunlight." Literally speaking, this image refers to a sharply delineated beam of light breaking through the clouds; metaphorically, to a sudden moment of clarity connecting heaven and earth. It is used in *Murder in the Cathedral* by the Women of Canterbury, who, in their opening chorus, foresee the terror associated with the return of Thomas.

> Some malady is coming upon us. We wait, we wait,
> And the saints and martyrs wait, for those who shall be martyrs and saints,
> Destiny waits in the hand of God, shaping the still unshapen:
> I have seen these things in a shaft of sunlight. (*CPP* 176)

"Sudden in a shaft of sunlight" is one of a cluster of meteorological images used in the *Quartets* to indicate a connection between heaven and earth, initiated from above. In *Burnt Norton*, sunlight fills pools with water and clouds empty them. In *East Coker* and *The Dry Salvages*, winter lightning is associated with the timeless moment, and in *Little Gidding*, the winter sun flames the icy pond. Significantly, the sun in the rose garden of Burnt Norton is associated with an illusion, but in the yard of Little Gidding, it is associated with the tongues of Pentecost.

The dialectical shape of *Burnt Norton* is doubly confirmed in the closing lines. First, the return to *Murder in the Cathedral* both frames the poem and, when combined with the allusion to the figure of the ten stairs from St. John of the Cross, integrates temptation into a pattern of the soul's ascent to God; second, the return to a rose garden, with hidden laughter coming from unseen children, but now purged of desire, highlights the necessity of transient moments in the achievement of transcendence. The presence of the thrush is signaled by the line "Quick now, here, now, always," but he has evolved from the deceptive bird in the rose garden and is on his way to becoming the bird of blessing at the end of *Little Gidding*, whose song blends with that of Julian of Norwich.

Moments on the Way to *Little Gidding*

We shall not cease from exploration
And the end of all our exploring
Will be to arrive where we started
And know the place for the first time.

Eliot, *Little Gidding* V

Burnt Norton first appeared in Eliot's *Collected Poems* in 1936 as a separate poem. Several years later, it was reconceived as the first of the sequence that was to become *Four Quartets*. The last three poems, composed on the *Burnt Norton* model, appeared during the early years of the war—*East Coker* in 1940, *The Dry Salvages* in 1941, and *Little Gidding* in 1942. Although clearly linked to *Burnt Norton*, the wartime *Quartets* have considerable integrity as a unit, due in large part to their shared context. They were all composed at a moment when Hitler was ascendant and victory uncertain. To a greater extent than *Burnt Norton*, they deal with big picture issues related to history (war, international order) and morality (good and evil). The crisis in *Burnt Norton* is personal; in the wartime *Quartets* it encompasses the survival of England and Europe. The wartime poems are linked to each other and to *Burnt Norton* thematically and imagistically. All deal with redeeming the time, and the last three recapitulate the symbols and images of their precursor. Timeless moments in sacred places occur in each of the *Quartets*, but although the moments are parallel, they are not replicas of the moment in the rose garden or of its spiritual successor at the still point of the turning world. Time does not exist in these moments, but they exist in time in that they are transitory and progressive, moving toward the Edenic moment in *Little Gidding*.

In *East Coker*, the images from *Burnt Norton* recur, not in the mind—as memories or as a reflection on the mechanics of redeeming time—but in the senses, as whispers and echoes. They arrive suddenly, involuntarily, as a gift.

Whisper of running streams, and winter lightning,
The wild thyme unseen and the wild strawberry,
The laughter in the garden, echoed ecstasy (III.29-32)

This passage is linked to *Burnt Norton* by the laughter in the rose garden, where "the leaves were full of children, / Hidden excitedly, containing laughter" (I.39–43). The echo of ecstasy is itself an echo, harking back to the hope in the *Burnt Norton* scene that the protagonist will come to understand the "new world" as completing the "partial ecstasy" of the old (II.31).

In *The Dry Salvages*, the images return, not as a memory or a whisper of ecstasy, but as a post-ecstatic rumination, an interpretation of a pregnant moment.

> For most of us, there is only the unattended
> Moment, the moment in and out of time,
> The distraction fit, lost in a shaft of sunlight,
> The wild thyme unseen, or the winter lightning
> Or the waterfall, or music heard so deeply
> That it is not heard at all . . .
>   . . . These are only hints and guesses,
> Hints followed by guesses . . . (V.23–28)

Earlier in the poem, the narrator muses that certain experiences can only be understood retrospectively; Eden can only be imagined after the fall and expulsion.

> We had the experience but missed the meaning,
> And approach to the meaning restores the experience
> In a different form, beyond any meaning
> We can assign to happiness. (II.45–48)

The struggle to interpret the experience in and out of time acknowledges its dialectical shape, in which the middle term, the felicitous moment, can only be known by a return that redeems it "in a different form." The images—the rose garden, wild thyme, winter lightning, and hidden waterfall—cease to be "mere sequence" and converge into a "sudden illumination" (II.38, 44): "The hint half guessed, the gift half understood, is Incarnation" (V.32).

In *Little Gidding*, Eliot reflects on the problem of evil in a time of global conflict, and I discuss the poem in that context in chapter 11. But to understand his claim that the end (goal and destination) of his journey has been to return to his first world and know it for the first time (*LG* V.27–29), one must have followed the unfolding presentation of the timeless moments that pave the path from the rose garden of *Burnt Norton* to the secluded chapel of *Little Gidding*. The "sudden illumination" that occurs at the end of the third quartet is that the significance of timeless moments is confirmed by religious experience. This illumination includes an awareness of the relation of his own exilic existence to that of the first Adam in the Genesis account of the expulsion and of the second Adam in the New Testament account of the Christ event, both of which are dialectical. In possession of this theological validation of his experiential moments, Eliot begins *Little Gidding* by describing a phenomenon used in Christian literature to symbolize the Incarnation.[7]

> Midwinter spring is its own season
> Sempiternal though sodden towards sundown,
> Suspended in time . . .
> . . . .
> . . . This is the spring time
> But not in time's covenant. (I.1-3, 13-14)

The snow-draped hedges and ice-glazed ponds are suddenly changed, not only by the shaft of winter sunlight but also by the transfigured imagination of the visitor to Little Gidding.

> The brief sun flames the ice, on pond and ditches,
> . . . .
> Stirs the dumb spirit: no wind, but pentecostal fire
> In the dark time of the year. (I.5, 10-11)

As the afternoon rays are reflected in nature's icy mirror, the observer sees them as tongues of fire, an allusion to the first Pentecost after the resurrection, when the Holy Spirit descended from Heaven and filled Jesus' followers (Acts 2:1-4). In the Jewish tradition of these disciples, Pentecost is the Festival of First Fruits, in which the new grain, that which augurs the harvest, is made into loaves to be presented at the altar (Num. 28:26). The timeless moments, though ephemeral, allow a similar foretaste, grounding faith that the moments are miniatures of a greater reality. Following the epiphany by the frozen pond, the pilgrim wonders when the Adamic curse will be lifted—"Where is the summer, the unimaginable/Zero summer?" (*LG* I.19-20).

The corollary of "living in time's covenant" is living in a particular place. As often noted, the final scene of *Little Gidding* incorporates place identifiers from the first scene in *Burnt Norton*—roses, children, a bird, a gate—and in both scenes, the images are perceived in part, not in whole—half-hidden, half-seen, half-heard. The reappearance of images and motifs suggests a dialectical movement that is foreshadowed throughout the sequence by the reciprocal play between beginnings and ends. That the two scenes have much in common, however, should not obscure their fundamental and revealing differences. The garden in *Burnt Norton* is the site of temptation and expulsion; the ground of *Little Gidding* is the site of mystical experience and reconciliation. In the first, a couple is trying to end their exile by turning back the clock; in the second, a pilgrim has accepted his exile and embraced the reality of an "unimaginable Zero summer." The most important difference is that in *Burnt Norton*, the timeless moment is triggered by memory and desire, whereas in *Little Gidding*, it comes as a moment of clarification unclouded by desire, a moment of *kairos*,[8] a definite and unrepeatable moment in time best described in *The Rock*:

> A moment not out of time, but in time, in what we call history:
> transecting, bisecting the world of time . . .
> A moment in time but time was made through that moment: (*VII*.19-20)

A comparison of the opening and closing scenes of the *Quartets* reveals a progression from the exilic to the Edenic imagination. The place in *Burnt Norton* is the rose garden of a vacant house; in *Little Gidding*, the grounds of a bygone community. Although the final meditation in *Little Gidding* contains garden imagery, it does not occur in a garden, but in a secluded family chapel. Moreover, the season is different. The garden experience occurs in late summer ("in the autumn heat"), and the chapel experience in midwinter (21 December, "the dark time of the year"), the season of Advent.[9]

> So, while the light fails
> On a winter's afternoon, in a secluded chapel
> History is now and England. (V.22-24)

Both places have gates: in *Burnt Norton*, a "first gate"; in *Little Gidding*, an "unknown, remembered gate." Both open onto a world of happiness, but whereas the joy in the first is transient and followed by exile, in the second, it is permanent with the permanence that time has. The latter gate is unknown, because when in one's first world, one is in a state of immediacy, in which knowing is subsumed in being; nevertheless, and paradoxically, the gate is remembered, because leaving it enables one to realize, however imperfectly, that one has been there. The epiphany regarding his first world enables the explorer to reconfigure himself as a pilgrim and to imagine the end (purpose, destination, and conclusion) of his long exile.

And the end of all our exploring
Will be to arrive where we started
And know the place for the first time. (V.27–29)

The cluster of exilic images in the first and fifth parts of *Burnt Norton*—a garden, a tempter, a lost world—recurs in the closing scene of *Little Gidding*, but although the images retain traces of their initial meaning, they have been transfigured. The bird that prompts the couple in *Burnt Norton* to enter the garden—"Quick, said the bird, find them" (*BN* I.19)—is succeeded in the coda of *Little Gidding* by a bird who begins with the "Quick now" tag line, but is a new creation. His predecessor is a deceptive thrush who needles the couple to "redeem the dream," to grasp the might-have-been happiness with might-have-been children. When they bite the apple, however, they discover that he is a trickster, and they are evicted—"Go, go, go"—with only their memories. In *Little Gidding*, the thrush returns.

Quick now, here, now, always—
A condition of complete simplicity
(Costing not less than everything) (V.39–41)

Transformed from tempter to comforter, he reassures the pilgrim in a time of war that God is aware of human suffering. Eliot emphasizes the theme by superimposing the image of a gray dove on the image of a gray German bomber.

The dove descending breaks the air
With flame of incandescent terror (IV.1–2)

The dove is the symbol of the Holy Spirit, the third person of the Trinity, who descended in the form of a dove at the baptism of Christ and who descended on the disciples at Pentecost. This dove is present in the "pentecostal fire" flaming the ice in the midwinter pond, but also, paradoxically, in the destructive fire falling from the bombers. In the final lines of *Little Gidding*, the Comforter, as the New Testament calls the Spirit, appropriates the words of Julian of Norwich to console uncomprehending suffering humanity, including the pilgrim.

And all shall be well and
All manner of thing shall be well

When the tongues of flame are in-folded
Into the crowned knot of fire
And the fire and the rose are one. (V.42-46)

The image of tongues of flame as petals of a rose is concrete, but the reconciliation of suffering and beauty that it projects is spiritual and aesthetic—"an abstraction / Remaining a perpetual possibility / Only in a world of speculation" (*BN* I.6-8). Although the conciliation is thoroughly grounded in the experience of reading, imagining, and believing, it still requires faith if it is to be fully realized.

11 War and the Problem of Evil in the Wartime *Quartets*

Reason, Love, Poetry

> The problem of conscience towards war is far too deeply rooted in the general problem of evil to be settled by letters to *The Times*.
>
> Eliot, "A Commentary" (1936)

The first of the *Four Quartets*, *Burnt Norton*, is in large part a meditation on time and memory, written in the aftermath of Eliot's visit to America and his reunion with his family and Emily Hale. The remaining three—*East Coker*, *The Dry Salvages*, and *Little Gidding*—are largely meditations on history and faith, written in London during the first two years of World War II (Ellis 103). Although *The Waste Land* is also a war poem, the focus is primarily on documenting a shattered world, whereas in the wartime quartets, the focus is on understanding the shattering. The Second World War began on 1 September 1939, with the German invasion of Poland; a year later, beginning on 7 September 1940, the *Luftwaffe* bombed London for fifty-seven consecutive nights and continued with intermittent raids through May 1941.[1] During this period, Eliot served as an air-raid warden, spending two nights each week on Kensington rooftops watching for fires. At dawn, he would walk through the smoky streets to his flat, a haunting experience that is recast in *Little Gidding* as a reference point in a meditation on being in time. As he makes his way through the fog, the weary watchman reflects on the dialectic between the immediate moment—"History is now and England" (V.24)—and the pattern that is "new in every moment"—"history is a pattern / Of timeless moments" (V.21-22).

War (especially "total war," which does not distinguish between civilians and combatants) is a circumstance that invites (for a Christian, compels) reflection on theodicy, defined as the conflict between the existence of evil and the existence of a good and all-powerful God. For nonbelievers, the issue often appears, if at all, as an ironic quip, as in Housman's "And malt does more than Milton can/To justify God's ways to man" (*Shropshire Lad* LXII.21-22). For Christians, it usually arises as a question, often a rhetorical question. In "The Tyger," Blake asks "Did he who made the lamb make thee?" to which the answer, as indicated in "The Lamb," is yes: God made both predator and prey—in Eliot's image, both the boarhound and the boar (*BN* II.13). It is clear from *Little Gidding* that the suffering of civilians during the Blitz inspired an analogous question for Eliot: "Who then devised the torment?" This difficult question runs throughout Western literature from Job to Elie Wiesel. Using reason, the master logician Augustine concludes that human beings are responsible for their own suffering. Drawing on spiritual intuition, the mystic Julian of Norwich suggests a different answer: Love is responsible. The tension between these ostensibly contradictory positions is caught in Eliot's line—"Who then devised the torment? Love" (*LG* IV.8). My argument in this concluding chapter is that the conflict between reason and love (intellect and feeling), represented in *Little Gidding* by Augustine and Julian of Norwich, is first pondered and then transcended in a move to poetry. As in Eliot's earlier triads, the move to language does not merge reason and love, but reinstates them as part of a higher entity in an ongoing process that is explored in part V of each of the quartets.

Eliot and the Problem of Evil

The sense of Evil implies the sense of good.

Eliot, "Baudelaire" (1930)

Eliot's interest in theodicy, like so much in his mature thought, can be traced to his graduate work in philosophy. In 1913-14, as a graduate assistant at Harvard, he taught a course on the history of philosophy from the Pre-Socratics to the Renaissance. His syllabus included two units dealing with the problem of evil. For 12 December, he assigned B. A. G. Fuller's *The Problem of Evil in Plotinus*, a book that is focused on the mystical understanding of good and evil. With Plotinus as his reference point, Fuller explains evil by explaining it away. For the following week, Eliot assigned Augustine's *Confessions* (*Prose* 1.776-82). With Genesis as his reference point, Augustine explains evil as the consequence of Adam's rebellion, a situation which, as Milton says in the opening lines of *Paradise Lost*, "Brought Death into the World and all our woe" (*PL* I.3). Milton, who has a cameo appearance in

Little Gidding (*LG* III.30), identifies the goal of Christian theodicy in the prologue to *Paradise Lost*—to "justify the ways of God to men" (*PL* I.26). In 1913, these two theodicies—the Augustinian and the Plotinian—were primarily intellectual positions juxtaposed for balance in a survey course, but over the next few years, as war swallowed millions, they became increasingly relevant to Eliot's daily life, culminating a generation later in the theodicy in *Little Gidding*. Of the two positions, the Augustinian is more fundamental in Eliot, but at least from the mid-1920s, the mystical understanding tempered his Augustinian leanings.

The contradiction between the idea (assumptions about God) and the reality (endless suffering, endless evil) suggests that God is either powerless or malevolent. Either he is unable to stop the trains to Auschwitz, or he doesn't care. The challenge for Christian thinkers is to defend God from the implications of this monstrous inconsistency. Augustine begins with a basic question—"Who is responsible for evil?" In order to convince others and himself that God is not to blame for history's horrors, he examines his own heart (primarily in the *Confessions*) and constructs a narrative (primarily in *The City of God*) informed by the account of the Fall in Genesis. Augustine argues that because God wants to be served by free agents (not by automatons or puppets), he gave his creatures a gift that even he could not retract—the gift of freedom. Augustine accepts the biblical position that Adam and Eve chose to rebel, the consequences of which included the corruption of their progeny and all creation. As children of Adam and cousins of Cain, all are rebels and thus, to varying degrees, responsible for human suffering. With this logic, Augustine is able to shift the blame to humankind and "justify" the ways of God.

In *Little Gidding*, as I maintain later in this chapter, Eliot shies away from the notion that any theodicy is satisfactory; in earlier work, however, he explicitly accepted the linchpin of Augustine's theodicy—the doctrine of Original Sin. Also a theological pillar of the *Divine Comedy*, the doctrine became part of Eliot's moral formation as early as 1911 and remained in place for most of his life. In the years surrounding his conversion, he wrote several essays on writers with a moral imagination informed by Augustine, the most significant of which are the three essays on Baudelaire. In 1927, in the second essay, he argues that the wellspring of Baudelaire's work was his "spontaneous" grasp of "the notion of Original Sin" (*Prose* 3.76). In the third, in 1930, he maintains that in spite of his addiction to romantic claptrap, Baudelaire understood that "so far as we are human, what we do must be either evil or good; so far as we do evil or good, we are human; and it is better, in a paradoxical way, to do evil than to do nothing: at least, we exist" (*Prose* 4.162). He concludes the third essay on Baudelaire with a lengthy quotation from T. E. Hulme on the importance of "Original Sin." In "Second Thoughts about Humanism," he endorses Hulme's position that the trouble with humanism is that it ignores this doctrine and thus "the problem of evil disappears; the concept of sin loses all meaning." Continuing, Eliot agrees with Hulme's definition of Original Sin as the position "that man is in no sense perfect, but a wretched creature, who can yet apprehend perfection" (*Prose* 3.621).[2] In these and other writings, Eliot is clearly echoing Augustine, and like him, is leaning on reason.

The Waste Land includes an example of Baudelaire's "spontaneous" grasp of Original Sin. At the end of "The Burial of the Dead," Eliot quotes a line from "Au lecteur," the prefatory poem of *Les Fleurs du mal*. After listing the deadliest of sins, Baudelaire suddenly assaults his reader with the charge of complicity: "You! *Hypocrite lecteur*!—*mon semblable*—*mon frère*!" (*WL* 76). The Augustinian understanding of human nature is even stronger in "The Fire Sermon," which concludes with the voice of Augustine himself.

To Carthage then I came

Burning burning burning burning
O Lord Thou pluckest me out
O Lord Thou pluckest

burning (*WL* 307-11)

This passage includes two quotations (in translation) from the *Confessions*. In the first, Augustine recalls his sexual desires as a university student: "To Carthage then I came, where there sang all around me in my ears a cauldron of unholy loves" (III.1). In the second, he confesses that he has surrendered to temptations that enter through the eyes: "I entangle my steps with these outward beauties; but Thou pluckest me out, O Lord, Thou pluckest me out" (X.34). Augustine's image, taken from the Old Testament, compares certain individuals to "brands plucked out of the fire" (Zech. 3:2; Amos 4:11). The figure is that of a partially consumed stick that is rescued from flames; although damaged, it survives in a chastened form. In recalling his youth, Augustine acknowledges that he is a brand plucked from the fires of sensuality.

Augustine's theodicy, broadly accepted in Christian theology, is assumed in numerous classics in English literature, notably Milton's *Paradise Lost* and *Paradise Regained*. The continuing power of this theodicy for Eliot is evident in the 1930s in *Murder in the Cathedral* and in the fourth lyric of *East Coker*, both of which deal with the suffering of Christ and draw on two paradoxes. The first is that of the "Fortunate Fall," outlined in the prologue to *Paradise Lost* (I.1-26), and the second is that of "Good Friday," represented in *Paradise Regained*. The argument is that Adam's disobedience led to the appearance of a second Adam, a man who did not rebel and whose suffering made possible the redemption of mankind and his elevation to a status above that of the first Adam, that is, of being "joint-heirs with Christ" (Rom. 8:17). The related argument of the second paradox is that the intense suffering of Christ on the cross can be pronounced "good" because it led to his resurrection on Easter and to mankind's redemption. In *Murder in the Cathedral*, these doctrines are dramatized in the characterization of Thomas Becket, whose death shows striking parallels to that of Christ. In *East Coker* IV, the theology of paradox is projected through a Good Friday lyric in which a "wounded surgeon" with "bleeding hands" uses the steel of "sharp compassion" to remove or neutralize the "distemper" inherited from Adam. The attendant nurse, herself dying, is assigned the twin duty of reminding the patient of "Adam's curse" and warning him that the cure involves suffering and death. Paradoxes abound as the patient acknowledges the connection between history and redemption, between Adam's curse and human suffering, between death and life.

> If to be warmed, then I must freeze
> And quake in frigid purgatorial fires
> Of which the flame is roses, and the smoke is briars.
>
> The dripping blood our only drink,
> The bloody flesh our only food:
> In spite of which we like to think
> That we are sound, substantial flesh and blood—
> Again, in spite of that, we call this Friday good. (*EC* IV.18-25)

As Whittier-Ferguson's illuminating close reading shows, this is a serious meditation on the sacrifice of Christ and its commemoration in the Eucharist (67-70). Given that *East Coker* is a war poem, this section is also a meditation on the service in both wars of field surgeons, who, though wounded themselves, continued to care for their brothers. It reverses the perception

—"April is the cruellest month"—of the ironic speaker in *The Waste Land.* Having witnessed the slaughter in the Great War, that speaker feels that April mocks the rituals of Christian burials; in 1918, April pointed to Good Friday without Easter.

Eliot's ability to accept the paradox of Good Friday is related to his reflections on mysticism. In the years following his conversion, Eliot began to reflect on English models of spirituality, including the fourteenth-century mystic Julian of Norwich, whose theodicy he first encountered when he read Evelyn Underhill's *Mysticism* at Harvard in 1913–14. Julian was horrified by the suffering that followed the religious wars and the Black Death, which historians estimate killed half (possibly more) of the population of England. Her response is contained in *A Revelation of Love*, the first book to survive by an Englishwoman and a classic in European spirituality. The origin of this book is described in the work itself. When she was thirty years old, Julian had a near-death illness. Her parish priest administered the last rites and then placed a crucifix before her eyes and instructed her to concentrate on the suffering of Christ. Between the hours of four and nine in the morning of 8 May 1373, she experienced in rapid succession fifteen visions, and the next night, she experienced one more (*A Revelation* 2, 3; *Writings* 125–35).[3] In the visions, which were not seen by others, the suffering Christ assured her that in ways she could not fathom, all would be well. Soon after her recovery, Julian described her visions in graphic detail. At some later time, she became an anchoress and was enclosed in a cell attached to a church in Norwich, where she remained for the rest of her life. In 1393, twenty years after her illness, she expanded the description of her experience, adding insights gleaned from thinking about the visions over time (*A Revelation* 51; *Writings* 277). This later version reveals that she was an informed theologian and an original thinker. Julian lived into her seventies, at least, for in 1416, she was named a beneficiary in a will.

Eliot's engagement with Julian was continuous from the early 1930s. His interest went through several stages. First, she was to him a symbol of continuity in the English Church. He said that he put Julian in the poem to give it "greater historical depth" by balancing his allusions to the seventeenth century with allusions to the fourteenth, the "other great period" in Church history (Gardner, 70). Second, Julian was a symbol of a vital connection between art and mysticism. Underhill praises her ability to convey truth in "homely images," quoting as an example: "A child, when it is a-hurt or adread, it runneth hastily to the mother for help, with all its might. So willeth He that we do, as a meek child" (*Mystics*, 130, 131). Third, Julian appealed to Eliot because of her philosophical imagination. In *Mystics of the Church*, Underhill maintains: "Apparently the most subjective, Julian is really the most philosophic of our early mystics." As an example, she quotes Julian's vision of God as a still point: "I saw God in a point . . . by which sight I saw that He is in all things . . . He is the mid-point of all things . . . He is the ground, He is the substance" (*Mystics*, 128–30). In *Murder in the Cathedral* and *Four Quartets*, Eliot uses this mystical symbol to suggest the point of intersection between time and eternity, as in *Burnt Norton*: "Except for the point, the still point, / There would be no dance, and there is only the dance" (II.20–21).

Finally, for Eliot, Julian was interesting because of her theodicy. She had trouble reconciling "all shall be well" with the suffering in her village and even more with the doctrine that suffering in this life would be followed by suffering in the next. "One point of oure faith is that many creatures shall be dampned [damned]: . . . man in erth that dyeth out of the faith of holy church . . . and also man that hath received cristondom [Christianity] and liveth uncristen life, and so dyeth oute of cherite. . . . And stonding alle this [this being so], methought it was unpossible that alle maner of thing shuld be wele" (*A Revelation* 32; *Writings* 223). Denise Baker makes a strong case that, in the process of trying to reconcile suffering with belief in God's goodness, Julian formulated "her own original response to . . . the problem of evil" (63). Her position, Baker argues, is a response to Augustine's. First, in changing the focus from God the Father to Christ the mother, she changes the focus from humanity as a morally responsible adult to humanity as a vulnerable child.

> Jhesu Crist . . . is oure very moder [mother]: we have oure being of him . . . with alle the swete keping of love that endlesly foloweth . . . oure moders bere us to paine and to dying . . . But oure very moder Jhesu, he alone bereth us to joye and to endlesse leving [eternal life]. . . . This fair, lovely worde, "moder," it is so swete and so kinde in itselfe that it may not verely be saide of none . . . but of him. (*A Revelation* 59, 60; *Writings* 309, 313)

In emphasizing the incarnate Christ, she brings the divine down to earth. Her Jesus is less abstract and more forgiving than Augustine's; her humankind is less culpable. The second point, a corollary of the first, is that she weakens Augustine's link between Original Sin and the existence of evil (Baker, 68–69). Julian concludes that Christ's saying "alle shalle be wele" must have two meanings. The first, which is clear, concerns salvation; the other, which is hidden, does not (*A Revelation* 30; *Writings* 216, 217). If it is true that all shall be well, then God must have "a secret," which she imagines as a "deed which the blisseful trinite shalle do in the last day . . . only knowen to himselfe, by which deed he shalle make all thing wele" (*A Revelation* 32; *Writings* 223). This conclusion acknowledges the limits of her own understanding, but it also skirts the edge of heresy by suggesting that all people will be saved.

At the time Eliot returned to reading Julian, he was living "*l'entre deux guerres*" (*EC* V.2) and attempting to balance his awareness of history with his faith. In *Little Gidding*, composed in 1942, he made his most compelling attempt to come to terms with the problem of evil. Given his emphasis on Original Sin as a touchstone for understanding history and human nature, it cannot be said that Julian replaced Augustine in his thinking, but it must be said that she forced a reexamination of his own moorings.

Little Gidding: Theodicy among the Flames

Who then devised the torment? Love.

Eliot, *Little Gidding* IV

The culmination of Eliot's exploration of theodicy occurs in *Little Gidding*. This is not surprising, for its context is a war involving massive suffering and genocide. Going back to his work in 1913, Eliot includes the two main streams of thought in Western theodicy—the Augustinian, which emphasizes man's sinfulness, and the mystical, which emphasizes God's sovereignty. Augustine's position is embedded in the remarks of the compound ghost of part II, and Julian of Norwich's riposte is quoted in III. The issue is raised explicitly in IV—"Who then devised the torment? Love"—and in the conclusion, both reason and love are transcended in an image of a rose with petals of flame, a symbol in art of a resolution that is incomprehensible in life.

The structure of *Little Gidding* is dialectical, juxtaposing rural peace with urban chaos, followed by meditations on the meaning of history. In part I, a refugee seeks sanctuary in the countryside, and in the phenomenon of sun reflected on ice, he experiences the presence of the Holy Ghost and of ghostly forerunners. In part II, an exhausted civilian in a burning metropolis concludes a night of watching for fires from aerial bombers, and on the way home, has a conversation with a compound ghost. In part III, the pilgrim beckons the spirit of Julian of Norwich to help him make sense of the horror. In part IV, directly concerned with theodicy, he assembles his theological ghosts for a question and answer session. The ghosts are less than objective but more than fanciful in that they are "familiar" spirits who pull him into a liminal zone, where he is forced to recall their relevance to the moral and philosophical puzzles at hand. In part V, which concludes both *Little Gidding* and *Four Quartets*, Eliot's narrator releases his ghosts—"See, they depart, and we go with them. / We are born with the dead: / See, they return, and bring us with them" (V.16-18), and moves to the "crowned knot of fire" that unites not only fire and roses but suffering and peace, as well.

The presiding Spirit of *Little Gidding*, introduced in the opening paragraph, is the third person of the Trinity, the Holy Spirit, who descended in tongues of flame on the day of Pentecost (Acts 2). In view of his impending death, Christ promised his disciples that "the Father . . . shall give you another Comforter, that he may abide with you forever; even the Spirit of truth" (John 14:16, 17). In the poem, this Spirit appears to a war-weary believer, not on Pentecost but in the midwinter of the year 1941 and the midwinter of Western civilization.

> When the short day is brightest, with frost and fire,
> The brief sun flames the ice, on ponds and ditches,
>
> . . . .
>
> Stirs the dumb spirit: no wind, but pentecostal fire
> In the dark time of the year. (I.4-5, 10-11)

As in the book of Acts, the tongues of flame appear suddenly, inexplicably in the form of a meteorological phenomenon that suggests an incursion from above. In the gospels, the Holy Ghost is symbolized by the dove that descended at the baptism of Christ. In *Little Gidding*, these two figures—the tongues of flame and the dove—are combined in the brilliant image of the German bomber as a "dark dove with the flickering tongue" (II.28), a monster that spits fire on civilians trapped in cities at war. The collocation of the two images is fundamental to the theodicy theme, in that it suggests the presence of the Holy Spirit in history and, as bombs are falling on London, the whisper of a connection between beauty and suffering, peace and terror.

In the second movement, the mise-en-scène changes from the icy garden at Little Gidding to the smoldering streets of London following a bombing raid. In the hour before dawn, the narrator, having finished his night's work as a fire watcher, is making his way home when he spies a stranger in the dusty ruins. In this hallucinatory twilight, the narrator catches the look of "some dead master / Whom I had known, forgotten, half recalled / Both one and many. . . . Both intimate and unidentifiable" (II.39-43). This dialectically perceived (known/forgot/half-recalled) "familiar compound ghost" represents, on one level, the narrator's divided self; on another, the victims of the bombing raids; and on still another, his "dead masters." Of these, Dante is paramount, because of the infernal nature of the scene, the imitation of the terza rima used in the *Commedia*, and the allusion to Dante's encounter with Brunetto Latini in *Inferno* XV. Although the constituent voices of the compound ghost are primarily those of literary masters, they also, both individually and cumulatively, project a moral imagination that comes from Augustine. Male and judgmental, the compound ghost scolds the pilgrim, reminding him of his responsibility for the pain he has suffered and caused others to suffer.

> Let me disclose the gifts reserved for age
>   To set a crown upon your lifetime's effort.
>   . . . .
>   First, the cold friction of expiring sense
> Without enchantment . . .
> . . . .
> Second, the conscious impotence of rage
>   At human folly, and the laceration
>   Of laughter at what ceases to amuse.
> And last, the rending pain of re-enactment
>   Of all that you have done, and been; the shame
>   Of motives late revealed, and the awareness
> Of things ill done and done to others' harm
>   Which once you took for exercise of virtue. (II.76-79, 82-89)

The emphasis here on moral responsibility is at the heart of Augustine's theodicy. His argument that humans are to blame for evil is the position of at least two of the figures included in Eliot's compound ghost—Swift and Dante. The Augustinian understanding of human nature is the reference point in satires such as "A Modest Proposal" and the basis of both theme and structure in the *Divine Comedy*.

In their commentaries on the war motif in *Little Gidding*, most critics focus on the encounter with the compound ghost on the bombed streets of Kensington in part II and the terror of the fire-spewing "dove descending" on the city in part IV. The attention to these sections is appropriate. But of even greater importance in grasping Eliot's struggle with words and meanings is the more prosaic meditation between the dramatization in II and the lyric in IV. In this intermediate passage (III), the poet reflects on the two elements at the heart of his theodicy—history and providence, specifically the conflict between fire raining down on civilians and belief in an omnipotent and loving God. In moving from the inferno of the compound ghost to the mind of a philosophical Christian poet, Eliot moves from an Augustinian perspective in which Original Sin is accepted as an explanation for the catastrophes of history to a counter perspective, which regards sin as in some way beneficial. It is a move from Augustine's "Who-done-it" to Julian's "What good can come of it?" The difference in emphasis issues from the metaphor used to understand the transcendent. Augustine thinks in terms of God the Father, tipping the scales toward justice, whereas Julian experiences Christ as a mother, tipping them toward mercy.

Part III of *Little Gidding* has two sections, the first a meditation on history as a chronicle of "Attachment to self and to things and to persons," which in time will evolve into detachment and be transformed into a pattern of timeless moments.

> Thus, love of a country
> Begins as attachment to our own field of action
> And comes to find that action of little importance
> Though never indifferent. History may be servitude,
> History may be freedom. See, now they vanish,
> The faces and places, with the self which, as it could, loved them,
> To become renewed, transfigured, in another pattern. (III.10–16)

The goal is "liberation" from attachment—"not less of love but expanding/ Of love beyond desire" (III.8–9).

In the second section of part III, Eliot frames his meditation on history with the theodicy of Julian of Norwich. She agrees with Augustine that suffering is caused by sin, but questions why God ever allowed sin to occur and fester: "Why, by the grete forseeing wisdom of God, the beginning of sinne was not letted [prevented]. For then thought me that alle shulde have be wele" (*A Revelation* 27; *Writings* 209). Eliot begins his meditation by quoting the reassuring words of Julian's Jesus:

> Sin is Behovely, but
> All shall be well, and
> All manner of thing shall be well. (III.17–19)

In theology, the idea that sin is "behovely" (necessary, inevitable, beneficial in the long run) is related to the paradox of the Fortunate Fall. Julian protests that she can understand how the suffering of Christ was redemptive and thus "behovely," but she cannot understand how the suffering in her village is beneficial. "Ther be many dedes evil done in oure sight and so gret harmes . . . that it semeth to us that it were unpossible that ever it shuld come to a good end" (*A Revelation* 32; *Writings* 221). She rejects the doctrine that suffering is punishment, and instead of counting "things ill done and done to others' harm," she counts possible goods: suffering leads to self-knowledge and to knowledge of God; pain provides the occasion for Christ's compassion for us and our compassion for others; suffering can purify our minds. As Baker notes, for Julian, sin is pedagogical (70). In the final lines of his meditation on history, Eliot returns to Julian's revelation.

> And all shall be well and
> All manner of thing shall be well
> By the purification of the motive
> In the ground of our beseeching. (III.47-50)

These lines combine two sayings of Julian's Jesus: "alle shale be wele" and "I am the grounde of thy beseking [beseeching]" (*A Revelation* 41; *Writings* 249). By quoting the words that Christ said to Julian during the vision, Eliot puts the narrator inside the drama. The verbatim quotations bridge the distance in time and space between Julian and the reader, enabling her to speak directly to readers in the Second World War and subsequent moments of turmoil in history.

Within this theodical frame, the narrator considers the relevance of Julian's visions to history. Her perspective requires him to take a more philosophical view of war, to consider the evolution of the here and now into a pattern of timeless moments, and to some extent, to attempt a God's-eye view. Beginning with "this place"—that is, Little Gidding—and the civil war that bloodied England in the seventeenth century, he ponders the situation of brothers killing brothers, both fighting for God and England. The "enemy brothers," to borrow a term from René Girard, "touched by a common genius," were not villains (59-65)—Charles I, who fled to Little Gidding for sanctuary, but eventually died on the scaffold; Cromwell, who led the parliamentarians, but whose death was followed by the restoration of the monarchy; Milton, Cromwell's Latin Secretary, "who died blind and quiet" after finishing his own theodicy, *Paradise Lost*.

These men, and those who opposed them
And those whom they opposed
Accept the constitution of silence
And are folded in a single party. (III.39-42)

As in his philosophical papers, Eliot shifts the focus from the antagonists to the relation between them. In one of his most meaningful dialectical images, the poet suggests that even in the moment of conflict, these men were "United in the strife which divided them" (III.25) and now, given the perspective of time, are "folded in a single party" (III.42).

Although Eliot's attention is primarily on a seventeenth-century war, his language brings in other times and other conflicts. His inclusion of Julian brings in the fourteenth century, with its "forgotten wars." "The spectre of a Rose" brings in the fifteenth-century Wars of the Roses. "Why should we celebrate/These dead men more than the dying?" is a reminder of the twentieth-century war then raging in Europe, with soldiers dying "here and abroad." The abandoned "king at night-fall" brings in the execution of Charles I and "three men . . . on the scaffold" brings in the crucifixion of Christ on Golgotha. This cruel history has left enduring scars, but for Eliot, as for Augustine, Julian, and Milton, something deep in the human spirit, inextricable from Providence, "Sings below inveterate scars/Appeasing long forgotten wars" (*BN* II.4-5). The detachment brought by time—"History may be servitude,/History may be freedom"—and the transfiguration into a pattern of timeless moments leads back to Julian's "all shall be well."

The climax of the struggle to frame the problem of evil in *Little Gidding* comes in part IV. In the first of two septets, Eliot conveys the historical reality of war by superimposing two images of the dove—one terrifying, the other comforting.

The dove descending breaks the air
With flame of incandescent terror
Of which the tongues declare
The one discharge from sin and error.
The only hope, or else despair
    Lies in the choice of pyre or pyre—
    To be redeemed from fire by fire. (IV.1-7)

The coalescence of the two doves is facilitated by visual overlap and supported by language, much of it associated with fire (incandescent, discharge, pyre), that can be applied simultaneously to the bomber and the Holy Ghost. Both generate "incandescent terror"—the bomber by falling fire, the dove by sudden epiphany. Both have tongues that declare "the one discharge from sin and error"—the bomber, ironically, by obliterating its victims; the Holy Ghost by pointing to Christ, who discharged the debts of mankind. The paradoxes ending the stanza highlight the reality of war and the inevitability of suffering—"pyre or pyre." At the same time, by using the language of redemption, the last three lines play with three meanings of fire—destructive, purgatorial, and refining. One of several reminders of the three-in-one motif, they suggest that, in ways yet to be revealed, fire is behovely.

The "what" of war is underscored in the first septet; in the second, the "who" and "why" are addressed. The second begins with the central puzzle in Christian theodicy: given that God is omnipotent and loving, why would he allow so much suffering?

> Who then devised the torment? Love.
> Love is the unfamiliar Name
> Behind the hands that wove
> The intolerable shirt of flame
> Which human power cannot remove.
> We only live, only suspire
> Consumed by either fire or fire. (IV.8-14)

The question of "who" is responsible for suffering comes from Augustine. The defensive nature of his position is caught in Eliot's diction. If God "devised" the pain of innocents, then he is a sadist. Augustine, like a premium lawyer, argues that God is not guilty; supported by history and scripture, he demonstrates that humans are responsible. Julian's response, supported by faith, is that Love is responsible. "What, woldest [wouldest] thou wit [know] thy lordes mening in this thing? Wit it wele, love was his mening" (*A Revelation* 86; *Writings* 379). This largely heterodox response is the heart of her "revelation." Accepting God's sovereignty, she has to admit, contra Augustine, that God is responsible for suffering—not God as avenger or judge, but God as Love. It is not surprising that modern critics are dismissive of Julian's faith that love is behind human suffering, nor is it strange that they attribute Eliot's meditation in *Little Gidding* IV to personal quirks. Bush, for example, suggests that "this fierce and uncomfortable theodicy" is evidence of Eliot's "insensitivity to others' suffering" and attributes its emphatic quality to "an overwhelming need to punish himself" (225); North regards it as a charade designed to convince readers of the redemptive value of the Blitz (126). The poem, however, must be allowed to speak and the poet at least to think about an issue that theists have grappled with for millennia.

To further illuminate Julian's argument, Eliot turns to Sophocles' *The Women of Trachis*, which tells the story of the "labors" of Heracles (Latin: Hercules). His labors ended, the hero returns home accompanied by a female captive. Years earlier, his wife, Deianira, had been raped by a centaur, who in turn had been shot by Heracles with a poisoned arrow. As he lay dying, the centaur told Deianira to save some of his blood, and if her husband should be unfaithful, she could use it to regain his love. To that end, she dipped a shirt in the centaur's blood, and she presents it to her husband as a homecoming gift. When he approaches the altar to perform the purification rites required of returning warriors, the sacred fires reactivate the poison in his shirt and make it impossible to remove. Caught between fire or fire, he ends the torment by immolating himself. The story contains several tenuous parallels to and contrasts with Julian's theodicy, one of which is paramount. In the Christian story, Love is the reason that Christ empties himself of divinity (*kenosis*) and dons the shirt of flesh in the Incarnation, a shirt that can only be removed by extreme suffering ending in death. In putting on the shirt of mortality, he burns in borrowed clothes that can only be extinguished by death. His larger suffering is the context for human suffering, including death of soldiers and civilians in war.

Eliot was not attracted to Julian because her position could be supported by reason or by analogies with classical literature. As one who had lived through one world war and was caught in a second, he valued her perspective because of her spiritual integrity. He identified with her view that one cannot make demands of God. Some things are and will remain hidden. The opening line of one of Eliot's earliest poems is "Hidden under the heron's wing," and in "Coriolan," written in the 1930s, he associates hiddenness with the still point, just as Julian does.

> O hidden under the dove's wing, hidden in the turtle's breast,
> Under the palmtree at noon, under the running water
> At the still point of the turning world. O hidden. ("Triumphal March" 32-34)

It does no good to assault the heron and the dove to find out what they are hiding. As Julian says, "the more we besy [busy] us to know his prevites [secrets] in that or in any other thing, the ferthermore shalle we be from the knowing" (*A Revelation* 33; *Writings* 227).

The End of Theodicy: Reason, Love, and Art

> For it is ultimately the function of art . . . to bring us to a condition of serenity, stillness, and reconciliation; and then leave us, as Virgil left Dante, to proceed toward a region where that guide can avail us no farther.
>
> Eliot, "Poetry and Drama"

Eliot's long reflections on the conflict between good and evil did not end in a resolution of the issue, but rather in a deeper awareness of the limits of human understanding and the importance of faith. In *Little Gidding*, preoccupied with the moral failures in his personal life and the horrific sequel to "the war to end all wars," Eliot summons the ghosts of mentors who had faced the problem of evil head on, thinkers who together point to the ancient understanding that God has two faces. Augustine emphasizes God's justice and power, whereas Julian emphasizes his mercy and love, antitheses roughly analogous to the fire and rose of his closing image. The conjunction of opposites—a rose with tongues of flame as petals—is sometimes interpreted as an indication that the contraries have been reconciled and sometimes as a demonstration that gaps cannot be bridged. Because of the Christian paradoxes that run through Eliot's later work, both interpretations are partially true and partially false. In part V of *Little Gidding*, the paradoxes are integrated into "the complete consort, dancing together" (V.10). The dialectical dance includes three steps. The first is that the contraries can be accommodated via a hermeneutical loop or return to the beginning. The second is that understanding comes from a crystallization of the mind that occurs in specific unrepeatable moments, and thus is inextricably linked to being in time. The third is that the reconciliation that in its fullness is unachievable in life can be prefigured in art, especially in the temporal arts of music, dance, and poetry. Eliot's emphasis on the place of poetry in the dialectical dance is not a celebration of art for its own sake, à la Mallarmé or Laforgue, but an extension of his early insight that faith is the sine qua non in philosophy and religion (*Prose* 1.186). Language, like all artifacts, is fallen; it can only take us to the Earthly Paradise on the banks of the river Lethe (*Purgatorio* 28–30). The ultimate reconciliation, symbolized by the smile of Beatrice, is on the other side of the river.

The epistemological significance of return, unambiguously stated in Eliot's early philosophical papers, is translated from prose to verse in the last section of *Little Gidding*.

> We shall not cease from exploration
> And the end of all our exploring
> Will be to arrive where we started
> And know the place for the first time. (V.26-29)

These lines constitute a performance in the sense that they are the return that they recommend. The point to which one returns, however, both is and is not the point from which one departed, for the pilgrim is in time and thus "not the same [person] who left that station/Or who will arrive at any terminus" (*DS* III.16-17). In returning, he brings everything accumulated in the three decades en route and experiences a "pattern that is new in every moment" (*EC* II.35). In regard to good and evil, the return includes Augustine's focus on justice and Julian's on mercy, his focus on history and hers on the future, his on freedom and hers on circumstances. The process of understanding does not end with the return to the beginning, but continues with a continuous interplay of beginnings and ends, of shadows and light. The pilgrim has learned that dualism is intractable and, moreover, that the meaning of pilgrimage is living in the in-between. The conflict between body and soul in the Prufrock poems and the shadow that bisects the abstract entities of *The Hollow Men* are not lost, but are transfigured among the stars.

The second principle underlying the culmination of Eliot's work in *Four Quartets* is the connection of illumination to specific moments in time: "Only through time time is conquered" (*BN* II.43). In his essays on thinkers such as Pascal and in his reflections on the Incarnation, Eliot insists on the connection between *chronos* (linear time, history) and *kairos* (a moment of crystallization that points beyond history and language). That unique "temporary crystallization of mind," that moment in history that enables one to imagine being redeemed from history, can only occur in time (*Prose* 4:340; Cullman, 39). The material world points to the immaterial, the natural to the supernatural; in Eliot's poignant phrase, nature bowers "echoed ecstasy." To pick up these echoes, one must tune in to the "Whisper of running streams, . . . The laughter in the garden" (*EC* III.29, 31).

In the final analysis, the attempt to construct a consistent theodicy in *Four Quartets* collapses in the face of history itself, which compels the recognition that good and evil (and other binaries) are woven into the "shirt of flame/Which human power cannot remove" (*LG* IV.10-11). The unity that is beyond the grasp of philosophers and theologians, however, can be imagined by the Christian artist, at least in a rudimentary way. The resolution that is achieved in *Four Quartets* exists only as an imaginative construct built of hints and guesses that cannot be reduced to logic but can be glimpsed in music, dance, and poetry. In all four poems in the sequence, the final movement emphasizes the potential of the arts for taking us to the frontier beyond which words fail, but meanings still exist.

> Words move, music moves
> Only in time; but that which is only living
> Can only die. Words, after speech, reach
> Into the silence. Only by the form, the pattern,
> Can words or music reach
> The stillness, as a Chinese jar still
> Moves perpetually in its stillness. (*BN* V.1-7)

As indicated by the title, *Four Quartets* contains an analogy between words and music, notes and harmony, conflict and attunement. The elegance of the form is corroborated by the exquisite balance of ideas (philosophical and theological, Eastern and Western, personal and impersonal). The musical analogy is corroborated by a running analogy with the dance. "Except for the point, the still point,/There would be no dance, and there is only the dance" (*BN* II.21). But most of all, it is the art of poetry, the dance of the words with the Word, that makes *Four Quartets* so endlessly suggestive. This dance with the still point, the Logos, is performed in part V of each of the four, culminating in the last movement of *Little Gidding*, where "every phrase/And sentence that is right (where every word is at home . . . The complete consort dancing together)" (*LG* V.3-4, 10).

The culmination of *Little Gidding* and of Eliot's career as a poet includes not only Augustine's fire but also Julian's roses, both caught in an image that transfigures them in another pattern.

> And all shall be well and
> And all manner of thing shall be well
> When the tongues of flame are in-folded
> Into the crowned knot of fire
> And the fire and the rose are one. (V.42-46)

The contraries that in his early work were experienced as a pendulum in his head are here resurrected in a new image, which embodies duality as essential to the choreography of the mortal dance. The image is easy to visualize because tongues of flame resemble petals of roses, but impossible to describe or even to comprehend as a reality apart from the image. A comprehensive figure, it collects and transcends the voices that sound throughout Eliot's oeuvre, which vanish and return "renewed, transfigured, in another pattern" (*LG* III.16). Dante had demonstrated how the incredible can be presented to the imagination by transforming the red rose of *eros* into the white rose of *agape* (*Paradiso* 31). Eliot's rose, unlike Dante's, is not celestial, nor is it white. It retains the red of blood and fire—the blood of Jesus and the victims of the Blitz, and the fire of the gray dove in the skies over London and on the frozen pond at Little Gidding. But the tongues of flame are more than fire and more than the lambent whispers of the Pentecostal Ghost or the poet's ghostly predecessors; they are also rose petals, transfigured into a new pattern. The tongues, moreover, are "in-folded" into a crown of fire, a dialectical image that suggests both the suffering endured by the incarnate Christ, mocked with a blood-soaked crown, and the transcendence of that horror by his resurrection and our redemption. By the end of *Little Gidding*, the fire and the rose, which Eliot has been using as separate images for three decades, have accumulated extraordinary resonance. When conjoined in the striking image that concludes the poem, they whisper of ecstasy and of atonement (at-one-ment), but they resist interpretation, remaining an image, a crowned knot of fire, at the apex of the poet's lifetime struggle with words and meanings.

Notes

Introduction: Logic and Longing in T. S. Eliot

1. Brooker and Schuchard, "Eliot's Apprentice Years," *Prose* 1.xxvii.

2. Quotations of Eliot's published letters are from *The Letters of T. S. Eliot*, edited by Valerie Eliot and Hugh Haughton or John Haffenden; for the occasional unpublished letter, forthcoming in a future volume of *The Letters*, quotation is from Eliot's typescript. All are quoted with the permission of Faber & Faber Ltd.

3. Aiken, More, Auden. In Brooker, *Contemporary Reviews*.

4. Quotations from Eliot's poems, identified in text by line number, are from *The Poems of T. S. Eliot*, edited by Ricks and McCue. Quoted by permission of Faber & Faber Ltd. and Johns Hopkins University Press.

5. Eliot often refers to James's novella *The Figure in the Carpet* (1896), as in his 1929 essay on Dante (*Prose* 3.707) and his 1941 introduction to Kipling's verse (*Prose* 6.217).

6. Quotations from Eliot's prose through 1946 are from the online edition of the *Complete Prose*; quotations of material published after 1946 are from the first publication.

Chapter 1. The Debate between Body and Soul in Eliot's Early Poetry

1. The epistemological crisis associated with modernism is outlined in Lovejoy (1–33) and in intellectual histories such as Quinones, *Mapping Literary Modernism*.

2. See David Spurr for an alternative but informed interpretation of Eliot's conflicts in consciousness.

3. The assumption that Eliot's early characters are essentially self-portraits is explored in several critical biographies, including those of Gordon and Bush.

4. *Trans.*: "Seething city, city full of dreams, / Where the ghost accosts passers-by in broad daylight."

5. I have been unable to locate Aiken's "Decadence," which may or may not have

been completed. Much later, Robert Sencourt, for decades a close friend, says in his memoir that Eliot brought back a Gauguin nude and displayed it in his rooms in Ash Street (34). It may be that Eliot also brought back one of Gauguin's Tahitian nudes, or it may be that this is a mistaken reference to *The Yellow Christ*.

6. It was presumably in reference to Fry's exhibition that Virginia Woolf, who attended in December, said in "Character in Fiction" that "on or about December 1910 human character changed." Originally published in the *Criterion* in July 1924 (2.8: 410), it was reprinted by the Hogarth Press in October as "Mr. Bennett and Mrs. Brown."

7. *Trans.*: "O Lord, give me the power and the courage/To regard my heart and my body without loathing."

8. This date is approximately the midpoint between his study of the symbolists in the spring and summer of 1909 and his voyage to Paris in October 1910.

9. For a modern example that preserves this objectivity and balance, see the debate between a milkweed and a stone in Richard Wilbur's "Two Voices in a Meadow."

10. For the textual description of Eliot's manuscript, see *Poems* 2.568–69.

11. Compare Wordsworth's *Prelude* and Shelley's "Ode to the West Wind."

12. *Trans.*: "Am I not a dissonance?"

13. Eliot's letter, dated 8 March 1946, as quoted in Pope (320): "I think that the passage beginning 'I am not Prince Hamlet,' a passage showing the influence of Laforgue, was one of these fragments which I took with me [to Paris], but the poem was not completed until the summer of 1911."

14. A year later, in 1912, Eliot copied into his notebook another section, "Prufrock's Pervigilium," which he added to the poem before giving it to Conrad Aiken to shop around in London. Aiken thought the new section was inferior; Eliot agreed and deleted it. Aiken, To *TLS*, 3 June 1960. The "Pervigilium" is printed in *Poems* 2.315–16.

15. See especially Smith, "Fascination of Hamlet," 43–59.

16. In a letter to H. Warner Allen dated 25 May 1960, Eliot said: "I wrote a poem when I was twenty-two which contains the line 'I grow old . . . I grow old.' That line, if I remember rightly, was borrowed from Sir John Falstaff." This memory conflates two of Falstaff's comments: "There lives not three good men unhang'd in England, and one of them is fat, and grows old" (*1 Henry IV*, II.iv) and "I am old, I am old" (*2 Henry IV*, II.iv).

Chapter 2. Eliot's First Conversion: "Rhapsody on a Windy Night" and the 1913 Critique of Bergson

1. This chapter is a revision of Brooker, "Eliot and Bergson." My quotations from Bergson, abbreviated in text, are from the authorized translations. Details in Bibliography.

2. Eliot to Eudo C. Mason, 19 April 1945. Forthcoming in *Letters*.

3. Eliot to E. J. Greene, 19 April 1940. Forthcoming in *Letters.*

4. Eliot, Notes on Bergson. Houghton Library, Harvard University.

5. Eliot's reference is to the Absolute of Bergson. He did not begin his study of F. H. Bradley until 1913.

6. Childs, Douglass, Habib, and Jain refer to this paper and comment at least briefly on its relevance to their readings of "Rhapsody on a Windy Night."

7. In this paper (a hand-written reading copy for his presentation), Eliot quotes Bergson in a mixture of French and English, as needed to make his point, and he consistently uses underlining for emphasis. The lecture is included in *Prose* 1.67–89.

8. The exact wording of Eliot's quotation from Bergson: "That which is given, that which is real, is something intermediate between divided extension and pure inextension. It is what we have termed the *extensive*" (*M&M* 326; Bergson's italics).

Chapter 3. Eliot's Debt to F. H. Bradley: Reality and Appearance in 1914

1. For an extended discussion of Eliot's education, see Brooker and Schuchard, *Prose* 1.xxvii–lxii.

2. See Jain, *Eliot and American Philosophy*, 60–111, and Kuklick, for excellent overviews of the department.

3. Henry Ware Eliot graduated with a Bachelor of Arts degree from Washington University on 18 June 1863. On that occasion, he delivered the commencement address, a "Philosophical Oration," entitled "Philosophy the Science of Truth." The holograph is in the Department of Special Collections in the Libraries of Washington University of St. Louis, which has kindly granted permission for my quotations. I am grateful to Timothy Materer for calling my attention to this document.

4. Eliot studied Joachim's epistemology, outlined in *The Nature of Truth*, in his Kant seminar in 1913.

5. The prototype of the 1914 "vigil poems" is "Prufrock's Pervigilium," composed in 1912 for inclusion in "The Love Song of J. Alfred Prufrock." These pervigilia were kept in Eliot's notebook and published in *Inventions of the March Hare*.

6. The Michaelmas essays are in *Prose* 1.65–92.

7. Capitalization as in Eliot's typescript.

8. See Joachim, *Nature of Truth*, §41, 113.

Chapter 4. The Poet and the Cave-Man: Making History in "Sweeney among the Nightingales" and *The Waste Land*

1. Virtually all studies of modernism, from *Dionysius and the City* (1970) by Monroe Spears to Marianna Torgovnick's *Gone Primitive* (1990), deal with the various dualities—cultural, racial, psychological, sexual—embedded in the topic. Most studies of Eliot acknowledge his indebtedness to the social sciences, and some include

extended treatment of the subject. Piers Gray, Richard Shusterman, Robert Crawford, Jeffrey Perl, and Marc Manganaro have discussed the importance of the social sciences in understanding Eliot's early criticism, and Gray, to whom I am especially indebted, has discussed the relevance of the 1913 essay on primitive ritual to an understanding of *The Waste Land*.

2. The seminar proceedings, as recorded by a student whom Royce designated as class secretary, were published in Costello, *Josiah Royce's Seminar, 1913–1914*.

3. Eliot's analysis of science and religion in this 1913 essay is extended in his 1927 review of Whitehead's *Science and the Modern World* ("The Return of Foxy Grandpa") and his 1932 article "Religion and Science: A Phantom Dilemma."

4. Eliot to H. Warner Allen, 25 May 1960. Forthcoming in *Letters*.

5. The fable is found in the *Brihadaranyake Upanishad*, v. 2, in Radhakrishnan, 289–90.

6. For a detailed exposition of the glosses, see Brooker and Bentley, 199–207.

Chapter 5. Individual Works and Organic Wholes: The Idealist Foundation of Eliot's Criticism

This chapter includes material from Brooker, "Dialectic and Impersonality" and "Writing the Self." Details in Bibliography.

1. Eliot to Henry Eliot, 1 January 1936. Forthcoming in *Letters*.

2. At the 139th meeting of the American Association for the Advancement of Science (1972), Lorenz presented a paper entitled "Does the Flap of a Butterfly's Wings in Brazil Set Off a Tornado in Texas?," http://eaps4.mit.edu/research/Lorenz/Butterfly_1972.pdf. See Hilborn for further discussion of chaos theory.

3. See "Eliot's Debt to F. H. Bradley," chapter 3 in this volume.

4. The crystallization of the story took about three months, not three days. However, since Eliot says this process can take years, the number of days or months does not affect my point about the artistic process in Conrad.

5. Quotations of Yeats are from *The Poems of W. B. Yeats* (new ed., 1983).

Chapter 6. Poetry and Despair: *The Hollow Men* and the End of Philosophy

1. In Sartre's *No Exit*, there are *three* damned souls.

2. Eliot discussed this process in his interview with Donald Hall, *Paris Review* (1959). The preexistence of *The Hollow Men* lyrics is described in detail in Ricks and McCue (*Poems* 1.711).

3. See the discussion in chapter 5 of the chemical analogy in "Tradition and the Individual Talent."

4. 1 January 1936. Forthcoming in *Letters*.

5. Eliot read both Baudelaire and Dostoevski in Paris during the winter and spring of 1911. He later indicated that *Crime and Punishment*, *The Idiot*, and *The Brothers Karamazov* made a lasting impression (Pope, 320). Here and elsewhere in this book, I use Eliot's preferred spelling for the Russian novelist: Dostoevski.

6. For discussion of Eliot's decision to replace the epigraph, see Brooker, "Dialectical Collaboration," 112–14.

7. See "Eliot's First Conversion," chapter 2 in this volume.

8. See discussion of Norbert Wiener and relativism in chapter 3.

9. In a review of Dowson's *Poetical Works* in the *TLS* (3 Jan. 1935), Goeffrey Tillotson suggested that "Cynara" was the source of Eliot's "Falls the Shadow." Eliot sent a letter to the editor (10 Jan. 1935) saying that, although "the derivation had not occurred" to him, he believed it "to be correct" because he had long been haunted by the lines Tillotson quoted: "Last night, ah, yesternight, betwixt her lips and mine/There fell thy shadow, Cynara! thy breath was shed . . ./But when the feast is finished and the lamps expire,/Then falls thy shadow, Cynara! the night is thine" (*Prose* 5.158). See *Poems* 1.723.

10. The implications of Eliot's view on James and intelligence are explored at length in Brooker, *Mastery and Escape*, chap. 1.

Chapter 7. Love and Ecstasy in Donne, Dante, and Andrewes

1. The Clark Lectures are published in full in *Prose* 2.609–761; the 1926 *TLS* essay, "Lancelot Andrewes," is in *Prose* 2.817–29.

2. This quotation is from the third paragraph of Meditation VI, translated by Haldane and Ross.

3. Eliot's Italian corrected. See *Prose* 2.623n1. Eliot used the translation by Rossetti; I am using the later and clearer translation by Musa.

4. Quotations of the poetry here analyzed by Eliot are printed as quoted in the Clark Lectures.

5. Translation: Musa.

6. Translation: Rossetti.

7. Translation: Musa.

Chapter 8. Eliot's Second Conversion: Dogma without Dogmatism

1. Forthcoming in *Letters*.

2. Forthcoming in *Letters*.

3. "Notes for a Talk to the Ecumenical Club." Forthcoming in *Prose* 8.

4. The typescript of "Journey of the Magi" that Eliot sent to his mother is a carbon, with annotations, now at Harvard's Houghton College Library.

Chapter 9. An Exilic Triptych: *The Waste Land, Ash-Wednesday*, "Marina"

1. Eliot to Ezra Pound, 11 November 1961. Forthcoming in *Letters*.

2. Dante, "Letter to Can Grande della Scala."

3. Quotations from the Bible are from the Authorized (King James) Translation, used by Eliot.

4. See headnote to Ezekiel in *New English Bible*, Oxford Study Edition.

5. The draft is at King's College, Cambridge. The conductor's call refers to cities along the Mississippi River: Natchez, Mississippi; Cairo, Illinois; and St. Louis, Missouri. This train call was used in a comedy routine by the Two Black Crows, an American blackface duo. According to I. A. Richards, Eliot often played recordings of their act for his English friends (6).

6. "Salutation" was probably begun in 1926 as part of a "Hymn to the Virgin." On 21 August 1926, Eliot wrote the editor of *Commerce* (Paris): "I have not got on with my Hymn to the Virgin." Haffenden's gloss: "The several verses that would ultimately comprise *Ash-Wednesday* (1930)" (*L*3.260).

7. Eliot to H. Warner Allen, 25 May 1960. Forthcoming in *Letters*.

8. Bratcher points out that the juniper tree also appears in a fairy tale.

9. Quinones, in an email to the author (6 June 2004), describes the significance of epiphany in literary modernism as its suggestion of "a sudden, unsummoned, adventitious appearance," with a "special claim on authenticity."

10. Seneca was much on Eliot's mind in the late 1920s. In 1927, he wrote an introduction to *Seneca his Tenne Tragedies*, published as "Seneca in Elizabethan Translation," and "Shakespeare and the Stoicism of Seneca," both in *Prose* 3.

11. Eliot to David Hoeniger, 28 October 1958. Forthcoming in *Letters*.

12. *Trans*: "The unique and supreme pleasure of making love lies in the absolute knowledge of doing evil." Baudelaire, *Intimate Journals* III.32.

13. Eliot to Hoeniger. In 1939, Eliot told John Hayward that he sometimes felt "acutely the desire for progeny" (*L*3.568n1).

14. *Social Register, Summer 1928/All Cities*. St. Louis section, p. 761.

Chapter 10. "Into our first world": Return and Recognition in *Burnt Norton* and *Little Gidding*

1. The nightingale in "Sweeney among the Nightingales" and in *The Waste Land*, similarly, sings from hiding and is associated with desire.

2. A revised version of "Two Masters" appeared as "The Modern Dilemma," in *The Christian Register*. In *Prose* 3.810–16. My quotations are from this version.

3. "I had not thought death had undone so many." *The Waste Land* (line 63), is a quotation from *Inferno* III.55–57.

4. Forthcoming in *Letters*.

5. A third way of redeeming the time, explored in part V of each *Quartet*, involves an analogy with poetry and the other arts. It is not part of the exilic dialectic and will be explored in my final chapter.

6. I am indebted to various readings of *Four Quartets*, of which the earliest and most formative were those by Helen Gardner, Harry Blamires, Lyndall Gordon, and Michael Edwards. Somewhat later, I read with appreciation the studies by John Paul Riquelme, Ronald Schuchard, Kenneth Paul Kramer, Steve Ellis, and John Whittier-Ferguson. My discussion in this chapter and the next is distinguished from these readings by a focus on the poem's dialectical structure, with special emphasis on the importance of the exilic imagination and the philosophical underpinning of his moral imagination.

7. The association of the Christ event with midwinter spring is caught in the 15th-century carol: "Lo, how a rose e'er blooming from tender stem hath sprung! / Of Jesse's lineage coming, as men of old have sung. / It came, a floweret bright, amid the cold of winter, / When Half spent was the night."

8. Cullman distinguishes between *chronos*, which refers to events as they occur, and *kairos*, which refers to a specific and unrepeatable point in time (39).

9. Eliot and Emily Hale visited Burnt Norton in September 1934; he visited Little Gidding in May 1936, with friends, not including Miss Hale.

Chapter 11. War and the Problem of Evil in the Wartime *Quartets*: Reason, Love, Poetry

This chapter includes material revised from Brooker, "The Fire and the Rose," and Brooker, "Alle shalle be wele."

1. See http://www.eyewitnesstohistory.com/blitz.htm.

2. Hulme's discussion of "Original Sin" is also quoted in "The Return of Foxy Grandpa" (1927; *Prose* 3.264).

3. Julian's "showings" (visions, revelations) survive in two versions. The "short text," written soon after her illness, contains a vivid description of each vision; the "long text," written twenty years later, adds her reflections on the meaning of her experience. Both are included in *The Writings of Julian of Norwich*. My in-text references are to the "long text," *A Revelation of Love*, and refer to the chapter numbers in *A Revelation* and the page numbers in *Writings*. (*Revelation* 2, 3: *Writings* 125–35) refers to chapters 2 and 3 in *A Revelation*, which are found on pages 125–35 in *Writings*. I retain Julian's medieval English in my quotations.

Bibliography

Works by T. S. Eliot

1. Collections and Critical Editions

The Complete Poems and Plays. London: Faber & Faber, 1969.

The Letters of T. S. Eliot. Vols. 1–2, 1898–1925. Edited by Valerie Eliot and Hugh Haughton. Vols. 3–7, 1926–1935. Edited by Valerie Eliot and John Haffenden. London: Faber & Faber, 2009–17.

The Letters of T. S. Eliot. Vol. 1: 1898–1922. Rev. ed. 2009.

Letters. Vol. 2: 1923–1925. 2009.

Letters. Vol. 3: 1926–1927. 2012.

Letters. Vol. 4: 1928–1929. 2013.

Letters. Vol. 5: 1930–1931. 2014.

Letters. Vol. 6: 1932–1933. 2016.

Letters. Vol. 7: 1934–1935. 2017.

On Poetry and Poets. London: Faber & Faber, 1957.

The Poems of T. S. Eliot. Edited by Christopher Ricks and Jim McCue. 2 vols. Baltimore: Johns Hopkins University Press, 2015.

T. S. Eliot: Apprentice Years, 1905–1918. Edited by Jewel Spears Brooker and Ronald Schuchard. Vol. 1 of *The Complete Prose of T. S. Eliot: The Critical Edition*. Baltimore: Johns Hopkins University Press; London: Faber & Faber, 2014.

T. S. Eliot: The Perfect Critic, 1919–1926. Edited by Anthony Cuda and Ronald Schuchard. Vol. 2 of *Complete Prose*, 2014.

T. S. Eliot: Literature, Politics, Belief, 1927–1929. Edited by Frances Dickey, Jennifer Formichelli, and Ronald Schuchard. Vol. 3 of *Complete Prose*, 2015.

T. S. Eliot: English Lion, 1930–1933. Edited by Jason Harding and Ronald Schuchard. Vol. 4 of *Complete Prose*, 2015.

T. S. Eliot: Tradition and Orthodoxy, 1934–1939. Edited by Iman Javadi, Ronald Schuchard, and Jayme Stayer. Vol. 5 of *Complete Prose*, 2017.

T. S. Eliot: The War Years, 1940–1946. Edited by David E. Chinitz and Ronald Schuchard. Vol. 6 of *Complete Prose*, 2017.

T. S. Eliot: A European Society, 1947-1953. Edited by Iman Javadi and Ronald Schuchard. Vol. 7 of *Complete Prose*, 2019.

To Criticize the Critic: Eight Essays on Literature and Education. New York: Farrar, Straus & Giroux, 1965.

The Waste Land: A Facsimile and Transcript of the Original Drafts, Including the Annotations of Ezra Pound. Edited by Valerie Eliot. New York: Harcourt Brace Jovanovich, 1971.

2. Individual Items

After Strange Gods: A Primer of Modern Heresy (1934). In *Prose* 5.15-55.

"The Art of Poetry, I: T. S. Eliot." Interview with Donald Hall. *Paris Review* (1959): [47]-70.

"Baudelaire" (1930). In *Prose* 4.155-67.

"Baudelaire in Our Time" (1927). In *Prose* 3.71-82.

"The Beating of a Drum" (1923). In *Prose* 2.471-75.

"Bergson" (1916). In *Prose* 1.425-27.

"A Brief Introduction to the Method of Paul Valéry" (1924). In *Prose* 2.559-66.

"Christianity and Communism" (1932). In *Prose* 4.422-31.

"The Clark Lectures" (Cambridge University, 1926). In *Prose* 2.609-761.

"A Commentary." *Criterion*: *A Literary Review* 12 (1933). In *Prose* 4.515-21.

"A Commentary." *Criterion*: *A Literary Review* 13 (1934). In *Prose* 5.80-83.

"A Commentary." *Criterion*: *A Literary Review* 15 (1936). In *Prose* 5.380-85.

"Dante" (1929). In *Prose* 3.700-745.

[Degrees of Reality] (1913). In *Prose* 1.57-66.

"The Development of Shakespeare's Verse" (1937). In *Prose* 5.531-61.

"Donne in Our Time" (1931). In *Prose* 4.369-82.

"Dowson's Poems" (1935). In *Prose* 5.158.

"Essays of a Catholic Layman in England, by Hilaire Belloc" (1931) [A review]. In *Prose* 4.320-22.

"Ezra Pound" (1946). In *Prose* 6.759-70.

"The Frontiers of Criticism" (1956). In *On Poetry and Poets*, 113-34.

"The Function of Criticism" (1923). In *Prose* 2.458-68.

[Inconsistencies in Bergson's Idealism] (1913). In *Prose* 1.67-89.

"In Memory of Henry James" (1918). In *Prose* 1.648-52.

"The Interpretation of Primitive Ritual" (1913). In *Prose* 1.106-19.

"An Interview." *Grantite Review* 24.3 (1962): 16-20.

"Introduction to *Revelation*, eds. John Baillie and Hugh Martin" (1937). In *Prose* 5.472-96.

Introduction to *Savonarola: A Dramatic Poem*, by Charlotte Eliot (1926). In *Prose* 2.771-76.

"Introduction to *Selected Poems*, by Ezra Pound" (1928). In *Prose* 3.517-33.
"Isolated Superiority. A review of *Personae*" (1928). In *Prose* 3.321-25.
"Kipling *Redivivus*" (1919). In *Prose* 2.33-39.
Knowledge and Experience in the Philosophy of F. H. Bradley (1916). In *Prose* 1.238-386.
"Lancelot Andrewes" (1926). In *Prose* 2.817-29.
"The Lesson of Baudelaire" (1921). In *Prose* 2.306-8.
Letter to Henry Eliot. 1 January 1936. Forthcoming in *Letters,* vol. 8.
Letter to Geoffrey Faber. 10 May 1936. Forthcoming in *Letters*, vol. 8.
Letter to E. J. H. Greene. 19 April 1940. Forthcoming in *Letters*, vol. 9.
Letter to Eudo C. Mason. 19 April 1945. Forthcoming in *Letters*.
Letter to David Hoeniger. 28 October 1958. Forthcoming in *Letters*.
Letter to H. Warner Allen. 25 May 1960. Forthcoming in *Letters*.
Letter to Ezra Pound, 11 November 1961. Forthcoming in *Letters*.
"Literature, Science, and Dogma" (1927). In *Prose* 3.44-50.
"London Letter: September, 1921." In *Prose* 2.369-74.
"Marie Lloyd" (1922). In *Prose* 2.418-23.
"The Metaphysical Poets" (1921). In *Prose* 2.375-85.
"The Method of Mr. Pound" (1919). In *Prose* 2.141-46.
"The Modern Dilemma" [originally "Two Masters"] (1933). In *Prose* 4.810-16.
"Modern Tendencies in Poetry" (1920). In *Prose* 2.212-25.
"Mr. Middleton Murry's Synthesis" (1927). In *Prose* 3.271-77.
"The Music of Poetry" (1942). In *Prose* 6.310-25.
"A Neglected Aspect of Chapman" (1924). In *Prose* 2.548-58.
"Notes for a Talk to the Ecumenical Club" (1955). Forthcoming in *Prose* 8.
Notes on the Lectures of Henri Bergson (1911). Houghton Library, bMS Am1691. Harvard University. Unpublished.
Notes towards the Definition of Culture. London: Faber & Faber, 1948.
"Paul Elmer More" (1937). In *Prose* 5.418-23.
"The *Pensées* of Pascal" (1931). In *Prose* 4.338-53.
"The Perfect Critic" (1920). In *Prose* 2.262-72.
"Philip Massinger" (1920). In *Prose* 2.244-59.
Philosophy A: Syllabus for an Introductory Course from the Pre-Socratics to the Renaissance (1913-14). In *Prose* 1.776-82.
"The Preacher as Artist" (1919). In *Prose* 2.165-69.
"A Prediction in Regard to Three English Authors: Writers Who, Though Masters of Thought, Are Likewise Masters of Art" (1924). In *Prose* 2.513-20.
"Preface to *Bubu of Montparnasse*" (1932). In *Prose* 4.417-21.
Preface to the 1928 edition of *The Sacred Wood*. In *Prose* 3.413-15.
"Reflections on Contemporary Poetry" (1919). In *Prose* 2.66-71.
[Relationship between Politics and Metaphysics] (1914). In *Prose* 1.90-105.
"The Relativity of the Moral Judgment" (1915). In *Prose* 1.197-215.

"Religion and Science: A Phantom Dilemma" (1932). In *Prose* 4.436-45.
"Report on the Ethics of Kant's *Critique of Practical Reason*" (1913). In *Prose* 1.49-56.
"Report on the Relation of Kant's Criticism to Agnosticism" (1913). In *Prose* 1.40-48.
"The Return of Foxy Grandpa" (1927). In *Prose* 3.261-66.
Review of *Baudelaire and the Symbolists*, by Peter Quennell (1930). In *Prose* 4.11-14.
Review of *The Study of Religions*, by Stanley A. Cook (1917). In *Prose* 1.562-63.
"The Search for Moral Sanction" (1932). In *Prose* 4.446-55.
"Second Thoughts about Humanism" (1929). In *Prose* 3.614-24.
[Self-realisation and Pleasure in the Ethics of Green and Sidgwick] (1914). In *Prose* 1.147-64.
A Sermon Preached in Magdalene College Chapel. Cambridge: Cambridge UP, 1948.
"Shakespeare and the Stoicism of Seneca" (1927). In *Prose* 3.245-60.
"Some Thoughts on Braille." *Books: The Journal of the National Book League* (London) 272 (1952): 176-77.
"Syllabus for a Tutorial Class in Modern English Literature" (1918). In *Prose* 1.754-59.
"Syllabus for a Tutorial Class in Modern English Literature, Second Year's Work" (1917). In *Prose* 1.589-93.
"TARR" (1918). In *Prose* 1.745-48.
"Thoughts after Lambeth" (1931). In *Prose* 4.223-50.
"Tradition and the Individual Talent" (1919). In *Prose* 2.105-14.
"*Ulysses*, Order, and Myth" (1923). In *Prose* 2.476-81.
The Use of Poetry and the Use of Criticism: Studies in the Relation of Criticism to Poetry in England (1933). New ed. London: Faber & Faber, 1964.
"The validity of artificial distinctions" (1914). In *Prose* 1.187-92.
"Views and Reviews [I]" (1935). In *Prose* 5.249-53.
"Virgil and the Christian World" (1951). In *On Poetry and Poets*, 135-48.
"War-Paint and Feathers" (1919). In *Prose* 2.137-40.
"Was There a Scottish Literature?" (1919). In *Prose* 2.92-96.
"What Dante Means to Me" (1950). In *To Criticize the Critic*, 125-35.
"What France Means to You" (1944) In *Prose* 6.512-15.
"What Is a Classic" (1944). In *Prose* 6.669-87.
"Why Mr. Russell Is a Christian" (1927). In *Prose* 3.160-63.
"William James on Immortality" (1917). In *Prose* 1.582-84.
"Wordsworth and Coleridge" (1932). In *Prose* 4.625-40.
"Yeats" (1940). In *Prose* 6.78-90.

General Bibliography

Aeschylus. *Agamemnon*. In *Oresteia*. Translated by Robert Fagles. New York: Penguin, 1977.

Aiken, Conrad. "King Bolo and Others." In *T. S. Eliot*, edited by Richard March and Tambimuttu, 20–23. Chicago: Henry Regnery, 1949.

———. Letter to Editor. *Times Literary Supplement*, 3 June 1960.

———. "The Scientific Critic." In Brooker, *Contemporary Reviews*, 61–64.

———. *Selected Letters of Conrad Aiken*. Edited by Joseph Killorin. New Haven, CT: Yale UP, 1978.

Alighieri, Dante. *See* Dante

Andrewes, Lancelot. *Ninety-Six Sermons*. Edited by John Posthumus Parkinson. Library of Anglo-Catholic Theology 5. Oxford: John Henry Parker, 1841.

———. *Seventeen Sermons on the Nativity*. Ancient and Modern Library of Theological Literature. London: Griffith, Farran, Okeden & Welsh, 1821.

Auden, W. H. "Port and Nuts with the Eliots" (1949). In Brooker, *Contemporary Reviews*, 506–8.

Augustine. *The Confessions of St. Augustine*. Translated by E. B. Pusey. New York: Collier, 1900.

Baker, Denise Nowakowski. *Julian of Norwich's Showings: From Vision to Book*. Princeton, NJ: Princeton UP, 1994.

Baudelaire, Charles. *Écrits sur la littératur*. Paris: Librairie générale française, 2005.

———. *The Flowers of Evil / Les Fleurs du mal*. English and French. Multiple translators. Edited by Marthiel and Jackson Mathews. New York: New Directions, 1955.

———. "Fusées," in *Journaux intimes*. In *Poison and Vision: Poems and Prose of Baudelaire, Mallarmé, and Rimbaud*. Dual language, translated by David Paul, 98–129. New York: Vintage Books, 1974.

Bell, Michael. *Literature, Modernism and Myth: Belief and Responsibility in the Twentieth Century*. Cambridge: Cambridge UP, 1997.

Bergson, Henri. *Creative Evolution* (1907). Translated by Arthur Mitchell. New York: Henry Holt, 1911.

———. *An Introduction to Metaphysics* (1903). Translated by T. E. Hulme. London: G. P. Putnam's Sons, 1912.

———. *Matter and Memory* (1896). Translated by N. M. Paul and W. S. Palmer. London: Allen & Unwin, 1911.

———. *Time and Free Will: An Essay on the Immediate Data of Consciousness* (1889). Translated by F. L. Pogson. London: George Allen, 1912.

The Bible. King James Version (1611). New York: Oxford UP, 1967.

Blake, William. *The Complete Poetry and Prose of William Blake*. Newly rev. ed. Edited by David V. Erdman. Berkeley: U of California P, 1982.

Blamires, Harry. *Word Unheard: Guide through Eliot's* Four Quartets. London: Methuen, 1969.

Bradley, F. H. *Appearance and Reality: A Metaphysical Essay* (1893), 2nd ed. London: Swan Sonnenschain; New York: Macmillan, 1908. Eliot's copy: 2nd ed. rev., 1908.

——. "On Our Knowledge of Immediate Experience." In *Essays on Truth and Reality*, 159-81. Oxford: Clarendon Press, 1914.

Bratcher, James T. "The Significance of the Juniper Tree Story in Eliot's *Ash-Wednesday*." *Notes & Queries* 58.1 (2011): 110-12.

Bronowski, Jacob. *The Common Sense of Science*. Cambridge, MA: Harvard UP, 1978.

Brooker, Jewel Spears. "Dialectic and Impersonality in T. S. Eliot." *Partial Answers* 3.2 (2005): 139-51. Reprinted as "Writing the Self: Dialectic and Impersonality in T. S. Eliot." In *T. S. Eliot and the Concept of Tradition*, edited by Giovanni Cianci and Jason Harding, 41-57. Cambridge: Cambridge UP, 2007.

——. "Dialectical Collaboration: Editing *The Waste Land*." In *Cambridge Companion to* The Waste Land, edited by Gabrielle McIntire, 102-15. Cambridge: Cambridge UP, 2015.

——. "Eliot and Bergson: 'Rhapsody on a Windy Night' and the Intractability of Dualism." *Partial Answers* 13:1 (2015): 1-17. Revision and expansion of "Seduction and Disenchantment." Lecture published in *Eliot, France, and the Mind of Europe*, edited by Jayme Stayer, 24-38. Cambridge: Cambridge Scholars Publishing, 1915.

——. "The Fire and the Rose: Theodicy in Eliot and Julian of Norwich." In *Julian of Norwich's Legacy: Medieval Mysticism and Post-Medieval Reception*, edited by Denise Baker and Sarah Salih, 69-86. London: Palgrave, 2010. A revision of "'Alle shalle be wele': Eliot and Julian of Norwich." *Explorations* 11 (2009 [2011]): 17-44.

——. *Mastery and Escape: T. S. Eliot and the Dialectic of Modernism*. Amherst: U of Massachusetts P, 1994.

——, ed. *T. S. Eliot: The Contemporary Reviews*. Cambridge: Cambridge UP, 2004.

—— and Joseph Bentley. *Reading* The Waste Land*: Modernism and the Limits of Interpretation*. Amherst: U of Massachusetts P, 1990.

—— and Ronald Schuchard. "Apprentice Years, 1905-1918." In Eliot, *Prose* 1.xxvii-lxii.

Brooks, Cleanth. "*The Waste Land*: An Analysis." *Southern Review* 3 (1937): 106-36.

Bush, Ronald. *T. S. Eliot: A Study in Character and Style*. New York: Oxford UP, 1983.

Childs, Donald J. *From Philosophy to Poetry: T. S. Eliot's Study of* Knowledge and Experience. New York: Palgrave, 2001.

——. *T. S. Eliot: Mystic, Son, and Lover*. New York: Palgrave, 1997.

Conrad, Joseph. *Heart of Darkness* (1899). Edited by Robert Kimbrough. 3rd ed. New York: W. W. Norton, 1988.

——. *The Secret Agent: A Simple Tale* (1907). London: J. M. Dent & Sons, 1923.

Cook, Stanley A. *The Study of Religions*. London: A & C Black, 1914.

Cooper, John Xiros. *T. S. Eliot and the Ideology of "Four Quartets."* Cambridge: Cambridge UP, 1995.

Costello, Harry T. *Josiah Royce's Seminar, 1913-1914, as Recorded in the Notebooks of Harry T. Costello*. Edited by Grover Smith. New Brunswick, NJ: Rutgers UP, 1963.

Crawford, Robert. *The Savage and the City in the Work of T. S. Eliot*. Oxford: Clarendon Press, 1987.

——. *Young Eliot: From St. Louis to "The Waste Land."* New York: Farrar, Straus & Giroux, 2015.

Cullmann, Oscar. *Christ and Time: The Primitive Christian Conception of Time and History*. Rev. ed. Translated by Floyd V. Filson. Philadelphia: Westminster Press, 1975.

Dante. *The Divine Comedy*. 3 vols. Temple Classics. London: J. M. Dent & Sons, 1909–1910. *The Inferno*. Translated by John Aitken Carlyle, 1909; *The Purgatorio*. Translated by Thomas Okey, 1910; *The Paradiso*. Translated by Philip H. Wicksteed, 1910.

——. *The Divine Comedy*. 3 vols. Translated by Mark Musa. New York: Penguin, 1984.

——. "Letter to Can Grande della Scala." In *Translations of the Later Works of Dante*. Translated by Philip H. Wicksteed. London: J. M. Dent & Sons, 1904.

——. *La Vita Nuova*. Translated by Mark Musa. Oxford: Oxford UP, 1992.

——. *La Vita Nuova*. Translated by D. G. Rossetti (1861). New York: Crowell, 1904.

Darwin, Charles. *On the Origin of the Species by Means of Natural Selection* (1859). New York: Signet Classics, 2009.

Descartes, René. *Meditations on First Philosophy* (1641). In *The Philosophical Works of Descartes*. Vol. 1. Translated by Elizabeth S. Haldane and G. R. T. Ross. Cambridge: Cambridge UP, 1967.

Douglass, Paul. *Bergson, Eliot, and American Literature*. Lexington: UP of Kentucky, 1986.

Durkheim, Émile. *The Elementary Forms of the Religious Life: A Study in Religious Sociology*. Translated by Joseph Ward Swain. London: Allen & Unwin, 1916.

——. *Les Règles de la méthode sociologique*. Paris: Alcan, 1895.

The Edinburgh Companion to T. S. Eliot and the Arts. Edited by Frances Dickey and John Morgenstern. Edinburgh: Edinburgh UP, 2016.

Edwards, Michael. *Eliot/Language*. Isle of Skye: Aquila Publishing, 1975.

Eliot, Henry Ware. "Philosophy, the Science of Truth." Commencement Address, Washington University of St. Louis. 18 June 1863. Special Collections, Washington University Libraries (MSS013-IV-Eliot). Unpublished. Quoted by permission.

Eliot, Henry Ware Jr. Letter to T. S. Eliot. 12 September 1935. In T. S. Eliot, *Letters* 7.748–63.

Ellis, Steve. "*Four Quartets*." In *The New Cambridge Companion to T. S. Eliot*, edited by Jason Harding, 103–15. Cambridge UP, 2017.

Frank, Joseph. "Spatial Form in Modern Literature." *Sewanee Review* 53 (1945): 221–40.

Frazer, Sir James George. *The Golden Bough: A Study in Comparative Religion*. 2nd ed. 3 vols. London: Macmillan, 1900.

Gallup, Donald. *T. S. Eliot: A Bibliography*. Rev. and extended ed. New York: Harcourt Brace & World, 1969.

Gardner, Helen. *The Composition of* Four Quartets. New York: Oxford UP, 1978.

Girard, René. *Violence and the Sacred*. Translated by Patrick Gregory. Baltimore: Johns Hopkins UP, 1977.

Gordon, Lyndall. *The Imperfect Life of T. S. Eliot*. Rev. ed. London: Virago, 2012.

Gourmont, Remy de. *Dante, Béatrice et la poésie amoureuse* (*Dante, Beatrice, and Love Poetry: An Essay on the Feminine Ideal at the End of the Thirteenth Century*). Paris: Mercure de France, 1908.

Gray, Piers. *T. S. Eliot's Intellectual and Poetic Development, 1909–1922*. Atlantic Highlands, NJ: Humanities Press, 1982.

Habib, M. A. R. *The Early T. S. Eliot and Western Philosophy*. Cambridge: Cambridge UP, 1999.

Hargrove, Nancy D. *T. S. Eliot's Parisian Year*. Gainesville: UP of Florida, 2009.

Hazlitt, Henry. "The Mind of T. S. Eliot" (1932). In Brooker, *Contemporary Reviews*, 200–202.

Hilborn, R. C. *Chaos and Nonlinear Dynamics: An Introduction for Scientists and Engineers*. Oxford: Oxford UP, 1994.

Housman, A. E. *The Poems of A. E. Housman*. Edited by Archie Burnett. Oxford: Clarendon Press, 1997.

Hulme, T. E. *The Collected Writings of T. E. Hulme*. Edited by Karen Csengeri. Oxford: Clarendon Press, 1994.

———. "Translator's Preface." In Georges Sorel, *Reflections on Violence*, translated by T. E. Hulme, v–xi. London: Allen & Unwin, 1916.

Jain, Manju. *A Critical Reading of The* Selected Poems *of T. S. Eliot*. Delhi: Oxford UP, 1991.

———. *T. S. Eliot and American Philosophy: The Harvard Years*. Cambridge: Cambridge UP, 1992.

James, William. *Pragmatism*. New York: Longmans, Green, 1907.

Joachim, Harold H. *The Nature of Truth*. Oxford: Clarendon Press, 1906.

Julian of Norwich. *The Writings of Julian of Norwich: A Vision Showed to a Devout Woman* and *A Revelation of Love*. Edited by Nicholas Watson and Jacqueline Jenkins. University Park: Pennsylvania State UP, 2006.

Knight, G. Wilson. *Myth and Miracle* (1929). In *The Crown of Life: Essays in Interpretation of Shakespeare's Final Plays* (1947). New York: Barnes & Noble, 1966.

Kramer, Kenneth Paul. *Redeeming Time: T. S. Eliot's* Four Quartets. Lanham, MD: Cowley Publications, 2007.

Kuhn, Thomas. *The Structure of Scientific Revolutions*. Chicago: U of Chicago P, 1962.

Kuklick, Bruce. *The Rise of American Philosophy: Cambridge, Massachusetts, 1860–1930*. New Haven, CT: Yale UP, 1977.

Levenson, Michael. *A Genealogy of Modernism*. Cambridge: Cambridge UP, 1991.

Lévi-Strauss, Claude. *The Raw and the Cooked* (1964). Mythologiques 1. Translated by John and Doreen Weightman. Chicago: U of Chicago P, 1996.

Lévy-Bruhl, Lucien. *Primitive Mentality* (1910). Translated by Lilian A. Clare. London: George Allen & Unwin, 1923.

Lorenz, Edward. "Does the Flap of a Butterfly's Wings in Brazil Set Off a Tornado in Texas?" http://eaps4.mit.edu/research/Lorenz/Butterfly_1972.pdf.

Lovejoy, Arthur O. *The Revolt against Dualism: An Inquiry Concerning the Existence of Ideas*. London: Allen & Unwin, 1930.

Maclaren, Alexander. *The Wearied Christ and Other Sermons*. London: Alexander & Shepherd, 1893.

Manganaro, Marc. *Myth, Rhetoric, and the Voice of Authority: A Critique of Frazer, Eliot, Frye, and Campbell*. New Haven, CT: Yale UP, 1992.

Marvell, Andrew. *The Poems of Andrew Marvell*. Edited by Hugh Macdonald. Cambridge, MA: Harvard UP, 1973.

Marx, William. "Paris." In *T. S. Eliot in Context*, edited by Jason Harding, 25-32. Cambridge: Cambridge UP, 2011.

Menand, Louis. *Discovering Modernism: T. S. Eliot and His Context*. New York: Oxford UP, 1987.

Milton, John. *Complete Poems and Major Prose*. Edited by Merritt Y. Hughes. New York: Odyssey Press, 1957.

More, Paul Elmer. "The Cleft Eliot" (1932). In Brooker, *Contemporary Reviews*, 214-17.

The New English Bible with the Apocrypha (1961, 1970). Oxford Study Edition. New York: Oxford UP, 1976.

North, Michael. *The Political Aesthetic of Yeats, Eliot, and Pound*. Cambridge: Cambridge UP, 1992.

Ovid. *Metamorphosis*. Translated by Rolfe Humphries. Bloomington: Indiana UP, 1955.

Patea, Viorica. "T. S. Eliot's *The Waste Land* and the Poetics of the Mythical Method." In *Modernism Revisited: Transgressing Boundaries and Strategies of Renewal in American Poetry*, edited by Viorica Patea and Paul Derrick, 91-111. Amsterdam: Rodopi, 2007.

Perl, Jeffrey M. "Disambivalent Quatrains." In *A Companion to T. S. Eliot*, edited by David E. Chinitz, 133-44. London: Wiley-Blackwell, 2009.

———. *Skepticism and Modern Enmity: Before and after Eliot*. Baltimore: Johns Hopkins UP, 1989.

Pilkington, A. E. *Bergson and His Influence: A Reassessment*. Cambridge: Cambridge UP, 1976.

Pope, John C. "Prufrock and Raskolnikov Again: A Letter from Eliot." *American Literature* 18 (1947): [319]-21.

Pound, Ezra. *Selected Letters: 1907-1941*. Edited by D. D. Paige. New York: New Directions, 1950.

———. *The Spirit of Romance* (1910). New York: New Directions, 1929.

Quinones, Ricardo J. *Mapping Literary Modernism: Time and Development*. Princeton, NJ: Princeton UP, 1985.

Radhakrishnan, S. *The Principal Upanishads*. The Muirhead Library of Philosophy. London: Allen & Unwin, 1953

Rainey, Lawrence. *Revisiting* The Waste Land. New Haven, CT: Yale UP, 2005.

Ribot, Théodule. *Diseases of Memory* (*Les maladies de la mémoire*, 1881). Translated by William H. Smith. New York: D. Appleton, 1882.

Richards, I. A. "On TSE." In *T. S. Eliot: The Man and His Work*, edited by Allen Tate, 1-10. New York: Dell, 1966.

Riquelme, J. P. *Harmony of Dissonances: T. S. Eliot, Romanticism, and Imagination*. Baltimore: Johns Hopkins UP, 1991.

Royce, Josiah. *The World and the Individual*. New York: Macmillan, 1900.

Russell, Bertrand. *The Autobiography, 1914-1944*. Vol. 2. Boston: Little, Brown, 1951.

——. "The Philosophy of Bergson." *Monist* 22 (1912): 321-47.

Sartre, Jean Paul. *No Exit* [1944] *and Three Other Plays. No Exit*. Translated by Stuart Gilbert. New York: Vintage Books, 1989.

Schlegel, Friedrich von. *The Philosophy of Language* (1820). In *The Philosophy of Life* and *Philosophy of Language*. Translated by A. J. Morrison. London: H. G. Bohn, 1847.

Schuchard, Ronald. *Eliot's Dark Angel: Intersections of Life and Art*. New York: Oxford UP, 1999.

Schwartz, Sanford. *The Matrix of Modernism: Pound, Eliot, and Early Twentieth-Century Thought*. Princeton, NJ: Princeton UP, 1985.

Sencourt, Robert. *T. S. Eliot: A Memoir*. New York: Dodd, Mead. 1971.

Shakespeare, William. *Complete Works*. Edited by Hardin Craig. Chicago: Scott, Foresman, 1961.

Shusterman, Richard. *T. S. Eliot and the Philosophy of Criticism*. New York: Columbia UP, 1988.

Singleton, Charles S. *An Essay on the Vita Nuova*. Baltimore: Johns Hopkins UP, 1949.

——. *Dante Alighieri, Inferno: Commentary*. Princeton, NJ: Princeton UP, 1970.

Smith, Grover C. "T. S. Eliot and the Fascination of Hamlet." In *The Placing of T. S. Eliot*, edited by Jewel Spears Brooker, 43-59. Columbia: U of Missouri P, 1991.

——. *T. S. Eliot's Poetry and Plays: A Study in Sources and Meaning*. 2nd ed. Chicago: U of Chicago P, 1974.

Social Register, Summer 1928/All Cities. Vol. 52:34. St. Louis section, p. 761. New York: Social Register Association, June 1928.

Sophocles. *The Women of Trachis*. In *Four Plays*. Translated by T. H. Banks. NY: Oxford UP, 1966.

Southam, B. C. *A Student's Guide to the* Selected Poems of T. S. Eliot. 6th ed. London: Faber & Faber, 1994.

Spears, Monroe K. *Dionysius and the City: Modernism in Twentieth-Century Poetry*. New York: Oxford UP, 1970.

Spurr, Barry. *"Anglo-Catholic in Religion": T. S. Eliot and Christianity*. Cambridge: Lutterworth Press, 2010.

Spurr, David. *Conflicts in Consciousness: T. S. Eliot's Poetry and Criticism*. Urbana: U of Illinois P, 1984.

Symons, Arthur. *The Symbolist Movement in Literature* (1899). 2nd ed. New York: Dutton, 1908.

Thormählen, Marianne. *The Waste Land: A Fragmentary Wholeness*. Lund Studies in English 52. Lund, SE: Liber Läromedel/Gleerup, 1978.

Timmerman, John H. *T. S. Eliot's Ariel Poems: The Poetics of Recovery*. Lewisburg, PA: Bucknell UP, 1994.

Torgovnick, Marianna. *Gone Primitive: Savage Intellects, Modern Lives*. Chicago: U of Chicago P, 1997.

Tylor, Edward Burnet. *Primitive Culture: Researches into the Development of Mythology, Philosophy, Religion, Language, Art, and Custom*. 2 vols. (1871). 3rd ed. London: John Murray, 1891.

Underhill, Evelyn. *Mysticism: A Study in the Nature and Development of Man's Spiritual Consciousness* (1911). New York: Dutton, 1961.

——. *Mystics of the Church* (1925). New York: Schocken, 1964.

Valéry, Paul. *Degas Manet Morisot*. Translated by David Paul. New York: Pantheon Books, 1960. Vol. 12 of *The Collected Works of Paul Valéry*.

Webb, C. J. J. *Group Theories of Religion and the Individual*. London: Allen & Unwin, 1916.

Whittier-Ferguson, John. "'Old Timbers to New Fires': T. S. Eliot's Christian Poetry." In *Mortality and Form in Late Modernist Literature*, 31-79. New York; Cambridge UP, 2014.

Wiener, Norbert. "Relativism." *Journal of Philosophy, Psychology, and Scientific Methods* 11.21 (1914): 561-77.

Wilbur, Richard. *New and Collected Poems*. New York: Harcourt Brace Jovanovich, 1988.

Wilson, Edmund. "The Poetry of Drought" (1922). In Brooker, *Contemporary Reviews*, 83-87.

Woolf, Virginia. "Character in Fiction." *Criterion* 2.8 (July 1924): 409-30.

Wundt, Wilhelm Max. *Elements of Folk Psychology: Outline of a Psychological History of the Development of Mankind*. London: Allen & Unwin, 1921.

Yeats, William Butler. *The Poems of W. B. Yeats*. New ed. Edited by Richard J. Finneran. New York: Macmillan, 1983.

Index